TOURISM MANAGEMENT: NEW RESEARCH

TOURISM MANAGEMENT: NEW RESEARCH

TERRY V. LIU
EDITOR

Nova Science Publishers, Inc.
New York

NOTICE TO THE READER

The Publisher has taken reasonable care in the preparation of this book, but makes no expressed or implied warranty of any kind and assumes no responsibility for any errors or omissions. No liability is assumed for incidental or consequential damages in connection with or arising out of information contained in this book. The Publisher shall not be liable for any special, consequential, or exemplary damages resulting, in whole or in part, from the readers' use of, or reliance upon, this material.

Independent verification should be sought for any data, advice or recommendations contained in this book. In addition, no responsibility is assumed by the publisher for any injury and/or damage to persons or property arising from any methods, products, instructions, ideas or otherwise contained in this publication.

This publication is designed to provide accurate and authoritative information with regard to the subject matter cover herein. It is sold with the clear understanding that the Publisher is not engaged in rendering legal or any other professional services. If legal, medical or any other expert assistance is required, the services of a competent person should be sought. FROM A DECLARATION OF PARTICIPANTS JOINTLY ADOPTED BY A COMMITTEE OF THE AMERICAN BAR ASSOCIATION AND A COMMITTEE OF PUBLISHERS.

Library of Congress Cataloging-in-Publication Data
Available upon request.

ISBN 1-60021-058-9

Published by Nova Science Publishers, Inc. ✛ *New York*

CONTENTS

PREFACE

The application of market segmentation techniques is long established in the tourism and hospitality literature, as discussed in chapter 1. Various methods have been proposed for dividing market segments into homogeneous or distinct groupings with regard to socio-demographic, travel characteristic, psychographic, geographic and behavioural characteristics. Amongst these approaches, the common ones are nationality, benefits sought, tourist role and social class, with nationality being the most important segmentation variable to be included. In the present study, nationality (cultural differences) in combination with visitor demographics and travel characteristics was used to investigate the similarities and differences of international tourists from China and the USA with regards to their perception towards the Vietnamese service provider's attributes and performances. It presents the findings of a self-administered survey administered to 170 American and 235 Chinese tourists visiting Vietnam during 2003 and 2004. The results have shown that there are more differences than similarities between the two samples in terms of cultural values and perceptions. Cultural values have strong impact on Chinese and American tourist perceived importance towards the Vietnamese hosts' attributes and performances. The implications for tourism industry management destination and marketers are presented. It is recommended that the Vietnamese tourism authorities target international tourism markets more precisely and improve the provision of tourism services in Vietnam.

Chapter 2 reviews that originated and refined in the West, community tourism started to draw Chinese researchers' attention in the last two decades of the twentieth century. However, there are essential differences, between the ideas of Chinese and Western researchers, regarding the concept of community tourism. Those differences basically hinge on two questions: is community tourism a democratic process or predominantly a planning strategy and; is sustaining the community or tourism the overall objective? To understand those differences, this study takes a detour through the modernization and [under]development theories so as to examine the contradictions manifest in China's modernization process and the implications for community tourism development. Three major criteria of contemporary modernity are adopted for the examination: the relationship between economy and politics, the question of civil society and public sphere, and the development towards democracy. The empirical study focuses on two cases of tourism development at two destinations – Sanya City in the island province of Hainan, and Huangshan City in the south Anhui Province. Hainan Island, once a marginalized provincial backwater, is now the centre of the whole nation's attention being China's largest special economic zone; while the south of Anhui, historically an important civilization center of

China, is increasingly marginalized in the country's modernization process, being a less developed inland region. Tensions between China's past tradition and contemporary impetus for 'modernization' manifest at the two destinations, thus offering typically exemplifying cases for the investigation. The study results indicate the transformation of Western ideas about community tourism to China is affected by the quality of false modernity. Such a quality prevails in China's current modernization campaign and creates a number of obstacles for actualizing Western concept of community tourism in the country.

The authors of chapter 3 state that research into local community attitudes has been on the rise for the past two decades and variety attempts have been made to cluster the community segments on the basis of their expressed attitudes. More than 80 research articles have so far been published in various research outlets. The researchers of the current research have in the past were involved in segmenting the Victorian community groups in various regional tourism product regions of Victoria in order to identify the profiles of the community segments on the basis of demographic variables. A well structured five part resident attitude questionnaire comprising of 35 statements highlighting attitudes, tourism activities, intention toward tourism and community development was used to generate the data. The employment of multivari ate statistics to the overall sample of 812 residents has yielded four distinct community clusters and they difered from each other on gender ratio, age, lifecycle stage, education, migration status, occupation and current involvement with regional tourism. Further a five factor resident attitudes were extracted from the results of the previous research in terms of exploring the underlying causes of both positive and negative attitudes of community towards tourism. In this research, the researchers have surveyed 1425 residents and attempted the overlay of the clusters on Victorian product regions with reference to the postal code of the residents to find out the differences in the spatial distribution of cluster profiles by using Map Info GIS. Also, the researchers have used the previously extracted attitude factors as a determining overlay on to the tourism product regions in order to measure their differences right across the tourism regions. The researchers have developed a set of resident attitudinal maps for the state of Victoria as a result of this spatial analysis and the implications of this will be discussed in light of advising the local governments, local tourism associations and tourism industry bodies on future tourism planning, marketing and resource allocation.

The existence of strong heterogeneous tourism demand looking for service provision adapted to its specific needs, along with the recent intensification of competition in the tourism market, has led to segmentation becoming fundamental to the marketing strategies of tourism organizations. Chapter 4 presents the innovation of identifying decision processes individual by individual, tourist by tourist. To achieve this, the authors propose a segmentation of the tourism market based on revealed preferences towards a destination at an individual tourist level; in other words, the real destination choices made by a tourist. These real choices reveal preferences in tourist destinations; the method has the twofold implication that it allows us to form groups of tourists with similar preferences or to treat them individually. Moreover, this analysis is based on *real choices* made by individuals, which avoids the measurement errors of segmentation criteria that use subjective variables, based on evaluations or declarations of intent. With this objective, the subsequent sections of this study are arranged as follows: The second section reviews the analysis of choice in tourism, in which the authors state the importance of studying the choice behavior of tourists, they examine the fundamentals of choice through *revealed preferences* and compare them to *stated preferences*, they study how to introduce heterogeneity into the modelization of tourist choice and they review the literature of destination choice in order to propose its determinant attributes. The third section presents the research design, in which they detail the methodology applied and the sample and data used. The fourth section shows the results obtained, both from the estimation of the utility function for each tourist and from the segmentation analysis. The fifth and final section summarises the main conclusions reached, the implications for management and future lines of research.

Adopting sustainable and strategic tourism planning perspective is imperative particularly for destinations in stagnation in order to better manage their efforts for rejuvenation. Carefully crafted and implemented vision can provide such destinations with many advantages, including community building and a long-term perspective, as discussed in chapter 5. Despite its importance, visioning exercises in the context of stagnated destinations are relatively rare. Drawing on Kusadasi case, this paper depicts the process of vision development. The experience has shown that it is not only the consensus-based vision but also the process followed in its generation matters.

Chapter 6 reviews that although tourism has been studied as a phenomenon by many different disciplines (sociology, anthropology, geography etc.), over the last few years one of the most incipient new research areas is tourism economics. The generalization of econometric software packages and the adaptation of economic theory have combined to offer a deeper insight into the economics of tourism. In this context, this study reviews the most popular aspects of tourism that have been analysed by economists in recent years. After a brief introduction, tourism demand modelling and forecasting techniques are evaluated as one of the most widely considered subjects in literature. Section three reviews studies of the tourism supply and structure of the tourist industry, followed in section four by an analysis of macroeconomic issues relating to tourism, like tourism's contribution to the GDP, tourism growth, employment and prices. In continuation, section five deals with the relationship between tourism and the environment, including non–economic impacts and sustainability, while section six concludes the paper.

Chapter 7 examines the different categories of cruise ship costs. Attention is focused upon capital, and running and operating costs, in the hope that they can be reduced to improve the performance of the company. The costs are examined in the context of the different cost categories aboard the cruise ship, including the five phases of cruise operation from the time the passengers embark to when they last depart. A cost-benefit analysis is carried out in order to identify the cost elements arising from each cost category involved in the examined operation phase, namely cruising, and to estimate the benefits for each cost element. Risk analysis is another issue that is examined. Risk assessment techniques are studied and the risk criteria for determining whether a risk is acceptable or not, are established. The proposed cost, benefit and risk assessment methodology is developed in the light of decisions of the cruise companies about the safe, economic, efficient and effective operation of their cruise ships. A test case is finally used to demonstrate the application of the proposed methodology.

Based on the survey data of Taiwan's international tourist hotels in 2002, chapter 8 first uses the DEA to access technical efficiency of each international tourist hotel, and then applies the Tobit censored regression model to investigate the relationship between technical efficiency and firm-specific characteristics. The DEA evaluation results show that international tourist hotels in Taiwan could have reduced inputs by at least 15 percent, on average, and still have produced the same level of outputs. The mean scale efficiency measure implies that the inefficiency is mainly from wasting resources instead of inappropriate production scale. The regression results show that an international tourist hotel's size has a positive impact on its technical efficiency. The impact of an international tourist hotel's service concentration on technical efficiency is positive. An international tourist hotel's degree of concentration in guest type is positively related with technical efficiency. International hotels located in Taipei are more technically efficient than those located in other areas. International hotels located in resort areas are more technically efficient than those located in other areas.

In: Tourism Management: New Research
Editor: Terry V. Liu, pp. 1-39

ISBN 1-60021-058-9
© 2006 Nova Science Publishers, Inc.

Chapter 1

AN ASSESSMENT OF SERVICE QUALITY IN VIETNAM: THE CROSS-CULTURAL PERSPECTIVES OF CHINESE AND AMERICAN TOURISTS

Thuy-Huong Truong[1] and Brian King[2]*
School of Hospitality, Tourism and Marketing
Victoria University, Australia

ABSTRACT

The application of market segmentation techniques is long established in the tourism and hospitality literature. Various methods have been proposed for dividing market segments into homogeneous or distinct groupings with regard to socio-demographic, travel characteristic, psychographic, geographic and behavioural characteristics. Amongst these approaches, the common ones are nationality, benefits sought, tourist role and social class, with nationality being the most important segmentation variable to be included. In the present study, nationality (cultural differences) in combination with visitor demographics and travel characteristics was used to investigate the similarities and differences of international tourists from China and the USA with regards to their perception towards the Vietnamese service provider's attributes and performances. It presents the findings of a self-administered survey administered to 170 American and 235 Chinese tourists visiting Vietnam during 2003 and 2004. The results have shown that there are more differences than similarities between the two samples in terms of cultural values and perceptions. Cultural values have strong impact on Chinese and American tourist perceived importance towards the Vietnamese hosts' attributes and performances. The implications for tourism industry management destination and marketers are presented. It is recommended that the Vietnamese tourism authorities target international tourism markets more precisely and improve the provision of tourism services in Vietnam.

Keywords: Vietnam, American tourists, Chinese tourists, Service Providers, Cultural values, Perception, Hosts and Guests

INTRODUCTION

The appeal of Vietnam as a tourism destination is based predominantly on its long history, culture and unique customs. The country is endowed with abundant historical and cultural heritage combined with a variety of beautiful and unspoiled natural attractions. Such attributes project its appeal to a wide cross-section of travellers. Vietnam's economic reforms have given further impetus to the growth of international tourism prompting the upgrading of tourism facilities and gradual relaxation of entry requirements.

As an emerging destination, Vietnam is experiencing a fast growth of international visitors from different cultural backgrounds, which places pressure on Vietnamese tourism professionals. If development is to be well managed, tourism professionals will need to broaden their understanding of both Western and Asian cultural differences, and managers will needed to encourage an atmosphere of familiarity and comfort amongst tourist groups, thereby contributing to enhanced visitor satisfaction. Appealing to the wide range of different tourists markets is however difficult because tourist needs are multiple and culturally determined. Despite Vietnam's previous contact with China and the USA, Vietnamese service providers still lack basic knowledge about the West and other Asian regions, their people and their value orientations, and they do not pay enough attention to the role of cultural understanding in promoting international tourism. Tourists will not be satisfied unless the tourism industry and front-line-staff in particular understand their cultural backgrounds. Tourism service providers contribute to the perceptions of each tourist which in turn influence tourist holiday satisfaction and repeat visitation. However, serving American tourists creates problems for Vietnamese service providers due to the large cultural differences between Western and Asian societies. Catering to Chinese tourists is also not an easy task for Vietnamese hosts, due to the slight cultural differences within the Asian societies. Vietnam is coping with a fast booming Chinese market with little prior experience.

As tourist destinations attract visitors from different cultures and countries, it is not reasonable to examine the satisfaction level of only one specific group of customers. Moreover, although the literature on customer perceptions and satisfaction has been dominated by the measurement of guest satisfaction with tourism and hospitality services, much past research is limited to homogeneous sample populations and sample destinations from Western countries. Additionally, little work has been done with regard to the assessment of cultural differences of international tourists visiting Vietnam. Therefore, a comparative analysis between tourists from different cultural backgrounds is required to better understand the importance of tourist product and services consumption at the destination. The objectives of this study are therefore to ascertain the similarities and differences in the perceptions of American and Chinese tourists holidaying in Vietnam.

The major objectives of this study are:

- To examine the different cultural values of Chinese and American tourists,
- To identify the effect of cultural differences between Chinese and American tourists on their perceptions of service quality in Vietnam with a particular focus on the attributes and performance of service providers, and
- To determine which cultural themes should be emphasized in tourism promotional strategies aimed at the Chinese and American tourism markets.

THE TOURISM INDUSTRY IN VIETNAM: CHALLENGES AND OPPORTUNITIES

Located in South East Asia, Vietnam is well place to integrate with wider tourism development trends both regionally and globally. The destination appeals to outsider because of its long history, its culture and its unique customs and habits. The history and development of Vietnam has produced a legacy of grand culture, history and artistic heritage yielding strong tourism attractions. In terms of potential tourist resources, the country is well endowed, and the market potential presents the country with good opportunities for tourism growth (Jansen-Verbeke et al, 1995). From a natural and cultural perspective, the country has much to offer to holidaymakers. It has beaches, caverns, marine lands and many places of unique and natural beauty including exotic plants and animals. It is also endowed with a rich cultural heritage including art, architecture, handicraft, customs and habits and tradition of ethnic groups. These characteristics or attributes form the basic potential of a diverse range of tourism products from coastal and beach tourism, through adventure and ecotourism to cultural heritage and urban tourism. Vietnam is therefore a destination appealing to a wide cross-section of travellers. Moreover, the strength of Vietnam also lies in its location in relation to neighbouring international gateways. This provides opportunities for the country to develop an intra-regional tourism strategy. According to Pookong and King (1999), all countries in the greater Mekong sub-region are endowed with abundant historical and cultural heritage, combined with a variety of beautiful and unspoiled natural environments. Those qualities combine to make the sub-region an attractive tourism destination.

Vietnam is a developing country where rural overpopulation and the demands of an emerging and diversifying urban economy are rapidly transforming economic and social relationships (Cooper and Hanson, 1997). With the growth of travel world wide, many underdeveloped countries around such as Vietnam have been able to improve their economies by increasing exports through low-cost production and also through tourism. Vietnam is the latest Asian country to declare the importance of tourism to National Development (VNAT, 1995). As tourism rapidly expands into Indo-China, Vietnam is trying to position itself to capitalize on this emerging industry.

The Vietnamese government's acknowledgement of tourism as a significant economic sector and accelerating economic reforms, have affected the development of tourism. The emergence of a free-market economy has created a more appropriate context for the development of a stable tourism industry. Favourable policies toward foreign investment have prompted a range of newly established international hotels thereby providing an increasing supply of rooms and an upgrading of tourism facilities. The continuous improvement in international relations and gradual relaxation of visa regulations have contributed to increased visitation. This, associated with attractions in terms of geography, economic position and international commodity exchange should create an impetus for tourism development in Vietnam and assist the country to follow the tourism development trends experienced in other parts of South East Asia.

Despite the opportunities, Vietnam has many challenges in terms of infrastructure and resources training and management. Due to many years of war and destruction, the country needs to pay urgent attention to maintaining and preserving its national heritage. According to Jansen-Verbeke and Go (1995: 315), Vietnam is not ready yet for a "large influx of tourists", particularly since the country still lacks suitable infrastructure, accommodation facilities, an appropriate tourism organisation and qualified staff to make a smooth change to a market economy tourism sector. Similarly, Theuns (1997) reported that there is an urgent need for upgrading the road infrastructure in order to be able to comply with increased tourist traffic. The level of service also needs to be improved to satisfy the expectations of international travellers and enable it to compete with other countries in the Southeast Asian region, especially Thailand Cooper (1997) has identified an urgent requirement for basic statistical information on visitor numbers and characteristics in order to obtain effective tourism's policy formulation.

The formulation of the "Doi Moi" policy, which brought privatization and Western management practices to the tourism industry has placed pressure on Vietnamese tourism and hospitality industries to improve their operations in response to rising guest expectations. The opportunity to act independently and the reality of having to satisfy customers or lose business are new and powerful motivations for many Vietnamese managers. Success has been accomplished more commonly in the larger cities where the local economy is stronger and visitation is higher. The challenge of joint venturing in Vietnam has been to develop a successful cross-cultural style. Evidence exists that the Vietnamese people are culturally dissimilar to Westerners, but are similar in some important ways. These and other cultural characteristics affect how they manage their businesses and how they interact with others. Over 30 years of oppressive Communist rule in Vietnam has left a foundation of distrust around unfamiliar people, especially foreigners. This leads to expressions of deeply held opinions on an individual rather than group basis and in a group only after sufficient time has passed. Vietnamese managers use a face-to-face style of interaction that enhances a top-down or vertical organization structure. This discourages the horizontal, networking relationships that are so characteristic of Western firms.

Since the introduction of the Open Policy (Doi Moi), the economy of Vietnam has faced political and consumer unrest in its difficult transition to a regulated market economy. Whilst most industries have experienced difficulties, the accommodation sector appears to have been an exception. This success has been influenced by the high expectations that international tourists and business travellers have of service standards. Increasing inbound travel, more foreign trade, and entrepreneurship have encouraged the success of Vietnam's tourism industry. However, the successes have come with challenges, especially in the area of human resources management. These challenges have arisen from differences in culture, political history, social systems, and the business practices between Vietnam and the West as well as with other developed Asian countries. Vietnamese tourism managers have shown a mixture of awareness and ignorance with commonly used management theory and its implementation. Front-line employees are more removed from the approaching changes. The absence of a developed labour market, coupled with the absence of tourism education provision further contributes to worker inexperience and lack of knowledge. Vocational training is a particular challenge due to years of entrenched, hard line government policies and attitudes. A key challenge for tourist service providers is how to accommodate the cultural backgrounds of different tourists with Vietnamese culture in order to achieve more effective management practices and to provide more efficient products and services for the international tourists.

The cross-cultural challenge is important for Vietnam's tourism industry. Vietnamese tourism service providers rely on a developed labour market that can be trained in the context of service, consistency, and quality and a known operational and physical environment. Yet they are limited by employee attitudes colored by the prevalence of communist ideas and Vietnam's subsequent, open policy-driven path to more open markets. And if these situations have led to differences between Eastern and Western culture, the question then is how tourist populations themselves differ in terms of culture and perception levels regarding tourist services received in Vietnam. Also how do Vietnamese service providers differ from their guests?

Since it already attracts a wide cross-section of holidaymakers, Vietnam has to some extent become accustomed to handling inbound travellers from different cultural backgrounds. The international tourism inherently involves an element of cross-cultural experience and experience gathering on the part of both the tourist and the tourism service providers. Given that the cultures of Asian travellers are very different from those of their Western counterparts; and particularly, since the various cultures within Asian societies are also dissimilar, an understanding of any cultural differences between international travellers, in terms of tourist perceptions of host attributes and performances is critical for Vietnam's tourism industry. Since the China and the USA are the leading tourist markets, it is important to look at cultural values which differ from those of Vietnamese, and being aware of these differences, help the Vietnamese hosts to understand the American and Chinese tourists and assess their perceptions towards the service quality on offer. An understanding of the potential dissatisfaction of international tourists in the area of service quality will help to eliminate negative perceptions, and provide them with experiences on holiday satisfaction. By taking cultural values into account and by analysing their influence on tourist perceptions towards service quality consumed in Vietnam, Vietnamese hosts could better understand the background of Western and other Asian tourists as well as their own background as well, and be better able to respond to Chinese and American tourist needs. Attention should be refocused on meeting culturally different tourist needs.

THE CHINESE AND AMERICAN INBOUND MARKETS

Courtesy of its natural scenery and exotic culture, Vietnam is becoming increasingly popular with international tour operators and whilst often being linked with tours to other countries in the region, it stands alone as a destination in the brochures of many major tour operators. The country is popular with both tourist groups and independent travellers and has become a popular destination on the East Asia back-packer route (Millington, 2001). With the growth in tourism receipts experienced since 1990, Vietnam's tourism industry has grown from a tiny base to become one of the country's most important. Tourism receipts have emerged as one of Vietnam's international trade major exports. According to official VNAT forecasts, international visitor arrivals are likely to grow at around 6 million in the year 2010 (2005). Vietnam is currently enjoying the attention of holidaymakers who are looking for new and exciting destinations. For many international tourists the country is still considered to be a new and popular destination. The main tourist markets over the next five years are expected to be China, North America, Japan, France, Korea, Germany, the UK, Taiwan, Thailand and Australia. If the trend continues over the next few years, Vietnam will be the next high-growth tourist destination after China. The steady growth of international tourist arrivals from various countries to Vietnam over the period from 2000 to 2005 is highlighted in Table 1.

Over the period from 1996, arrivals by air and land have grown faster than those by sea, thus highlighting the increasing popularity of Vietnam to local markets, especially China. The need to cater for both long haul markets (such as the USA) and short-haul market (such as China) makes the subjects of the present research particularly relevant. China and the USA have strong historical and cultural links with Vietnam. Air transport links have been fully re-established between the three countries, and cross-border transportation by train and bus is now well established between Vietnam and China. It is likely that Vietnam will continue to enjoy more advantages with respect to the Chinese and US leisure, business and VFR markets. Furthermore, the corresponding deflationary influence on the Vietnamese Dong relative to the USA and China currencies has made Vietnam a more affordable destination for tourists from these markets. The combination of affordability and overseas promotion by the government over the past few years has stimulated strong inbound tourism growth.

Table 1. International Tourist Arrivals to Vietnam by Major Countries (2000-2005)

Nationality	2001	2002	2003	2004	2005
China	672,846	724,385	639,423	778,431	684,054
Japan	204,860	279,769	209,730	267,210	298,979
Taiwan	200,061	211,072	207,866	256,906	260,987
USA	230,470	259,967	218,928	272,473	299,442
France	99,700	111,546	86,791	104,025	114,779
Australia	84,085	96,624	93,292	128,661	132,398
Britain	64,673	69,682	63,348	71,016	73,828
Thailand	31,789	40,999	40,123	53,682	77,599
Total	1,588,484	1,794,044	1,559, 501	1,932,404	1,942,066
Grand Total	2,330,050	2,627,988	2,073,433	2,927,876	3,140,426

Source: VNAT (2005)

CHINESE TOURISTS IN THE ASIA CONTEXT

Asia has long been an attraction for international tourists and more recently has become the world's fastest growing destination region. Located in Asia and possessing abundant tourism potential, Vietnam has the potential to participate fully and actively in wider regional development trends. A number of treaties have been signed between Vietnam and other ASEAN regional countries including Thailand, Singapore, Indonesia, the Philippines, China, Indonesia, Malaysia, Myanmar (Burma) and Laos. These will allow for the movement of tourists between the nations. Beside Western markets, another target group for Vietnam is Asia's growing middle class. The destination is suitable for Asians seeking relaxation but unable to afford to travel long haul. On the one hand, the large regional market made up of neighbouring countries such as Cambodia, Lao PDR, Thailand and particularly China will continue to growth. On the other hand, Japan, Taiwan, Korea, Singapore, Malaysia and Thailand offer great potential for tourism in Vietnam as well as in terms of investment.

According to the World Tourism Organisation (WTO, 2000), China will be the world's fourth largest outbound tourist generating country by 2020. The growth in outbound tourism from China is due to three main factors. These are firstly sustained economic growth, secondly the change of lifestyle for Chinese people, and finally the relaxation of Chinese government policy towards outbound travel. Fourteen other countries within the Pacific Asia region have recorded annual increases of Chinese mainland visitors of more than 10% since 1996. China will remain among the main sources of tourists to Vietnam and it will account for an even larger proportion of international tourists by 2010 (VNAT, 2005). For this reason, China still seems to be the single most important market for Vietnam tourism, even though other Asian countries have recently increased most quickly.

For Chinese travellers, China' border provinces have emerged as major destinations. Yunnan, a Southwest China's province that borders the three ASEAN Member States of Vietnam, Lao PDR and Myanmar, has attached great importance to trade, economic cooperation and tourism with Southeast Asian countries. In addition, a tourism belt is taking shape along the boundary between the Guangxi Zhuang Autonomous Region in South China and Vietnam. This is likely to bring more opportunities for the burgeoning border trade and tourism between Vietnam and China as well other countries thanks to its attractive features such as interesting customs of diverse minority communities, mysterious frescoes and ancient battlefields.

Most Chinese tourists arrive in Vietnam by land. Along the several thousand kilometers of the Sino-Vietnamese border, many Chinese travel through the port to Ha Long Bay for sightseeing purposes. Travel from China has also increased since the launch of direct air links between Hanoi and Ho Chi Minh City and Guangzhou, Beijing and Shanghai. The Chinese travellers who can best afford international air travel are however likely to be households concentrated along China's eastern seaboard in urban areas such as Shanghai and the Pearl River Delta. Thanks to the familiar culture, relatively short distances, affordable prices and particularly the relaxed travel policies between Vietnam and China over the past years, the Chinese tourist market will continue to perform well and provide much needed volume of activity for Vietnam's tourism industry.

As China is currently an emerging fast growing outbound countries, a number of studies have investigated the travel behaviour of Chinese tourists when travelling overseas (King and McVey, 2003). In their study of travel from China to Australia, Pan et al. (2004) identified the Chinese preferences as all-inclusive package tours including sightseeing excursions, local guides, accommodation and meals with mainly Chinese food with some Australian-style meals. The Chinese appear to prefer to travel in groups, enjoying the most popular itinerary or visiting the most impressive places in Australia and using budget hotels. Regarding the perceptions and preferences of Chinese visitors, Yu and Weiler (2001) mentioned that Australia is perceived as most attractive to Chinese visitors for its scenic beauty, safety, famous attractions and different cultures.

WESTERN MARKETS AND U.S. TOURISTS

Based on the VNAT report (2005), Western markets are the other major source of international tourists to Vietnam with about 40 per cent market share. These markets will account for the second largest source of international tourists to Vietnam after China by the year 2010 and will contribute an even larger proportion of international tourists by 2020. Americans will remain among the major sources of Western tourists to Vietnam. Arrivals from the USA doubled from 147,982 in 1997 to 272,473 in 2005. American sources are likely to stabilize as the second important market for Vietnam, despite the recent growth coming from other Western countries such as France, Australia, Britain, Austria and Germany. VNAT has increased its promotional activities in the USA in the hope of gaining increasing market share.

Over the past few years, there has been a marked change in the preferences of American travellers away from longer and more expensive travel to Europe towards shorter and cheaper trips to Asia. Tourists are constantly looking for new destinations that offer the opportunity to experience a wide range of activities and attractions, often with the added feature of encountering a new culture. Moreover, the changing ethnic composition of American society and particularly since the big flow of Vietnamese immigration to USA in the 1970 has expanded American's awareness of the diversity of Asian cultures. The interest in Asia correlates strongly with the educational attainment of American travellers. This intellectual bent is borne out by their high interest in educational trips in general, and the cultural and historical offerings of Vietnam, in particular.

As a tourist destination, Vietnam came late to the American market and remains relatively underdeveloped. During the previous two decades, the borders of Vietnam were closed to American citizens. Many previous visits to Vietnam were not legal due to trade sanctions and the "Dealing with the Enemy Act" which was passed at the end of the Vietnam conflict. However, the re-establishment of diplomatic ties between America and Vietnam has initiated a new era of commercial and cultural relations between the two nations. According to Caruso (1994), "although the recent end to the long standing American embargo has the Vietnam government planning lucrative joint business ventures with giant multinational corporations, its biggest potential may be in tourism". Vietnam has received more press coverage in the last few years than in the past. Although not all of the coverage has been favourable, it has served to keep Vietnam "top of mind" for American tourists. Beautiful attractions, an interesting history and exotic culture have attracted American travellers to Vietnam. Furthermore, attractive prices, are one of the factors stimulating American travellers who have always had an interest in the country but were deterred by the cost.

Ruppel et al. (1991) have mentioned that Americans seldom travel to poor, developing countries except in the case of Mexico. However, Vietnam is different because it prompts Americans to return to a part of their past. Since the lifting of the embargo, the flow of American tourists has continuously increased. Vietnam is now open to American pleasure holidaymakers, business as well as visiting friends and relatives travel and the travel industry is free to engage in marketing. A study by Agrusa (1994) has confirmed that Americans exhibit a high level of interest in returning to Vietnam as tourists. The primary areas of interest were found to be cultural and natural sightseeing. Moreover, the pleasure market has been enhanced further by the business travel market because many American business travellers have added a pleasure component to their Vietnam trips. The potential market for business extenders is substantial. It is likely that the strength of the dollar and the lower costs of lodging in Vietnam will entice more business travellers to the region to add a pleasure component to their trips.

Since Americans have a high degree of familiarity with Vietnam, there appears to be considerable potential for marketing tourism packages with American veterans as the target market (Agrusa, 1994; Bone, 1995). The military connection provides Vietnam with some prospect of building tourism. Hundreds of thousands of American soldiers have been stationed throughout the country during peacetime. Many of them, motivated by nostalgia or curiosity about how things have changed, may be interested in revisiting Vietnam. Vietnam has a plethora of sites from the War that are of interest not just to veterans but also to veterans' families, uninvolved service and others interested in military history. Vietnam can take steps to attract those Americans interested in exploring sites of military significance. U.S. military personnel and their families are thus a bright market prospect for Vietnam. Many who were there during the Vietnam War are anxious to go back under different conditions. However, the U.S. market is extremely complex and heterogeneous, and the potential market for Vietnam is a relatively small subset of all travellers. Therefore, it is necessary for Vietnam's tourist authorities to focus more promotional efforts on those markets segments most likely to visit. Vietnam will certainly continue to enjoy more advantages with respect to the pleasure, business and visiting friends and relatives (VFR) travel markets once the air transport links between two countries are fully re-established.

The foregoing discussion suggests that limited research has been undertaken on the Chinese and American outbound market travels. To date literature regarding the travel behaviour of Chinese and American travellers to Vietnam appears virtually non-existent. Beside Truong's (2005) study no research has been conducted to examine the needs, perceptions and satisfaction levels of international tourists in Vietnam. An examination of the behaviour and perception levels of tourists from different nationalities will help to profile these markets. Identifying salient activity preferences and travel characteristics will assist the development of design strategies for competitive advantage. Investigating the cultural differences and perceptions of American and Chinese tourists toward services will help to develop an understanding of the needs and expectations of tourists from different cultural backgrounds with implications for staff training, service improvement and product development.

LITERATURE REVIEW

Culture

Culture is a broad and complex multidimensional phenomenon which is very difficult to define (Edelstein et al., 1989). According to Kroeber and Kluckhohn (1952), there are over 160 definitions of culture presented in the literature. Culture has been defined and conceptualized by countless researchers in a diversity of social science disciplines, including anthropology, sociology, psychology, intercultural communication, marketing and management. These definitions range from viewing culture as "is everything", to those that adopt a narrower view.

In its "broad" sense, most studies refer to culture in psychological terms such as values, norms, rules, behaviour, perceptions, attitudes, beliefs, symbols, knowledge, ideas, meanings and thoughts (Bennett and Kassarjian, 1972; Argyle, 1990; Peterson, 1979; Leighton, 1981; Camilleri, 1985; Ember and Ember, 1985; Mill and Morrison, 1985; Moutinho, 1987; Robinson and Nemetz, 1988; Kim and Gudykunst, 1988). Individuals reflect that culture in their thinking and lifestyle, through their personal morality and behaviour. Cultures differ in their assumptions about the obligations of its members to one another and about the basis for community. People from the same culture typically share the same cultural variables and people from different cultures differ in terms of cultural variables. Since cultures vary, it is possible to identify individuals from similar and distinct cultural backgrounds. By analysing the correlations between various cultural variables, it is possible to distinguish various cultures because the elements that constitute culture are independent variables of culture (Segall, 1984) and they are separated and often based on the correlated factors (Munroe and Munroe, 1980; Samovar and Porter, 1991). However, despite the various definitions found in the literature, culture has been generally agreed as a "theory" (Kluckhohn, 1944), an "abstract" or a "name" for a very large category of phenomena (Moore and Lewis, 1952).

In the present study, all of these definitions have been used to analyse the national culture of Vietnamese hosts and international tourists. Special emphasis is placed on Kroeber and Kluckhohn's (1952) definition which referred to culture as an inclusion of most of the major elements of culture. This most comprehensive and generally accepted definition of culture was reconfirmed by Adler (1997) as:

> "Culture consists of patterns, explicit and implicit, of and for behaviour acquired and transmitted by symbols, constituting the distinctive achievement of human groups, including their embodiment in artifacts; the essential core of culture consists of traditional (i.e., historically derived and selected) ideas and especially their attached values; culture systems may, on the one hand, be considered as products of action, on the other, as conditioning elements of future action" (Kroeber and Kluckhohn, 1952, p.181).

Kroeber and Kluckhohn's definition of culture has created a foundation for the development of the current study's objectives as it refers to culture as values, rules of social behaviour, perceptions, and differences and similarities between people. This definition of culture was chosen because it seems that the cross-cultural satisfaction of tourists and the service providers is influenced by the differences and similarities in the tourists' and hosts' cultural values and perceptions.

The Relationship between Culture and Perceptions

Perceptions are based on physiology (the five senses) and also have characteristics related to demography, behaviour, society, culture, economics and psychology (Usunier, 2000). Culture is particularly important as a determinant of perceptions (Samovar and Porter, 1991). It has a great influence on how experiences are perceived and also on the interpreted meaning. McCracken (1986) has referred to "culture" as a lens through which people view the world. Cultural influences may be viewed as how people perceive and assimilate phenomena. Wei et al (1989) observed that cultural differences lead to different perceptions of what constitutes appropriate behaviour (p. 329). Since views about the world differ, it is unsurprising that perceptions also differ (Krech and Crutchfield, 1948; Robertson, 1970). Perceptions rely on cultural values, expectations, experiences and interests and are culturally determined.

Referring to culture as perception, McCort and Malhotra (1993) noted that "culture is the shared, consumption relevant knowledge system necessary to operate in a manner acceptable to one's society. This knowledge system, though the formation of culturally learned rites of perception and interpretation imbues objects and behaviours with meanings for its members".

Urriola (1989, p.66) indicated that culture is "the sum of peoples' perceptions of themselves and of the world...". Triandis (1972) defined the main elements of subjective culture are values, role perceptions, attitudes, stereotypes, beliefs, categorizations, evaluations, expectations, memories, and opinions. He mentioned that the similarities in subjective culture lead to frequent interaction among members of similar cultural groups. He also reported that "when the similar behaviour patterns obtained in one culture differ from the similar patterns obtained in another, we infer the existence of some differences in subjective culture" (Triandis, 1972, p.9). This definition was confirmed by the work of Samovar et al., (1981) who noted that the members of a similar subjective culture have similar values, conform to similar rules and norms, develop similar perceptions, attitudes and stereotypes, use common language, or participate in similar activities.

Culture affects each stage of the process of perception. Initially, it provides patterned material for perception (e.g. architecture, the aroma of foods, and the sound of music). Later, through verbal and nonverbal means, it suggests the proper labelling of and responses to perceptions of patterns. The relationship between culture and perceptions has been frequently noted. Several empirical studies have identified the influence of culture on perceptions (Mayo and Jarvis, 1981; Schneider and Jordan, 1981). Redding (1980) and Mayo and Jarvis (1981) pointed out that culture causes different nationalities to perceive differently with those growing up in different environments perceiving differently because they interpret causes differently (Segall et al., 1990). Richardson and Crompton (1988) attributed the different perception of French and English Canadians to cultural differences which elicit different responses to market strategies. Singer (1982) pointed out that different cultural values lead to different perceptions. One example is aesthetic values which are culturally determined and influence the perception of physical appearance and attractiveness. Keown et al. (1984) reported cultural influences on the differences between tourist perceptions of retail stores in 12 countries. Ritchie (1974) found significant differences in individual perceptions of leisure activities prompted by different personal values and cultural backgrounds. People with significantly diverging personal values exhibited significantly different perceptions.

Tourist perceptions have become a focus for researchers who are involved in examining the various dimensions of the tourist perspective. The findings of previous cross-cultural research has confirmed that tourist perceptions of a destination or hospitality businesses may vary on the basis of country of origin (Richardson and Crompton, 1988; Catalone et al., 1989; Luk et al., 1993; Huang et al., 1996; Armstrong et al., 1997). Pizam and Sussmann (1995) investigated tour guide perceptions of similarities and differences between tourists from four countries. The same survey was subsequently repeated among Israeli tour guides (Pizam and Reichel, 1996). In both studies, tour guides perceived that different behavioral characteristics were evident amongst tourists from different nationalities.

A number of studies have examined host perceptions of tourists. Brewer's (1984) study of Mexico concluded that local residents have "general" stereotypes of all Americans, which lead to "specific" stereotypes which are then applied to American tourists. Pi-Sunyer (1978) found that Catalans stereotype English tourists as stiff, socially conscious, honest, and dependable. Boissevain and Inglott (1979) observed that the Maltese characterized Swedish tourists as misers, and the French and Italians as excessively demanding. Other studies found that residents of tourist destinations perceived tourists to be different from themselves in a variety of behavioural characteristics and lifestyles. Pizam and Telisman-Kosuta (1989) found that in the destinations where a majority of tourists were foreigners, the residents perceived the tourists to be different from themselves in a variety of behavioural characteristics, such as attitudes or morality. In destinations where the majority were domestic tourists, the differences between the tourists and the residents were perceived as minimal. Similarly, Wagner (1977) in a study of charter tourism to the Gambia noted that the locals saw Scandinavian tourists as a "clearly demarcated group, whose dress, behaviour and life-style set them apart" (p. 43).

Culture has also been empirically proven to have an impact on the formation of expectations (Armstrong et al. 1997) as well as quality expectations (Luk et al., 1993). The cultural differences in expectations regarding service levels between hosts and visitors left many with negative impressions" (1989, p. 3). In the same vein, Befu (1971) reported that Japanese hosts take good care of the affairs of their guests in advance, anticipate the guests' needs and believe that they know best what the guests' needs are. However such an attitude may also be frustrating for Western tourists who think they know best what their needs are. Western tourists may regard Japanese hospitality as uncomfortable. On the other hand, the Western tradition of not anticipating the guests' needs in advance may negatively impact on the satisfaction of Japanese tourists with the hospitality of Western hosts.

Moreover, the relationship between culture, perception and interaction was also highlighted in a number of studies. Sheldon and Fox (1988) noted that there are many cultural differences in relation to interaction patterns between guests and service providers. These differences may lead to different perceptions about what constitutes proper treatment of guests and shapes different attitudes of hosts towards tourists (Richter, 1983). Wei et al. (1989) emphasized the influence of cultural differences on the interaction processes between service providers and visitors. They reported that poor quality service may lead to unpleasant encounters between tourists and hosts, low morale, and unfriendly attitudes. They indicated that "interacting with service personnel is a primary way in which visitors form an impression and make judgments about their hosts. In Reisinger and Turner's (2003) study, cultural value is seen to impact on interaction behaviour which is important in services given the nature of the service encounter, which is a dyadic interaction between Asian tourists and Australian service provider. File et al. (1995) have argued that the service encounter is a social process and is apt to be affected by differences in cultural perceptions and values, thus strengthening the need to consider customer participation in light of cultural values.

There appear to be a number of factors creating serious problems for how tourists and host perceive each other. It is important to determine how tourists perceive hosts and vice versa particularly in the cross-cultural context of the tourism industry. Cultural differences mean that there is a considerable negative perception arising amongst Western and Eastern tourists, as well as amongst Western tourists of Eastern hosts and vice versa. Insensitivity to these differences may cause misunderstanding and interaction difficulties between tourists and hosts. Although there are many other cultural differences between members of Western and Eastern societies that have impacted on their perceptions and social interaction, it can readily be seen that members of Western and Eastern cultures have totally opposite cultural orientations and expectations from the perceptions and social interactions. These cultural differences may have a negative influence on how people perceive others.

There is a significant relationship between culture and perceptions since perceptions of the world around are influenced by the culture into which one has been socialized. It is important to understand cultural value orientations that affect perceptions. Most tourism and hospitality industry employees appear to implicitly or explicitly acknowledge the existence of tourist cultural differences in terms of interests, needs, expectations, destination or hotel selection and preferred activities. Clearly destination image and perceptions influence vacation choice decisions and national cultural characteristics affect tourist perceptions. To date there has been little cross-national research undertaken in order to explore the potential impact of culture on tourists' perceived importance of host attributes and performance. No study has investigated tourist evaluations of service quality in Vietnam. For the chapter, it is important to analyse the cultural differences and determine which of them have the most detrimental effects on the cross-cultural perception of the Chinese and American tourists of Vietnamese hosts' attributes and performances.

Service Quality - Host Attributes and Performance

Service may be defined as "any activity or benefit one party can offer to another that is essentially intangible and does not result in the ownership of anything. Production may or may not be tied to a physical product" (Kotler et al., 1989, p.725). According to Parasuraman et al (1988), it is more difficult for the purchasers of services, such as tourists, to evaluate quality, than it is for the purchasers of tangible products. This is because services have three main unique features. The first is intangibility reflecting that services deliver performances and experiences rather than the objects. The second is heterogeneity, which acknowledges that service delivery may not be consistent across individuals, time, and situations. The third is inseparability. Unlike the production of tangible goods, the purchaser is usually involved in the service production process and quality of service is often determined by service delivery. In other words, a service is consumed while it is produced.

Parasuraman et al. (1985) noted that service quality is an "elusive and indistinct construct, often mistaken for imprecise objectives" and "not easily articulated by consumers" (p. 41). Lewis and Booms (1983) drew attention to the subjective character of service quality and argued that the evaluation of service quality depends upon "what is acceptable and what is not" (p. 100). Parasuraman et al. (1988) expanded upon this notion and reported that service quality is the result of a subjective customer perception of service. Consequently, service quality is often related to the perception of service by a customer. Service perception is often referred to as the perception of the interaction between a customer and a service provider.

Service quality has various dimensions. Gronroos (1982, 1990) has proposed that service quality is made up two components namely technical quality and functional quality. Technical quality refers to the performances visitors receive, for instance a withdrawal transaction at a bank. Functional quality refers to the process of service delivery, for instance the withdrawal service may be provided through the ATM or by the teller in person. Similarly, Lehtinen and Lehtinen (1982) recommended three quality dimensions including physical, corporate and interactive quality. While physical quality relates to the technical aspects of the service, the latter two dimensions emphasize the corporate image of the service organization and the interactive processes that occur between a tourist business and its visitors. As service quality occurs during the service encounter between a consumer and a service provider, the interactive dimension of service quality is central to service. Consequently, the quality of this interaction is essential in the assessment of total service quality (Parasuraman et al, 1985; Solomon et al., 1985; Urry, 1991). Martin (1987) differentiated the procedural and convivial as the two dimensions of service quality. The former deals with systems of selling and distributing a product to a customer and is mechanistic in nature. The latter highlights service provider behaviour, courtesy, attentiveness, friendliness, their verbal and non-verbal skills and positive attitudes or personal interest towards their customers such as being appreciative of the customer or being able to fulfil the customer's psychological needs. This convivial dimension according to Martin (1987) will give emphasis to the customer's need to be respected, relaxed, feel comfortable, important, pampered, and welcomed.

Evaluations of service quality embrace not only the service delivered, but also the manner in which it is delivered. In the tourism and hospitality sector, perception of service quality relies very heavily on the development of positive perceptions of hosts (service providers), as perceptions of hosts are part of the overall perceptions of a tourism product. The attributes of hosts are the fundamental aspects of service quality. For instance, providing prompt and courteous service to clients or smiling in a pleasant and involved way to customers are the important attributes of service quality. Crompton and MacKay (1989) defined service quality as the quality of service attributes. Service attributes are the constituent elements of the opportunities that management provides for tourists or recreationists. These are controlled and manipulated by tourist suppliers. To reflect this perspective, Crompton and Love (1995) renamed service quality in the tourism field as "quality of opportunity". Quality of opportunity or performance quality of the tourism entity is defined as the quality of service attributes that are under the control of service suppliers. It is operationalized as the disparity between the desired level of service and perceptions of the performed level of service. Pizam et al. (1978) highlighted the friendliness and courtesy of employees towards tourists as well as their willingness to help tourists as the important hospitality characteristics in the service delivery process. Callan (1997) mentioned service quality as "staff who get things done promptly and provide honest answers to problems"; as "a responsive, caring and attentive staff" who "making the recipient feel thoughtful, efficient, correct and magnanimous"; or as "a hospitality which leads the guest to feel at home" (p. 48). Saleh and Ryan (1992) also emphasised that "appearance is not only important but to some extent is more important than the range of facilities being provided" (p. 168).

Pearce (1982) demonstrated that the overall tourist perceptions of service will be determined by interactions with a variety of people within the tourism and hospitality industry. These include hoteliers, restaurateurs or other employees who contribute to the overall tourist perceptions of service. Sutton (1967) reported that competency in providing services is an important element influencing positive tourist perceptions of service. The negative perceptions of tourists arise because of the impoliteness of service providers, their feeling of discontent or because of not being able to achieve a certain standard of service. Therefore, the positive perceptions of the service such as the service providers' friendliness or politeness encourage both repeat consumption of that product and repeat visitation to the host region. By way of contrast, tourist negative perceptions of the service created by variables such as impoliteness or annoyance at poor service, will lead to the opposite effect.

Since service quality is a multidimensional concept, it is very difficult to evaluate. With its subjective characteristic in nature, each dimension of service quality can be perceived differently, depending whether it is perceived by a visitor or by a service provider particularly in the cross-cultural context. According to Gee (1986), tourist perceptions of hosts are the most important of the various tourist perceptions. There have been studies investigating customer evaluations of service quality conducted for tourist destinations but little cross-national exploration has been undertaken on the influence of cultural values on tourist evaluations of service attributes and performance. To date, no study has investigated tourist cross-cultural perceptions in term of service quality in Vietnam. For the current study, tourist perceptions of hosts will be assessed in terms of service providers' attributes and performance. An examination of tourist perceptions of host attributes and performance should enable the detection of better negative perceptions, change or modify them if necessary, and therefore, respond better to the diverse cultural needs of tourists. Assessing the various perceptions of the Chinese and American travellers towards Vietnamese hosts should be valuable, enabling the salient attributes and the re-evaluated image to be incorporated into tourism marketing planning.

METHODOLOGY

The chapter reports part of a large empirical research project involving four samples identifying the cultural differences between Asian and Western visitors in Vietnam. The quantitative survey has investigated Chinese and American tourists with regard to their perceptions of service provider attributes and performances. Interviews were undertaken with 235 Chinese and 170 US tourists.

Questionnaire Design

Self-completion questionnaires are widely regarded as generating the most reliable responses, since respondents have the opportunity to review the completed questionnaire or revisit questions that were not initially answered. Once the researchers had identified themselves, respondents were provided with information about the intent and content of the survey. Respondents were assured that the survey was anonymous, confidential and voluntary. All questionnaires were returned, whether complete or incomplete. The interview was designed to solicit a wide range of information. The structured interview-based questionnaire attempted to capture complex group measurement of Chinese and American tourist socio-demographics, travel characteristics, cultural values and perceptions of service. Most questions were identical for the two samples in order to facilitate comparison. The questionnaire composed consisted of four parts:

- The first part collected socio-demographic and travel characteristics information from the two respondent groups.
- The second part of the questionnaire drew upon Rokeach's Value Survey (RVS). The RVS (Rokeach, 1973) was chosen as the most appropriate means of measuring human values because of its widespread recognition as a reliable and valid measurement of cultural values (Kamakura and Mazzon, 1991). Using a 6-point scale, respondents were asked to rate 18 terminal and 18 instrumental values, with 1 indicating 'Completely Unimportant' and 6 meaning 'Extremely Important'.

- The third part of the questionnaire measured perceptions of service and consisted of twenty-nine items. This part drew upon Parasuraman et al's 10 service quality criteria (1985, 1988). The ten dimensions composed of tangibles, reliability, responsiveness, communication, credibility, security, competence, courtesy, understanding, knowing the customer, and access. A number of items were adapted from Parasuraman et al.'s (1985) study on service quality dimensions in recognition that they cover the most important service quality criteria. However, the SERVQUAL instrument was initially designed for a generic measurement of service quality and does not make adequate provision for the criteria contributing to the overall quality of tourism services. The original scale was modified and supplemented using additional categories that could measure both the Chinese and American Western perceptions of service quality. Some additional variables were added to the questionnaire such as knowledge of American culture and customs and knowledge of Chinese history and culture. It was predicted that these variables would be useful for measuring tourist perceptions of the attributes and performance of Vietnamese service providers. The measuring items for the perceptions of service were rated on a 6-point scale according to their importance with 1 representing 'Completely Unimportant' and 6 to an item rated as 'Extremely Important'.

The first draft of the questionnaire was piloted among a group of forty American and Chinese subjects (20 in each group) who had previously visited Vietnam. The aim of the pilot study was to determine appropriate questions for measuring the relevant concepts and to assess the reliability and validity of the questionnaire. Subjects were asked to evaluate the questionnaire in terms of meaningfulness, style, clarity and difficulty or ease of completion. The questionnaire was originally designed in English and was then translated into Chinese by a professional translator. Finally it was back translated from Chinese into English to achieve equivalence of concepts. The two versions were used to survey both the American and Chinese tourists.

Data Collection

The full survey was conducted between 2003 and 2004, and the questionnaires took respondents 20 minutes to complete. The Chinese and American tourists were approached in locations within Vietnam, where large concentrations of Western and Asian tourists are to be found. These included major attractions, restaurants, shops, hotels, bars in the cities of Ho Chi Minh City, Danang, Hoi An, Hue, Hai Phong and Hanoi. One hundred and ninety questionnaires were collected from American respondents. Twenty cases had missing data and 170 responses were fully completed and usable. Two hundred and sixty questionnaires were collected from the Chinese tourists. Twenty-five cases had missing data and 235 responses were complete and usable.

Methods of Analysis

Version 12 of SPSS was used for the purposes of data input. A descriptive analysis was used to analyse respondent's socio demographic and travel characteristics. A Principal Components Analysis with orthogonal varimax rotation was used to determine the major cultural dimensions and any key indicators where the American and Chinese cultures appeared to differ. The varimax approach was used in order 1) to maximize the variance of factor loadings across variables and for each factor to make high loadings higher and low loadings lower; 2) to achieve a clearer separation of the factors; and 3) to identify the variables most representative of these factors (with the highest loadings).

RESULTS

Socio-Demographic Profiles of American and Chinese Tourists

The socio-demographic profiles of American and Chinese tourists are illustrated in Table 2. These highlight age, gender, education and occupation differences between the two respondent samples.

The gender distribution differed between the Chinese sample (53.6% of males and 46.4% of females), and the American sample (45.9% of males and 54.1% of females). The age of the American sample is close to normally distributed with a tendency towards older age. Approximately 70% of respondents were aged between 39 and 60 years. The Chinese sample tended to be younger with more than 67% being under 38 years old, 29.3% between 39 to 52 and only 3.4 % between 53 to more than 60.

The American sample was generally more highly educated than the Chinese sample. A high proportion of the former hold a university degree (28.2%) or post-graduate degree (23.5%). These results indicate that over 51% of US respondents had a university or post-graduate degree compared with 48.3% who had a college or high school qualification. In the case of the Chinese sample, 32.8% of respondents had completed a university degree, 11.9% had post-graduate degrees followed by those with college degree (27.2%) and 28.1% of those with high school and primary education.

A wide range of occupational groupings was evident within the Chinese and American samples. Amongst the American respondents, the largest group (45.9%) consisted of retirees with 31.8% being professionals followed by administrators and managers (20.6%), technicians (11.2%), tradespersons (9.4%), students (7.6%) and labourers or workers (5.9%). In the case of Chinese sample, the largest group of respondents was tradespersons (21.3%), followed by technicians (19.1%), professionals (18.3%), labourer or worker (16.6%), manager or administrator (14%) and student (9.4%). It is interesting to note that the number of retired Chinese is very low with only 1.3 % of the total sample compared with their American counterparts (45.9%).

Table 2. Socio- Demographic Profile of Chinese and American Tourists

Socio-Demographic Profile	Chinese Tourists (N=235)	American Tourists (N=170)
Gender		
Male	53.6	45.9
Female	46.4	54.1
Age		
18-24	16.2	12.4
25-31	26.0	7.10
32-38	25.1	10.6
39-45	15.7	17.1
46-52	13.6	20.0
53-59	1.70	8.80
More than 60	1.70	24.1
Education		
Primary School	5.50	00.0
High School	22.6	22.4
Non Degree (College)	27.2	25.9
University Degree	32.8	28.2
Post-Graduate	11.9	23.5
Occupation		
Manager / Administrator	14.0	20.6
Professional	18.3	7.60
Student	9.40	9.40
Tradesperson	21.3	11.2
Technician	19.1	5.90
Laborer / Worker	16.6	13.5
Retired	1.30	45.9

Source: Survey Results 2004

The Travel Characteristics of American and Chinese Tourists

The following section outlines respondent travel characteristics such as travel purpose, travel mode, travel companion, length of stay, number of trips to Vietnam and the use of different information sources for preparing their holiday. Table 3 provides a breakdown of the responses.

The majority of respondents travelled to Vietnam for pleasure purposes (74.7% of American respondents and 50.6% of Chinese respondents). Besides that, a high percentage of Chinese respondents travelled to Vietnam for business purpose (46.4%). The Americans visited Vietnam with other purposes such as visiting friends and relatives (9.4%), education (8.2%), business (5.3%) and conference (2.4%).

In response to the question "How many times have you holidayed in Vietnam?", the majority of respondents reported that their holidays to Vietnam were their first trips with 60% of Chinese tourists and 58.8% of American tourists responding in this way. The Chinese sample was also higher for second time visits to Vietnam (23.4%) in comparison with their American counterparts (21.2%).

The majority of respondents used an escorted tour (88.9% of Chinese respondents and 58.8% of American respondents). Given the sampling frame, it is not surprising that respondents demonstrated a strong preference for escorted tours. A similar tendency for group rather than for individual travel is evident in the case of other Western and Asian outbound travel markets to Vietnam. A desire for fewer hassles, convenience and reasonable prices may be reasons for choosing escorted tours amongst respondents. When selling package tours to Chinese and American tourists, tour operators may be well advised to emphasize the benefits of fewer problems, greater convenience and reasonable prices. In addition, they might promote values such as quality service and variety of tour options to increase their market share.

A relatively high proportion of American tourists (41.2%) and only 11.1% of Chinese travelled to Vietnam as free independent travellers. Although the percentage of Chinese independent travellers is very low in comparison with Americans, it still shows the growing interest of independent travel to Vietnam. The opening up of Vietnam to individual travellers in the early 1990s offered a rare opportunity to witness both the speed and adaptation processes of development of low-budget accommodation infrastructure. A significant number of backpackers discovered Vietnam as a newly accessible destination. The relatively high percentage of independent travel has been probably the result of visa relaxation over the last few years, especially during the promotion of Vietnam as a "destination for the New Millennium". Such features may guide the Vietnamese tourism industry when marketing or promoting their products. It may be worth emphasising the backpacker segment which allows tourists to explore, sightsee and undertake a variety of activities independently.

With regard to party composition, 57.6% of respondents travelled alone while more than 35.3% travelled with two persons as a couple and 7.1% with three persons as with friends in the case of American tourists. For Chinese group tourists, 57.5% of the respondents were travelling with four, five and six persons as with friends or colleagues while 19.6% of respondents traveled with two persons as a couple, and 14.9% of respondents with three persons as with family. The interpersonal relationship that respondents enjoy with family and friends during their trip, and the friendly relationship created with others whilst on holiday were also another interesting experience reported by many respondents. Escorted tours would usefully feature activities that allow tourists the opportunity to enjoy the company of fellow travelers.

The typical duration of American vacations to Vietnam was two to three weeks. Some 36.5% of respondents holidayed in Vietnam more than two weeks, 32.4% for one to two weeks, 11.2% for more than four weeks, 8.8% for between two to three weeks, 7.6% for between three weeks to four weeks and 3.5% for less than one week. The duration of trip seems to be longer than expected relative to other long haul destinations. The duration of Chinese vacations in Vietnam was predominantly one week (71.9%), 20.4% from one week to two weeks and only 7.8% from over two weeks to four weeks. As China is very close to Vietnam, it is not surprising to see a high percentage of Chinese tourists are visiting Vietnam for the second or third time and have a short length of stay since they can access to the country conveniently across the border by train or by bus.

Regarding information, the majority of Chinese respondents (27.1%) used information supplied by their families and relatives, though most also used other sources. Some 22.3%

had used media, 13.4% used travel agents, 13.0% used previous travel experience to Vietnam, 9.3% used newspaper, 7.5% used Internet and 7.3% used guidebooks. In the case of American respondents, (20.5%) cited Internet as the most important source of information, though most had also used other sources. Some 19.1% had used guidebooks while 13.6% used travel agents. Other sources included 12.3% who obtained information from their families and relatives, and 12.3% from newspaper, 11.1% from with previous travel experience to Vietram, and 11.0% from the media. The results show that Chinese and American travellers have accessed to a wide range of sources of information when preparing for a holiday in Vietnam. These findings are in line with other studies which indicate that tourists who plan their travel well in advance usually search for detailed information. The sources of information and types of promotional tools have an influence over destinations images (Telisman-Kosuta, 1989; Butler, 1990; Bojanic, 1991; Gartner, 1993). The outcomes confirm that the information obtained from family, relatives and friends, media (in the case of Chinese) and that the Internet, guidebooks and travel agents (in the case of American) were the most prominent means of forming the perceptions of Vietnam.

The above evaluation has shown that there are significant differences in the socio-demographic profiles of the two groups of tourists. The Chinese and American tourists travelling to Vietnam exhibit distinctive socio demographic characteristics that need to be considered when tour operators are designing new products. The research has indicated that a preponderance of Chinese respondents are in the younger age group and are in the workforce. These respondents can afford to travel overseas as they possess discretionary income relative to older and retired Chinese people. Nearly 60% of Chinese respondents are tradespersons, technicians and labourers or workers. By way of contrast, the American counterparts tend to be older and more educated. This result is in overall agreement with the study undertaken by PATA (1999) which pointed out that older and retired American can afford overseas holidays. Vietnamese inbound tour operators should design appropriate types of products that could satisfy the needs for each market, ensuring that there is minimal risk and that comfort and heath considerations are paramount. This recommendation is confirmed by the work of Collins and Tisdell (2000) who also found that older travellers tend to be less risk-taking and more concerned about heath and comfort than travellers in general.

The emerging travel profiles have also highlighted the substantial differences between Chinese and American tourists in term of travel purpose, length of stay, number of trips to Vietnam and particularly with travel mode, travel companion and the use of different information sources for preparing their holiday. From a marketing perspective there is evidence that different cultures do attach different levels of significance to travel mode, travel companion and particularly the use of information. These findings have illustrated the impact of cultural values on each nationality. Coming from a collectivist culture, the Chinese appear to prefer travelling in group, using information supplied by their families and relatives, while Americans with their individualist culture, favour more with individual travel and enjoyment, and used more information accessed from the Internet.

These outcomes are in line with the findings from other research which has indicated that tourists from different nationalities and cultural backgrounds use different types of information and with varying frequency. For instance, Uysal et al. (1990) discovered that the information search behaviour between German, French, British and Japanese tourists are different when they travel to the USA. Similarly, Gursoy and Chen (2000) reported that the information search behaviour of British, German French tourists is also different.

Table 3. Travel Characteristics of Chinese and American Tourists

Travel Characteristics	Chinese Tourists (N=235)	American Tourists (N=170)
Purpose of Trip To Vietnam		
Holiday	50.6	74.7
Education	0.00	8.20
Conference	0.00	2.40
Business	46.4	5.30
Visiting Friends and Relatives	6.00	9.40
Sources of Information about Vietnam		
Family/ Relatives/ Friends	27.1	12.3
Media	22.3	11.0
Previous experience	13.0	11.1
Guide books	7.30	19.1
Travel agents	13.4	13.6
Newspaper	9.30	12.3
Internet	7.50	20.5
Number of Trips to Vietnam		
First time	60.0	58.8
Second time	23.4	21.2
Third time	12.8	11.2
Fourth time	1.70	3.50
Fifth time	1.70	2.40
Six time and more	0.40	2.90
Length of Holiday in Vietnam		
Less than one week	71.9	3.50
From one week to two weeks	20.4	32.4
More than two weeks	2.60	36.5
From two weeks to three weeks	2.60	8.80
From three weeks to four weeks	0.90	7.60
More than four weeks	1.70	11.2
Travel Mode to Vietnam		
Escorted Tour	88.9	58.8
Independently	11.1	41.2
Travel Companion		
Alone	8.10	57.6
Two Person	19.6	35.3
Three Persons	14.9	7.10
Four Persons	13.2	0.00
Five Persons	17.9	0.00
Six Persons	26.4	0.00

Source: Survey Results 2004

Results of the Principal Components Analysis

A Principal Components Analysis with varimax rotation was conducted in an attempt to establish the dimensions of the identified cultural differences and any representative group variables which might be expected to cause dysfunction between population cultures. The information contained within the 36 cultural value variables, and the 29 perceptions of services variables which differed between Chinese tourists and American tourists were summarised and then transformed into a smaller set of new composite dimensions. These revised dimensions define the fundamental constructs which are assumed to underlie the differing variables. A variable was included within a factor in instances where the factor loading was reported as been greater than 0.50. As a general rule, loadings of 0.50 or greater were considered to be significant. The fairly large number of factors which were extracted necessitated the larger size of the loadings on later factors to be considered significant. Dimensions with Eigenvalues of greater than 1 were considered to be significant.

Cultural Values

For the purposes of measuring cultural values, the Measure of Sampling Adequacy is 0.791 in the case of Chinese tourists and 0.649 in the case of American tourists. This confirmed that the analysis of particular samples was significant.

In the case of the Chinese sample, 11 factors were extracted with an Eigenvalue of greater than 1, comprising 63.71% of the explained variance. Factor F7 was eliminated from consideration since it could cause problems with interpretation. Three factors F8, F10 and F11 were eliminated from analysis because their definition and correlation was confined to a single variable. The seven-factor solutions (F1, F2, F3, F4, F5, F6 and F9) for the 36 cultural values variables in the Chinese sample were retained for further analysis since they were well defined by two or more variables. The seven-factor solution identified in Table 4 can be summarized as follows:

- Factor 1: *Interpersonal Relationship* refers to variables that describe indicators associated with having true friendship, a world of beauty, loving, a sense of accomplishment, an exciting life and salvation.
- Factor 2: *Competence* refers to personal meaning in life such as being intellectual, independent, independent, mature love and imaginative.
- Factor 3: *Ability-Cheerfulness* refers to variables that describe the cues associated with being capable, cheerful, forgiving, courageous and broaded-minded.
- Factor 4: *Integrity* reflects the inner cues associated with being honest and helpful.
- Factor 5: *Politeness* consists of variables reflecting the importance of to be polite and responsible.
- Factor 6: *Obedience* consists of variables reflecting the importance of being obedient and self-respect.
- Factor 9: *Safety-Security* consists of variables reflecting the importance of being self-controlled and maintaining the security for family.

Table 4. Results of the Varimax Rotated Component Matrix for Cultural Values

Chinese Tourists (N=235)	LD	American Tourists (N=170)	LD
KMO= 0.791 Bartlett'sTest = 2931.984 Sig. = 0.000		KMO = 0.649 Bartlett'sTest = 1313.241 Sig. = 0.000	
F1: Interpersonal Relationship True friendship A World of Beauty Loving A Sense of Accomplishment An Exciting Life Salvation (saved, eternal life) E%V = 10.68	 0.70 0.62 0.62 0.60 0.58 0.57	**F1: Equality Accomplishment** Equality A Sense of Accomplishment Helpful A World of Beauty E%V = 7.73	 0.70 0.69 0.64 0.55
F2: Competence Intellectual Independent Logical Mature Love Imaginative E%V = 10.18	 0.78 0.75 0.61 0.55 0.54	**F3: Esteem-Personal Contendness** Freedom A World of Peace E%V = 5.50	 0.70 0.66
F3: Cheerfulness-Forgiveness Capable Cheeerful Forgiving Courageous Broaded-minded E%V = 9.14	 0.78 0.75 0.64 0.63 0.52	**F4: Integrity** Self-controlled Honest E%V = 5.13	 0.84 0.51
F4: Integrity Helpful Honest E%V = 5.60	 0.66 0.57	**F5: Competence** Intellectual Logical E%V = 4.92	 0.77 0.65
F5: Politeness Polite Responsible E%V = 4.59	 0.83 0.56	**F6: Forgiving** Forgiving Salvation E%V = 4.48	 0.73 0.71
F6: Obedience Obedient Self-respect (self-esteem) E%V = 4.27	 0.50 0.50	**F8: Sense of Self** A Comfortable Life Responsible E%V = 4.20	 0.69 0.65
F9: Safety-Security Self-controlled Family security E%V = 3.94	 0.76 0.54	**F13: Idealism-Quality of Life** Independent Pleasure E%V =3.84	 0.79 0.60

Source: Survey Results 2004

Within the American sample, 14 factors were found with an Eigenvalue of greater than 1, comprising 65.87% of explained variance. Four factors were subsequently eliminated from the analysis (F7, F11, F12 and F14) because each was defined with only one variable. Three factors were also eliminated from analysis (F2, F9 and F10) as it was anticipated that they could cause interpretation problems. The seven-factor solution for the 36 cultural values variables in the American sample (F1, F3, F4, F5, F6, F8 and F13) were retained for further analysis as they were well defined by two or more variables. The following labels have been applied to the factors identified in Table 4.

- Factor 1: *Equality and Accomplishment* refers to variables that describe the cues associated with self-fulfillment through equal opportunity, a sense of accomplishment contributing to society and a wish to work for the welfare of others in a world of beauty of nature and arts.
- Factor 3: *Esteem and Personal Contendness* refers to personal meaning in life such as exercising a freedom of choice, having affection and tenderness with others and a desire for a world that free of war and conflict.
- Factor 4: *Integrity* reflects the inner cues associated with being honest, sincere and truthful as well as being self-controlled and self-disciplined.
- Factor 5: *Competence* refers to variables that describe indicators associated with intelligence, logic and consistency.
- Factor 6: *Forgiveness* consists of variables reflecting the importance of a willingness of forgive others and the search for eternal life (salvation).
- Factor 8: *Sense of Self* refers to personal meaning including a search for a prosperous and comfortable life and the attitude to be dependable, reliable and responsible.
- Factor 13: *Idealism and Quality of Life* reflects the inner cues associated with being independent or self-reliant, and a search for an enjoyable leisurely life.

Perceptions of Service

In terms of service perceptions, the Kaiser-Meyer-Olkin Measure of Sampling Adequacy resulted in a figure of 0.913 for Chinese tourists and 0.908 for American tourists. This provided assurance that the analysis was significant for the sample given.

Four factors have been extracted for the Chinese sample with an Eigenvalue of greater than 1, comprising 57.65% of explained variance. Factor F5 was eliminated from analysis since it was anticipated that it could cause interpretation problems. The four-factor solution (F1, F2, F3 and F4) for the 29 perceptions of service variables in the Chinese sample was retained for further analysis. The four-factor solution identified in Table 5 can be summarized as follows:

- Factor 1: *Promp-Punctual Service and Smart* reflects the ability of hosts to behave toward tourists in a specific way indicative that they are able to solve problems quickly, to perform punctual service and to provide accurate information. It also reflects that hosts are responsive to tourist needs, able to answer all the questions requested by guests. It also refers to the intangible cues associated with hosts' smart appearance.

- Factor 2: *Intercultural Competence and Well Mannered* relates to the ability of hosts to anticipate tourists' needs, to be familiar with guest culture and customs in order to offer personalized attention, to be familiar with guest culture and customs in order to offer personalized attention to tourists. This also entails the capacity of the host to understand tourists by being respectful and being able speak the foreign languages required for the relevant tourist market (Chinese language in this case).

- Factor 3: *Communicative* reflects tourist expectation that hosts are easy to talk to , easy to find when needed and are able to keep tourists informed.

- Factor 4: *Courtesy and Friendliness* refers tourist expectation that hosts are approachable and behave towards tourists with a polite, friendly and confident manner. It also required hosts' knowledge of their own history and culture.

Table 5. Rotated Component Matrix for Perceptions of Service

Chinese Tourists (N=235)	LD	American Tourists (N=170)	LD
KMO = 0.913 *Bartlett'sTest = 3466.463* *Sig. = 0.000*		*KMO = 0.908* *Bartlett'sTest = 3067.216* *Sig. = 0.000*	
F1: Prompt-Punctual Service-Smart		**F1: Understanding Tourists**	
Solve Problems Quickly	0.79	Give Adequate Explanations to Tourists	0.79
Capable of Performing Service	0.78	Keep Tourists Informed	0.69
Punctual-Perform Services On Time	0.75	Answer all Questions	0.63
Provide Accurate Information	0.73	Easy to find when needed	0.62
Responsive to Tourists' Needs	0.73	Listen to Tourists	0.61
Answer all Questions	0.72	Understand Western and Asian Tourists' Needs	0.61
Provide Prompt Service	0.65	Approachable	0.61
Neatly Dressed	0.52	Provide Accurate Information	0.55
		Solve Problems Quickly	0.50
E%V = 19.72		*E%V = 17.27*	
F2: Intercultural Competence-Well Mannered		**F2: Courtesy-Friendliness**	
Anticipate Western and Asian Tourists' Needs	0.70	Respectful	0.76
Know Asian and Western Culture and Customs	0.67	Considerate	0.75
Offer Individualized Attention to Tourists	0.63	Polite	0.73
Understand Western and Asian Tourists' Needs	0.62	Treat Tourists as Guests	0.62
Respectful	0.59	Confident	0.61
Speak English, French, Chinese Languages	0.59	Friendly	0.55
		Easy to talk to Tourists	0.51
E%V = 13.18		*E%V = 16.22*	
F3: Communicative		**F3: Responsive-Punctual Service**	
Easy to talk to Tourists	0.74	Responsive to Tourists' Needs	0.85
Easy to find when needed	0.70	Helpful	0.79
Keep Tourists Informed	0.59	Punctual, Perform Services On Time	0.75
		Capable of Performing Service	0.74
		Provide Prompt Service	0.55
E%V = 10.08		*E%V = 14.67*	

Table 5. Rotated Component Matrix for Perceptions of Service (Continued)

Chinese Tourists (N=235)	LD	American Tourists (N=170)	LD
F4: Courtesy-Friendliness		F4: Intercultural Competence	
Approachable	0.63	Know Asian and Western Culture and Customs	0.79
Polite (Well-Mannered)	0.61	Anticipate Western and Asian Tourists' Needs	0.60
Friendly	0.56	Offer Individualized Attention to Tourists	0.59
Confident	0.54	Speak English, French, Chinese Languages	0.59
Know Vietnamese History and Culture	0.51		
E%V = 9.34		E%V = 7.97	

Source: Survey Results 2004

Six factors have been extracted for the American sample with an Eigenvalue of greater than 1, comprising 64.76% of explained variance. Two factors were eliminated from the analysis (F5 and F6) because they were only defined with one variable each. The four-factor solution (F1, F2, F3 and F4) for the 29 perceptions of service variables in the American sample was retained for further analysis. The four-factor solution identified in Table 5 can be summarized as follows:

- Factor 1: Un*derstanding Tourists* entails the capacity of the host to understand tourists by giving adequate explanations, providing accurate information, keeping tourists informed and answering all questions. It also expects that the hosts are approachable, easy to find when needed and are able to solve problems quickly.
- Factor 2: *Courtesy and Friendliness* describes the hosts' ability to treat tourists as guests, to behave towards tourists in a respectful and polite manner. It entails the need to be considerate, confident, friendly and to talk to tourists with easy.
- Factor 3: *Responsive and Punctual Service* reflects the hosts' ability to behave toward tourists in a specific way indicative that they are responsive to tourist needs, able to perform and provide prompt service.
- Factor 4: *Intercultural Competence* relates to the ability of hosts to speak the foreign languages required for the relevant tourist market that (English in this case) to be familiar with guest culture and customs in order to offer personalized attention and anticipate the needs of each tourist market being handled.

DISCUSSION

Chinese and American Cultural Values

A significant aspect of China is its long cultural and national history. Throughout the long Chinese history, the Confucian ideology has been firmly established as an undeniable system governing nearly all aspects of Chinese lives. Based on Confucian philosophy, the conception of "Wu Lun" (the five cardinal relationships) is highly valued in Chinese society as the stability of society is based on unequal relationships between people. This concept invocated the ideal social order between a king and his subjects, father and son, husband and wife, older brother and younger brothers, and among friends governs all aspects of human life and behaviour for the Chinese. Consequently, the *Interpersonal Relationships* between people are based on mutual and complementary obligations: the junior partner owes the senior respect; the senior owes the junior partner protection and consideration (Hofstede and Bond, 1988; Lau and Kuan, 1988).

In Chinese culture an individual is not complete unless defined by a person's surrounding relations. This is similar to the Confucian principle of a person being defined by his or her kinship networks and the Confucian value of interpersonal harmony and knowledge and acceptance of one's place in society and family (Uba, 1994). As can be seen by this definition of the self, the Chinese self is integrally related to one's *Interpersonal relationships;* the importance of others means that a person adjusts his or her actions in accordance with external expectations or social norms, rather than with internal wishes or personal integrity, so that he or she can function as an integral part of the social network (Yang, 1981). *Gan Qing, Ren Qing* and *Lian* are considered as the three major interpersonal concepts in the Chinese society. *Gan Qing* is similar to the concept of "interpersonal emotions," but it also represents mutual good feelings, empathy, friendship and support, and love between two people without sexual connotations. *Ren qing* represents another important dimension of interpersonal transactions in the Chinese culture. Similar to the definition *of Gan qing,* "human feeling" is the literal translation *of Ren qing;* however, *Ren qing* also involves a person's natural affective responses and interpersonal resources (Gabrenya and Hwang, 1996). *Ren qing* can be given and taken as interpersonal resources, which helps to build a relational bond between the parties. The virtue of *Xiao* (filial piety) is based on this concept of reciprocating *Ren qing.* A child owes his or her parents *Ren qing* for conceiving and raising him or her (Gao, 1996). This feeling of indebtedness serves as a control mechanism in dictating a Chinese person's behaviour within a family.

The traditional values that demonstrate a strong interpersonal focus in Chinese culture include maintaining harmony and the Confucian concept of the Golden Mean in every *Interpersonal Relationship*. Golden Mean refers to avoiding confrontation in a situation of potential controversy. In other words, one should not stubbornly hold on to opposing opinions but should avoid confrontations and achieve moderation (Chu, Hayashi and Akuto, 1995). Moreover, *Obedience* and deference to authority is a behavioural expression of maintaining interpersonal harmony. Although seemingly unrelated to interpersonal orientation, deference to authority and following the Golden Mean are very much tied to interpersonal harmony in the Chinese culture. This is consistent with what Gabrenya and Hwang (1996) have referred to as the "harmony within hierarchy" that characterizes many Confucian societies. Therefore, behaving according to the roles of hierarchical positions is also how Chinese display, enhance, and protect the image of their hierarchical position and maintain the status quo and harmony in the society (Chu, Hayashi and Akuto, 1995). These Chinese interpersonal cultural norms and the consciousness of hierarchies and harmony maintenance are in stark contrast to the American values of independence, competition, and equal rights.

Predominantly influenced by Confucianism, Chinese culture also emphasizes the value of education and a desire for accomplishment. Scholarship is the most important criterion for people in the highest social class as it brings power, prestige, and wealth (Hsu, 1972). Virtue with regard to people's tasks in life consists of working hard and trying to acquire education, skills and *Competence* and not spending more than necessary, being patient, and persevering, moderation is enjoined in ail things (Chiu, 1990). This is in line with Feather's (1986) study which reported that the Chinese assigned more importance to respect, hard work, scholarship wisdom, being capable, imagination, intellect, and logic.

Confucianism advocates a common set of presumptions and values. It values *Safety and Security*. It emphasizes an obligation to family therefore Chinese life is centered around the extended family which is important in all major life events. Very close relationships are maintained between all the members of the family and all its members financially support the family. Family affairs and security is a primary concern of all its members. People support respect for parents, tradition, duty, obligations, and the getting of wisdom. As a result, the Americans who are taught to be independent and self-reliant might not understand the Chinese type of family life. Confucianism also gives emphasis to *Integrity and Politeness*. It encourages people to work hard, be responsible, be knowledgeable, be self-esteem and self-controlled and help others but places a lower emphasis on personal advancement. This is in line with Hsu's (1972) study which reported that people are more emotionally restrained, situation-oriented, and more concerned with appropriate behaviour in relation to others. They are more socially and psychologically dependent on others and they form a big network of relationships.

In Chinese society, the element of conformity is constantly emphasized under the influence of collectivism. The priority of the group as opposed to the individual's interest gives birth to the strong notion of conformity (Bond and Hwang, 1986). The importance of *Cheerfulness and Forgiveness,* of keeping harmony in interpersonal relations, both within and outside the family, seriously limits any expression of hostility and aggressiveness. Compliance to social pressure and norms is encouraged at all times. Another product of collectivism and high-power distance is the notion of harmony. The value *Zhong wong* or *Ho* (Golden Mean or harmony) is the concept in all relationships between nature and humans and among fellow humans. If people adhered to the doctrine of the Golden Mean they would achieve the desired and harmonious balance, which was essential for a harmonious society. Therefore, the central thrust of *Li* (propriety and tempered human behaviour) actually is the achievement and maintenance of *Ho* (Chiu, 1992). Thus, to achieve *Ho* among humans, an adequate Chinese adult must conform to the demands of *Li* and *Hsiao* (filial piety) in all forms of interpersonal relationships as a manifestation of having the cultivation of *Jen* (humanism).

A by-product of conformity and the need for social acceptance is the notion of saving face (*Lian*). Face is an image of self-delineation in terms of approved social attributes (Bond and Hwang, 1986). The concept of saving face represents another way that a Chinese person's behaviour may be regulated in an interpersonal context. In Chinese society, inappropriate behaviour often results in negative comments and loss of face in one's community. The need for face, therefore, helps to dictate how a person behaves. Chinese people are particularly concerned with losing face not only for themselves but also for other people (Chiu, 1992). For instance, a person would constantly monitor his or her own behaviour to follow social norms such as being filial to one's elderly relatives; deferring to the male authority in the family, typically the father; maintaining a harmonious relationship between husband and wife. Otherwise, one may encounter ridicule and would bring loss of face to one's family. The family is the prototype of all social organizations. A person is not primarily an individual; rather, he or she is a member of a family. Children should learn to restrain themselves, to overcome their individuality so as to maintain the harmony in the family (Bond and Wang, 1983; Ko et al., 1990). For that reason, *Cheerfulness and Forgiveness* is very important value in Chinese society in order to keep harmony and to save face amongst people.

In contrast to Chinese people, the Americans exhibit a Western mindset and *Equality-Accomplishment* is ranked as most important. American society is relatively egalitarian and values achievement. Social recognition is linked to the need to work hard, demonstrating capability and logic. These values are perceived in terms of individual freedom and happiness, consistent with the conclusion that Americans are more achievement oriented (Lipset, 1963). They have a high need for achievement and want to excel (McClelland, 1981). They believe that all people have a right to succeed in life and be materially well off. They believe in another chance, achievement and goals attainment (Samovar et al., 1991). Personal fulfilment is achieved through dedication to their job and performing to the best of their ability. Accomplishment is associated with hard work and capability and social recognition is attained through hard work and personal achievement. They value humanitarianism and egalitarian relationships between people (Dodd, 1995).

Americans attach considerable importance to having *Esteem-Personal Contendness, Integrity* and *Idealism-Quality of Life*. These values can be found in Western societies more generally and in the United States in particular. Recognition of these values could derive from the emphasis on the individual and from the individual's need to define himself or herself independently of a group or collective. The Chinese type of family orientation is seldom understood by Americans who are taught to be self-reliant and independent. They are concerned about their individual feelings, comfort, needs, and responsibilities. They focus on materialistic and hedonistic values such as comfort, enjoyment, fun and pleasure. They are particularly concerned with their personal moral responsibility for actions. This is in line with Dodd's (1995) study on American cultural determinants, which identified a strong emphasis on individualism, individual opinions, individual creativity and achievement. Americans value personal freedom, independence, directness, honesty, work, time, success and material well-being. They attach great importance to learning individuality, independence, self-motivation and an achievement orientation. They think that human nature can be changed and education is an important element in improving human nature (Jandt, 1998).

The findings of the present research indicate that Chinese and American tourists attach particular importance to *Competence*. Although they rank the factors differently, similarities are evident between the two groups, possibly attributable to the strong impact of the Confucian and Protestant faiths. For both American and Chinese, personal fulfilment is achieved through dedication to their job and performing to the best of their ability. However, while the social recognition of the American culture is only attained through hard work and personal achievement; accomplishment in Chinese society is not only associated with hard work or collectivism but also relies strongly on good connection "*Quanxi*" amongst the group members. Moreover, the Chinese way of *logic* is intuitive and elastic. The Chinese believe in a universe-energy wisdom that can be gained by meditating, opening minds and communicating with the cosmic world. In contrast, the American way of thinking is objective and absolute. Traditionally, social status in China has been determined by having the right social position and belonging to the "right group" rather than financial wealth, as is the case in United States. Consequently, little emphasis was placed on intellectual achievements and professional competence in China. However, since the Open Door and Reform Policy in 1978 advocated by Deng XiaoPing, many Chinese have achieved upward social mobility by seizing the available opportunities and independence, financial success and intellectual achievement makes an absolute necessity in the Chinese life-style. In China today, status is gained from having attended a prestigious university, or being employed by a leading company or ministry. The high income that such employment guarantees also brings financial wealth. Consequently with the raised income and improved quality of life style, outbound travel from China has become a form of luxury consumption available to people who possess obtainable financial resources which enabling them to enjoy the benefits.

Chinese and American Perspectives Towards Service Quality

The American respondents expected precise and accurate information. In contrast, Vietnamese hosts are less concerned with providing such details and are not worried if problems are not resolved immediately. Coming from an egalitarian society with a strong focus on logic and science, the Americans are more direct and open. While the straightforwardness is absolute for them, truthfulness is relative for the Vietnamese hosts. For American tourists *Understanding Tourist* involves an expectation that their hosts are informative and adequate in the information provided, are trustworthy, approachable and easy to find when needed.

For the Vietnamese hosts, time is stretchable and as a result time commitments do not have to be kept. People are usually flexible about time, appointments and the provision of service. Except for the services offered in some 4 or 5 star hotels or resorts, most activities including the service provided by other sectors like restaurants and retail shops may occur over an extended time period, continuing for at least twice as long as the corresponding Western activity. This may be part of the concept in Vietnamese culture that being in a hurry and looking for quick solutions to problems is an indication of impatience. The Vietnamese style of perceiving time is more flexible and involves a more relaxed manner rather than the American idea of "time is money" and "a time and place for everything". For American guests, time commitments are important and must be kept. Therefore, *Responsive and Punctual Service* from the American perspective involves host responsiveness to tourist needs and the capability to perform and provide prompt service. The focus is on punctuality and efficiency of service provision responding to clients' needs in a satisfactory manner.

Relative to their American counterparts, Chinese tourists possess some similar cultural values as the Vietnamese, thought their concept of time is very different. Chinese people are concerned about punctuality. They expect people to be on time or early for meetings and appointments. They expect to adhere to a full, heavy schedule and get their best and as much as possible out of every activity. Being late is regarded as lacking concern for the other and is regarded as unprofessional. Their expectations towards the attributes and performance of Vietnamese service providers' are very high. *Prompt Service and Smart* involves an expectation amongst Chinese tourists that their hosts are capable of providing prompt service and solving problems quickly. This also relates to host responsiveness towards tourist needs. It entails the prompt response to tourist requests and implies the need to handle tourist queries promptly. This is different to the Vietnamese style of work which is more flexible, relaxed, and in which delays can sometimes be justified. Moreover, the traditional customs concerning physical appearance and appropriate dress are deeply embedded in Chinese culture with different styles, colours and materials that were strictly prescribed by law for different social classes. In Chinese culture the traditional customs concerning with physical appearance and appropriate dress are deeply embedded through different styles, colours and materials which at were strictly prescribed by law for different social classes. For this reason, Vietnamese hosts need to relate to tangible cues associated with the service such as professional physical appearance is considered as very important for Chinese tourists. However, this is in contrast to American culture in which clothing style is more casual and depends less on social position or age.

In Chinese society, a complex system of grading is evident based on age, occupations, and positions. This requires correct behaviour and respect to be shown towards all of higher social standing within the vertical social hierarchy. Within this highly complex system of deference to hierarchical authority, customary laws and standards specify how each community member should react to others, the nature and forms of obligations within and outside kin groups. Each age group must, for example, be addressed by the correct terminology and language. Therefore *Courtesy and Friendliness* according to Chinese tourists' expectations that they should being treated by hosts with a polite and well-mannered attitude as an expression of etiquette, but not only with the friendly and approachable manner. For Americans, certain principles of social stratification and age grading within Chinese and Vietnamese society may not be readily understood. Being accustomed to greater egalitarianism, Americans are more casual and their behaviour depends less on social position and age. Therefore, the American expectation of *Courtesy and Friendliness* involve being treated by their hosts with a friendly, considerate, confident and polite manner (as an expression of respect and kindness) but not with the politeness as an expression of etiquette.

Regarding *Intercultural Competence*, although American tourists enjoyed the distinctive Vietnamese culture, they were unhappy about the inability of Vietnamese to communicate with them in some retail shops or restaurants. As members of high uncertainty avoidance cultures, the Vietnamese worries about being exposed to language difficulties when serving foreign tourists. Beyond a certain point, this may become annoying for American visitors. For instance, the sellers follow every step of tourists in their shops as a signal of personalized attention to guests, but may appear as untrustworthy and adopting a pushy manner from the tourist perspective. Enquiries about people's age and earnings are acceptable in Vietnamese society and are viewed as signs of thoughtfulness. However, they are considered to be impolite in the individualist American culture where personal privacy is respected. For that reason, the inherent need to care about foreign visitors in Vietnamese culture results in a national responsibility for giving constant attention to and helping foreigners to cope with the different customs, to a degree that may become annoying for American tourists as they might feel uncomfortable when someone else decides about fulfilling their needs. As a result, it is imperative to have knowledge of guest cultures and languages amongst the Vietnamese hosts when responding to guest standards of behaviour and needs.

In contrast with their American counterparts, the *Intercultural Competence* according to Chinese tourist expectations is very different. They expected that their hosts are easy to find and easy to talk to them. As members of high uncertainty avoidance cultures, they expected that their hosts would be *Communicative* and able to speak with them respectfully and in a correct Chinese dialect. The importance of a person depends on the social position, age and gender. Social rank determines the manner in which people will be perceived and treated. Social respect is gained through status and age which are symbols of experience and wisdom. Respect and deference is given to authority and high hierarchy positions. This is in contrast to the egalitarian American society in which social recognition is gained through hard work and achievement.

Furthermore, coming from a society with dependent relationships such as China, people with lower social and economic standing are often dependent on others for security and protection. Therefore, Chinese tourists do not like to be left on their own and require constant care and attention from their hosts. As a result, the needs of Chinese guests must be anticipated, understood and fulfilled by Vietnamese hosts. This type of dependency does not occur among Americans. In an individualistic society such as the United States, people know best what their needs are and how these needs can be satisfied. The need to think and behave like individuals and to preserve one's privacy cannot be understood by the Vietnamese and Chinese societies because even the concept of privacy does not exist in these cultures.

CONCLUSIONS

The Principal components analysis was successfully used to determine whether or not the basic factoral structure of cultural differences between the Chinese and American tourists in term of the perceived importance of Vietnamese host attributes and performance. The research has clearly identified the existence of cultural differences between Chinese and American tourists and these form two distinct groups indicative of cultural values and perceptions of services. The variables that loaded significantly on the above dimensions are the key cultural determinants of perception towards the attributes and performances of the Vietnamese hosts from the Asian and Western guest perspectives.

The major cultural difference arises because the Chinese have been educated on the basis of Confucian thought. Most US residents have been brought up in a predominantly Protestant and Christian religious background. The cultural differences identified between the Chinese and American tourists are closely related to the findings of the literature and substantiate some popularly held views about cultural differences between Chinese and American tourists.

Tourism marketers would be well advised to consider American cultural differences affecting perception of service quality when marketing to other Western tourists. It is clear that Vietnamese tourism marketers cannot rely exclusively on perceptions of service quality such as Understanding Tourists, Courtesy and Friendliness, Responsive and Punctual Service and Intercultural Competence to address all Western tourists markets (American tourists) perceptions towards service quality. To influence American (or Western) tourist perception and satisfaction directly, marketers need to address such cultural values as Equality and

Accomplishment, Esteem and Personal Contendness, Integrity, Competence, Forgiveness, Sense of Self and Idealism and Quality of Life.

In the case of the Chinese market, there are several differences between how Chinese tourists and Vietnamese hosts perceive each other despite the obvious cultural similarities with Vietnam. Serving the Chinese market is a great challenge for Vietnam's tourism industry. Firstly, cross-cultural communication and interaction problems occur between hosts and guests as a result of the Chinese language dialects. Secondly, Vietnamese hosts still lack knowledge about human resources training and management as well as the amenities necessary for catering such an emerging but fast booming tourist market like China. As a result, tourism marketers would be well advised to consider Chinese cultural differences on perception of service quality when marketing to other Eastern tourist market. It is obvious that Vietnamese tourism marketers cannot rely exclusively on perceptions of service quality such as Prompt Service and Smart, Intercultural Competence and Well Mannered, Communicative and Courtesy and Friendliness to generate Asian tourists markets (Chinese tourists) perceptions towards service quality. Marketers can best influence Chinese (or Asian) tourist perceptions and satisfaction directly through issues associated with cultural values such as Interpersonal Relationship, Competence, Cheerfulness and Forgiveness, Integrity, Politeness, Obedience and Safety and Security.

The various cultural differences and similarities identified between Chinese and American societies must be considered in tourism marketing strategies because the by-products of these cultural differences are perceptions which determine tourist behaviour and decision-making. In the case of developing countries such as Vietnam and its neighbours, cultural training programs may assist service providers to understand their own culture and the culture of the tourist generating countries and to appreciate cultural differences. Such cultural awareness will enhance host understanding to develop a good understanding amongst international tourists from different cultural backgrounds. This should minimise any negative perceptions and dissatisfactions occurring because of misunderstandings or misconceptions of tourist psychological needs and experiences.

A number of conclusions can be drawn from the findings of the study. Firstly, the results do support the notion that there are cultural differences between the Chinese and American populations in the tourism context in comparison with the outcomes from previous studies. Secondly, the study indicates that cultural differences are very useful constructs for international tourism promotion since they can provide correct criteria for targeting and positioning new tourists markets. Consequently, tourism marketers should take account of differences in cultural values of international tourists in order to identify the niche markets appropriate to their tourism products and services. For the developing tourism destinations particularly in Asia and Africa, it is necessary to go beyond the established socio-demographic and travel characteristics. Nationality could be used as the most controversial segmentation variable for creating specific market profiles, and for determining how a destination should be positioned or repositioned itself in order to make it appeal towards the international tourist markets. Based on the noted reasons, the current study could contribute to the body of knowledge concerning cross-cultural differences between Eastern and Western tourist markets.

As the extent of influences varies from market to market, it would be useful to replicate the study on samples of various Asian and Western nationalities to determine these influences and form a basis for appropriate promotional strategies. An important implication of this finding is that it becomes increasingly important for tourism marketers to have knowledge of cultural differences in values to create service quality perceptions. This may in turn lead directly to overall satisfaction. The significance of the study lies in highlighting the need for further exploration the cultural differences amongst international tourists from diverse cultures and developing culture-oriented marketing strategies.

REFERENCES

Adler, N. J. (1997). *International Dimensions of Organisational Behavior*. Cincinnati, Ohio: International Thomson Publishing.

Agrusa, J. (1994). *The analysis of "Since the life of the U.S. embargo: The tourism potential of American Vietnam War Veterans in Vietnam"*. Paper presented at the 1994 STTE Conference Proceedings, Lexington.

Armstrong, R., Mok, C., and Go, F. (1997). The Importance of Cross-Cultural Expectations in the Measurement of Service Quality Perceptions in the Hotel industry. *International Journal of Hospitality Management, 16*(2).

Befu, H. (1971). *Japan: An Anthropological Introduction*. New York: Harper and Row.

Bennett, P. D., and Kassarjian, H. J. (1972). *Consumer Behavior*. Englewood Cliffs: New York: Prentice Hall.

Boissevain, J., and Inglott, P. (1979). Tourism in Malta. In E. DeKadt (Ed.), *Tourism: Passport to Development?* Oxford: Oxford University Press.

Bojanic, D. C. (1996). Consumer perception of price, value and satisfaction in the hotel industry: An exploratory study. *Journal of Hospitality and Leisure Marketing, 14*(1), 5-22.

Bond, M. H., and Wang, S. H. (1983). Aggressive behaviour in Chinese society: The problem of maintaining order and harmony. In A. P. Goldstein and M. Segall (Eds.), *Global perspectives on aggression* (pp. 58-74). New York.

Bond, M. H., and Hwang, K. K. (1986). The social psychology of Chinese people. In M. H. Bond (Ed.), *The psychology of the Chinese people*. London: Oxford University Press.

Bone, W. (1995). *An Assessment of the Potential Impact of American Vietnam War Veterans on the Emerging Travel Industry of Vietnam: A Case Study of Hawaii*: University of Hawaii, Travel Industry Management.

Brewer, J. D. (1984). Tourism and Ethnic Stereotypes: Variation in a Mexican Town. *Annals of Tourism Research, 11*(3), 487-501.

Butler, R. (1990). Alternative Tourism: Pious Hope or Trojan Horse? *Journal of Travel Research, 28*(3), 40-45.

Callan, R. J. (1997). An attributional approach to hotel selection. Part 1 the managers' perception. *Progress in tourism and hospitality research, 3*, 333-349.

Camilleri, C. (1985). La Psychologie Culturelle (Cultural Psychology). *Psychologic Francaise, 30*, 147-151.

Carusa, M. (1994, April 1). Napalm and Nostalgia: The War Lives on as a Tourism Attraction. *Conde' Nast Traveler*, 76-78.

Catalone, R. J., Di Benedetto, C. A., and Bojanic, D. C. (1989). Multiple Multinational Tourism Positioning using Correspondence Analysis. *Journal of Travel Research, 28*(2), 25 - 32.

Chiu, R. (1990, November). *Sources and management of organizational stress: A Hong Kong case.* Paper presented at the Eighth Association of Psychological and Educational Counsellors of Asia Biannual Conference, Kuala Lumpur, Malaysia.

Chiu, R. (1992, March). *Understanding organizational stress; A cultural perspective.* Paper presented at the Annual Conference of the Midwest Society for Human Resources/Industrial Relations, Chicago, IL.

Chu, G. C., Hayashi, C., and Akuto, H. (1995). Comparative analysis of Chinese and Japanese cultural values. *Behaviormetrika, 22*, 1-35.

Collins, D., and Tisdell, C. (2000). Changing patterns with age: Australian evidence and the need to modify current theories. *Australian Journal of Hospitality Management, 17*, 15-25.

Cooper, M., and Hanson, J. (1997). Where there are no tourists...yet. A Visit to the Slum Brothels in Ho Chi Minh city, Vietnam. In M. Oppermann (Ed.), *Sex Tourism and Prostitution: Place, Players, Power, and Politics.* New York: CCC.

Cooper, M. (2000). Tourism in Vietnam: Doi Moi and the Realities of Tourism in the 1990s. In C. M. Hall (Ed.), *Tourism in South and South East-Asia: Issues and Cases.* Oxford: Butterworth-Heinemann.

Crompton, J. L., and MacKay, K. J. (1989). Users' Perceptions of the Relative Importance of Service Quality Dimensions in Selected Public Recreation Programs. *Leisure Sciences, 11*, 367-375.

Crompton, J. L., and Love, L. L. (1995). The Predictive Validity of Alternative Approaches of Evaluating Quality of a Festival. *Journal of Travel Research, 34*(1), 11-24.

Dodd, C. (1995). *Dynamics of Intercultural Communication.* Boston: MA: McGraw-Hill.

Edelstein, A. S., Ito, Y., and Kepplinger, H. M. (1989). *Communication and Culture: A Comparative Approach.* New York: Longman.

Ember, C. R., and Ember, M. (1985). *Anthropology* (4th ed.). New York: Englewood Cliffs. Prentice-Hall.

Feather, N. T. (1986). Value Systems Across Cultures: Australia and China. *InternationalJournal of Psychology, 21*, 697-715.

File, K. M., and Prince, R. A. (1995). Positive word-of-mouth: customer satisfaction and buyer behaviour. *International Journal of Bank Marketing.*

Gabrenya, J. W. K., and Hwang, K. (1996). Chinese social interaction: Harmony and hierarchy on the good earth. In M. H. Bond (Ed.), *The handbook of Chinese psychology* (pp. 309-321). Hong Kong: Oxford University Press.

Gao, G. (1996). *Communication in personal relationships across cultures.* Thousand Oaks: CA: Sage Publications, Inc.

Gartner, W. C. (1993). Image formation process. *Journal of Travel and Tourism Marketing, 2*(3), 199-212.

Gee, C. (1986). *Marketing to International Visitors.* Unpublished Manuscript. Hawaii: University of Hawaii.

Gronroos, C. (1982). A Service Quality Model and Its Marketing Implications. *European Journal of Marketing, 18*(1), 36-44.

Gronroos, C. (1990). *Service Management and Marketing.* Lexington: Lexington Books.

Gursoy, D., and Chen, J. S. (2000). Competitive analysis of cross cultural information search behavior. *Tourism Management, 21*(6), 583-590.

Hofstede, G., and Bond, M. H. (1988). The Confucius connection: from cultural roots to economic growth. *Organizational Dynamics, 16*, 5-21.

Huang, J. H., Huang, C. T., and Wu, S. (1996). National Character and Response to Unsatisfactory Hotel Service. *International Journal of Hospitality Management, 15*(3), 229-243.

Hsu, F. L. K. (1972). *Americans and Chinese.* New York: Doubleday Natural History Press.

Jandt, F. (1998). *Intercultural Communication: An Introduction.* Thousands Oaks: CA: Sage Publications.

Jansen-Verbeke, M, and Go, F. (1995). Tourism development in Vietnam. *Tourism Management, 16*(4), 315-325.

Kamakura, W., and Mazzon, J. (1991). Value Segmentation: A Model for the Measurement of Values and Value System. *Journal of Consumer Research, 18*(2), 208-218.

Kim, Y. Y., and Gudykunst, W. B. (1988). *Theories in Intercultural Communication. International and Intercultural Communication Annual 12.* Newbury Park, CA: Sage Publications.

Keown, C., Jacobs L., and Worthley, R. (1984). American Tourists' Perceptions of Retail Stores in 12 Selected Countries. *Journal of Travel Research, 22*(3), 26-30.

King, B. E. M. and McVey, M. (2003). China Outbound. *Travels and Tourism Analysis* (1), 1-32.

Kluckhohn, C. (1944). *Mirror For Man.* New York: McGraw-Hill.

Ko, A., Chiu, R., and M., W. (1990, December). *Significance of cultural change and its implications to management Practices.* Paper presented at the First International Organizational Behavior Teaching Conference, Singapore.

Kotler, P., Chandler, P., Gibbs, R., and McColl, R. (1989). *Marketing in Australia* (2nd ed.). New York: Prentice Hall.

Krech, D., and Crutchfield, R. S. (1984). *Theory and Problems of Social Psychology.* New York: McGraw-Hill.

Kroeber, A., and Kluckhohn, C. (1952). Culture: A Critical Review of Concepts and Definitions. In *Peabody Museum of American Archaeology and Ethnology Harvard University Press* (Vol. 47, pp. 223). New York: Random.

Lau, S. K., and Kuan, H. C. (1988). *The ethos of the Hong Kong Chinese.* Hong Kong: The Chinese University Press.

Lehtinen, U., and Lehtinen, J. R. (1982). *Service Quality: A Study of Quality Dimensions.* Helsinki Finland: Service Management Institute.

Leighton, A. H. (1981). Culture and Psychiatry. *Journal of Psychiatry, 26*, 522-529.

Lewis, R. C., and Booms, B. (1983). The Marketing Aspects of Service Quality. In L. L. Berry, L. Shostack and G. Upah (Eds.), *Emerging Perspectives on Services Marketing.* Chicago: American Marketing Association.

Lipset, S. (1963). The Value Patterns of Democracy: A Case Study in Comparative Analysis. *American Sociological Review, 28*, 515-531.

Luk, S., De Leon, C., Leong, F. W., and Li, E. (1993). Value Segmentation of Tourists' Expectations of Service Quality. *Journal of Travel and Tourism Marketing, 2*(4), 23-38.

Martin, W. B. (1987). A New Approach To The Understanding and Teaching of Service Behavior. *Hospitality Education and Research Journal, 11*(2), 255-262.

Mayo, E. J., and Jarvis, L. P. (1981). *The Psychology of Leisure and Travel Behaviour, Boston: CBI Publishing Massachusetts*. Boston: CBI Publishing Massachusetts.

McClelland, D. (1981). Childrearing versus Ideology and Social Structure as Factors in Personality Development. In R. H. Munroe, R. L. Munroe and B. Whiting (Eds.), *Handbook of Cross-Cultural Human Development* (pp. 73-90.). New York: Garland STPM.

McCort, D. J., and Malhotra, N. K. (1993). Culture and Consumer Behaviour: Toward an Understanding of Cross-Cultural Consumer Behaviour in International Marketing. *Journal of International Consumer Marketing, 6*(2), 91-127

McCracken, G. (1986). Culture and Consumption: A Theoretical Account of the Structure and Movement of the Cultural Meaning of Consumer Goods. *Journal of Consumer Research, 13*, 71-84.

Mill, R. C., and Morrison, A. M. (1985). *The Tourism System: An Introductory Text*. Englewood Cliffs, New Jersey: Prentice Hall.

Millington, K. (2001). Vietnam: Country Report. *EIU Travel and Tourism Analysis, 2*, 87-97.

Moutinho, L. (1987). Consumer Behaviour in Tourism. *European Journal of Marketing, 21*(10).

Moore, K., and Lewis, D. J. (1952). Learning Theory and Culture. *Psychological Review, 59*, 380-388.

Munroe, R. H., and Munroe, R. L. (1980). Perspectives Suggested by Anthropological Data. In H. C. Triandis (Ed.), *Handbook of Cross-Cultural Psychology* (pp. 253-318.). Boston: Allyn and Bacon.

Pan, G. W. (2004). *Business Partnership Relationships in the Chinese Inbound Tourism Market to Australia*. Unpublished PhD, Griffith University.

Parasuraman, A., Zeithaml, V. A., and Berry, L. L. (1985). A Conceptual Model of Service Quality and its Implications for Future Research. *Journal of Marketing, 49*(Fall), 41-50.

Parasuraman, A., Zeithaml, V. A., and Berry, L. L. (1988). SERVQUAL: A Multiple-Item Scale for measuring Consumer Perceptions of Service Quality. *Journal of Retailing, 64*(Spring), 12-37.

PATA. (1999). *Hotel Online Special Report*: PATA Strategic Information Centre.

Pearce, P. L. (1982). Tourists and Their Hosts: Some Social and Psychological Effects of Inter-Cultural Contact. In S. Bochner (Ed.), *Cultures in Contact: Studies in Cross-Cultural Interaction*. Oxford, New York: Pergamon Press.

Peterson, R. A. (1979). Revitalizing the Culture Concept. *Annual Review of Sociology, 5*, 137-165.

Pi-Sunyer, O. (1978). Through Native Eyes: Tourists and Tourism in Catalan Maritime Community. In V. Smith, L. (Ed.), *Host and Guests: The Anthropology of Tourism*. Philadelphia: University of Pennsylvania Press.

Pizam, A. (1978). Tourism's Impacts: The Social Costs to the Destination Community as Perceived by its Residents. *Journal of Travel Research, 16*(4), 8-12.

Pizam, A., and Telisman-Kosuta, N. (1989). Tourism as a Factor of Change: Results and Analysis. In J. Bystrzanowski (Ed.), *Tourism as a Factor of Change: A Socio-Cultural Study 1* (pp. 149-156). Vienna: European Coordination

Pizam, A., and Sussmann, S. (1995). Does nationality affect tourist behavior? *Annals of Tourism Research, 22*(4), 901-917.

Pizam, A., Neumann, Y., and Reichel, A. (1996). The Effect of Nationality on Tourist Behaviour: Israeli Tour-Guides Perception. *Journal of Hospitality and Leisure Marketing, 4*(1), 23-49.

Pookong, K., and King, B. (Eds.). (1999). *Asia-Pacific Tourism Regional Co-operation Planning and Development* (1st ed.). Melbourne: Hospitality Press.

Redding, S. G. (1980). Management Education for Orientals. In B. Garratt and J. Stopford (Eds.), *Breaking Down Barriers - Practice and Priorities for International Management Education*. London: Gower Press.

Reisinger, Y., and Turner, L. (2003). *Cross-cultural behaviour in tourism: concepts and analysis*: Buttterworth-Heinemann.

Richardson, S. L., and Crompton, J. L. (1988). Cultural Variations in Perceptions of Vacation Attributes. *Tourism Management, 9*(2), 128-136.

Ritchie, B. J. R. (1974). An Exploratory Analysis of the Nature and Extent of Individual Differences in Perception. *Journal of Marketing Research, 11*(1), Journal of Marketing Research.

Richter, L. K. (1983). Political Implications of Chinese Tourism Policy. *Annals of Tourism Research, 10*, 347-362.

Robertson, T. S. (1970). *Consumer Behavior*. Glen view, Ill.: Scott: Foresman and Company.

Robinson, G. L. N., and Nemetz, L. (1988). *Cross-Cultural Understanding*. UK: Prentice Hall International.

Rokeach, M. (1973). *The Nature of Human Values*. New York: Free Press.

Ruppel, F., Blaine, T. W., and Peterson, W. (1991). U.S. Tourism in the Socialist Republic of Vietnam Voices. *The Art and Science of Psychotherapy, 27*(1), 189-199.

Saleh, F., and Ryan, C. (1992). Client Perceptions of Hotels: A Multi-Attribute Approach. *Tourism Management, 13*(2), 163-168.

Samovar, L. A., Porter, R. E., and Jain, N. C. (1981). *Understanding Intercultural Communication*. Belmont, CA: Wadsworth Publishing Company.

Samovar, L. A., and Porter, R. E. (1991). *Communication between Cultures*. Belmont, CA: Wadsworth Publishing Company.

Schneider, M., and Jordan, W. (1981). Perceptions of the Communicative Performance of Americans and Chinese in Intercultural Dyads. *International Journal of Intercultural Relations, 5*(1), 175-191.

Segall, M. H. (1984). More Than We Need to Know About Culture but Are Afraid Not to Ask. *Journal of Cross-Cultural Psychology, 15*, 153-162.

Segall, M. H., Dasen, P. R., Berry, J. W., and Poortinga, Y. H. (1990). *Human Behavior in Global Perspective: An Introduction to Cross-Cultural Psychology*. London: Pergamon: Pergamon Press.

Sheldon, P. J., and M., F. (1988). The Role of Foodservice in Vacation Choice and Experience: A Cross-Cultural Analysis. *Journal of Travel Research, 27*(3), 9-15.

Singer, K. (1982). Culture Learning: The Fifth Dimension in the Language Classroom. In L. Damen (Ed.), *Second Language Professional Library: Reading Mass* (pp. 54-55). Addison- Wesley Publishing.

Solomon, M. R., Surprenant, C., Czepiel, J. A., and Gutman, E. G. (1985). A Role Theory Perspective on Dyadic Interactions: The Service Encounter. *Journal of Marketing, 49*(1 Winter), 99-111.

Sutton, W. A. (1967). Travel and Understanding: Notes on the Social Structure of Touring. *International Journal of Comparative Sociology, 8*(2), 218-223.

Telisman-Kosuka, N. (1989). Tourist destination image. In S. F. Witt and L. Moutinho (Eds.), *Tourism Marketing and Management Handbook* (pp. 557-561). New York: Prentice Hall.

Theuns, H. (1997). Vietnam: Tourism in an Economy in Transition. In F. Go and C. Jenkins (Eds.), *Tourism and Economic Development in Asia and Australasia.* London: Pinter.

Triandis, H. C. (1972). *The Analysis of Subjective Culture.* New York: Wiley-Interscience.

Truong, T. H. (2005). Assessing Holiday Satisfaction of Australian Travellers in Vietnam: An Application of the HOLSAT Model. *Asia Pacific Journal of Tourism Research, 10*(3), 227-246.

Uba, L. (1994). *Asian Americans: Personality Patterns. Identity, and Mental Health.* New York: The GUI I ford Press.

Urriola, 0. (1989). Culture in the Context of Development. *World Marxist Review, 32,* 66-69.

Urry, J. (1991). The Sociology of Tourism. In C. P. Cooper (Ed.), *Progress in Tourism, Recreation and Hospitality Management 3* (pp. 48-57). England: The University of Surrey.

Usunier, J.-C. (2000). *Marketing across cultures* (3rd ed.). New York: Financial Times Prentice Hall.

Uysal, M., McDonald, C. D., and Reid, L. J. (1990). Sources of Information by International Visitors to U.S. Parks and Natural Areas. *Journal of Parks and Recreation Administration., Vol 8 (1),* 51-59.

VNAT. (2005). Vietnam National Administration for Tourism: *Tourist Statistic Visitors. Available from* www.vietnamtourism.com

Wagner, U. (1977). Out of Time and Place - Mass Tourism and Charter Trips. *Ethnos, 42,* 38-52.

Wei, L., Crompton, J. L., and Reid, L. M. (1989). Cultural Conflicts: Experiences of US Visitors to China. *Tourism Management, 10*(4), 322-332.

WTO. (2000). *Tourism 2020 Vision: East Asia and Pacific.* Madrid: WTO.

Yang, K. S. (1981). Social orientation and individual modernity among Chinese students in Taiwan. *Journal of Social Psychology, 11*(3), 159-170.

Yu, X. L. (1999). *Chinese pleasure travellers in Australia: A leisure behaviour analysis.* Unpublished Master, RMIT Univeristy, Australia.

In: Tourism Management: New Research
Editor: Terry V. Liu, pp. 41-63

ISBN 1-60021-058-9

Chapter 2

CONTRADICTIONS OF MODERNIZATION IN CHINA AND THE IMPLICATIONS FOR COMMUNITY TOURISM DEVELOPMENT

Yiping Li

Department of Geography,
The University of Hong Kong, China

ABSTRACT

Originated and refined in the West, community tourism started to draw Chinese researchers' attention in the last two decades of the twentieth century. However, there are essential differences, between the ideas of Chinese and Western researchers, regarding the concept of community tourism. Those differences basically hinge on two questions: is community tourism a democratic process or predominantly a planning strategy and; is sustaining the community or tourism the overall objective? To understand those differences, this study takes a detour through the modernization and [under]development theories so as to examine the contradictions manifest in China's modernization process and the implications for community tourism development. Three major criteria of contemporary modernity are adopted for the examination: the relationship between economy and politics, the question of civil society and public sphere, and the development towards democracy. The empirical study focuses on two cases of tourism development at two destinations – Sanya City in the island province of Hainan, and Huangshan City in the south Anhui Province. Hainan Island, once a marginalized provincial backwater, is now the centre of the whole nation's attention being China's largest special economic zone; while the south of Anhui, historically an important civilization center of China, is increasingly marginalized in the country's modernization process, being a less developed inland region. Tensions between China's past tradition and contemporary impetus for 'modernization' manifest at the two destinations, thus offering typically exemplifying cases for the investigation. The study results indicate the transformation of Western ideas about community tourism to China is affected by the quality of false modernity. Such a quality prevails in China's current modernization campaign and creates a number of obstacles for actualizing Western concept of community tourism in the country.

INTRODUCTION

The concept of community tourism emerged decades ago, and has been defined and redefined in the context of developed countries. In the last two decades of the 20th century, tourism scholars in China started their attempts to apply the concept in Chinese context. However, there are some essential differences, between the perspectives of the Chinese and the Western scholars, regarding the concept of community tourism. The differences, more or less, are reflected in their attempts to answer these questions. Is community tourism a democratic process or predominantly a planning strategy? Should sustaining the community or tourism be the overall objective? To appreciate the difference, this research takes a detour through the modernization and [under]development theories. The major reason for taking such an approach is the sheer size and diversity of its land and people set China apart from many other less developed societies. Having a long feudalist history and currently under a single-party rule, China has highly centralized bureaucracy which, more than in many other less developed societies, has exercised a high degree of economic and social control, and has taken a major role in national policy-making. This research aims to examine some contradictions associated with China's current modernization campaign. Three major criteria of contemporary modernity [Chamberlain, 1994; Granovetter, 2001; Hollingworth and Boyer, 1997; Whyte 1992] are adopted for the examination. They are the relationship between economy and politics, the question of civil society and public sphere, and the development towards democracy.

The examination concentrates on the contradictions associated with China's current modernization campaign. It especially focuses on two cases: the Nanshan Cultural Tourism Zone (hereafter Nanshan) in Sanya City of Hainan Province and the Wan'an Ancient Street (hereafter Wan'an) in Huangshan City of Anhui Province (see Figure 1)

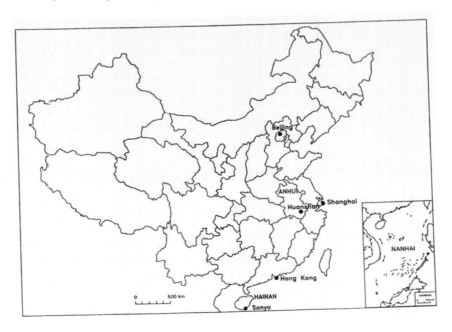

Figure 1. Location Map of Sanya and Huangshan

They are selected because, firstly, both Hainan Island (where Nanshan is located) and south Anhui Province (where Wan'an is located) are China's important tourist destinations. Secondly, Hainan, once a marginalized provincial backwater, is now the centre of the whole nation's attention being China's largest special economic zone (hereafter SEZ); while south Anhui, historically an important civilization center of China, is now increasingly marginalized by the country's modernization agenda, being a less developed inland region. It is believed the two destinations where manifests the tension between China's past tradition and contemporary impetus for 'modernization' offers an significant field for the investigation. Two major objectives are attempted: 1) to analyse the obstacles to actualizing community tourism in China and; 2) to propose an approach for studying community tourism that will enhance future research of similar issues regarding China. The potential contributions to be made are, firstly, a much-needed examination of the obstacles to actualizing community tourism in China will be accomplished. Secondly, the research findings will be insightful for future studies of community tourism in China and for other less developed societies as well.

LITERATURE REVIEW

An Evolutionary Perspective of Community Tourism

The studies of community tourism begin with the research into the social impacts of tourism (Butler, 1980; Keller, 1987; Keogh, 1990; Murphy, 1985; Smith, 1989). They suggest community participation in the tourism development process be crucial to maximizing the various socio-economic benefits while minimizing the negative impacts of tourism (Fallon et al., 2003; Inskeep, 1991; Ryan and Montgomery, 1994). A sustainable approach to development, community tourism, or community involvement in the tourism development process, promotes a dynamic tourism-community relationship that can only be established in a modernized civil society where individuals confront opportunities and responsibilities of citizenship (Stone, 1989). Such a concept originates in the developed Western countries, and has been developed in both theoretical and practical terms.

The most simultaneously accepted concept of community tourism is perhaps the well-known advocacy of 'community involvement'. That is, destination communities should get involved in, rather than being excluded from, tourism development within the boundary of the destination area where they are settled. This advocacy can be justified, first of all, by the fact that destination community creates the base for the community tourism development, because its nature, culture, society and even economy constitute the major, if not all components, of the tourism products (Fry, 1977; Hatton, 1999; Horn and Simmons, 2002). Such dependency may vary according to the type of community, but destination communities should not be excluded from participating in the tourism development process. Secondly, it is the destination community that suffers most the negative impacts of tourism, such as congestion, soaring price, deteriorated environment, and cultural assimilation (Donald et al., 2004). Therefore, the community must have a say in any kind of development at its own backyard in order to protect the rights of the community. Finally, if the host community is excluded, conflicts may occur, bringing detrimental impacts to the sustainable tourism development at the destination level. Arguably, exclusion of the host community may create more and more antagonistic 'hosts', leading to a 'lose-lose' result to both the community and the industry (Body and Singh, 2003).

Such justification for the advocacy of community involvement in the tourism development process seems to be indisputable. In practice, however, local communities, especially those in rural and peripheral regions, are relatively disadvantaged in terms of education, social class, power, resource, and information. As a result, the benefits of tourism development are pocketed by outside operators and the government, while local people must deal with diminished livelihood (Bell, 1987), and suffer the negative social and environmental impacts even though they are benefiting, in economic terms, from tourism (Scheyvens, 2003). Some destination communities do participate in the decision-making process and share the benefits, yet can hardly exert real influence on and concrete control over the tourism development. In order to reverse such treatment to the destination community, Stakeholder concept is applied (Getz and Timur, 2004; Timothy, 1999) for balancing all legitimate voices in community destinations. Stakeholders of community-based destinations may include local residents, governments and private investors – at the primary level; and any party potentially affected by the development – at the second level (Clarkson, 1995). The importance of each stakeholder should not be determined by its possession of critical resources, such as money, information, and personnel. Any legitimate voice deserves an equal weight regarding chance of participation and benefits sharing in the tourism development process. To achieve this, empowerment of local communities is considered most crucial.

It appears that both the advocacy of community involvement and the disciples of stakeholder concept support the participation of local communities in the tourism development process. On one hand, 'equitable involvement' will ensure not only the chance of participation be fairly given to all concerned in the destination, but also the benefits be distributed to the population as a whole not the individual speculators. On the other hand, only when local communities share equally the economic, social, psychological and political benefits will they actively support the development. This benign circulation can foster a mechanism effective to sustain both the community and the industry (Mason and Mowforth, 1995). Although it is highly risky to make generalization towards the concept of community tourism because one community is seldom like another, 'equitable involvement' proves to be a very basic concept of such. It has served as a key standard germane to judge if tourism practices in community destinations accord with the spirit of community tourism.

Theories of Modernization and [under]Development

Predominantly a Western concept, community tourism has been upheld as one of the so-called 'new directions in tourism' for the less developed non-Western societies. Researchers (Brohman, 1996; Hatton, 1999; Mitchell, 2001) have studied community tourism issues in the less developed world, mainly from the perspective of community involvement in economic terms. Their studies have not addressed the complexity of applying the concept, which Timothy (1999) believes to be partially caused by the various local socio-cultural and economic conditions associated with the modernization process at destinations. It is argued that, the contemporary tourism development approaches developed by taking into account the socio-economic, political and human resources conditions of the developed Western societies may not be directly transferable to the less developed world without considerable adaptations

(Tosun and Jenkins, 1998). The argument is supported by the studies on the cases from Turkey (Göymen, 2000; Tosun et. al., 2003). They indicate the modernization the less developed societies hope to achieve by prioritizing tourism development places those societies in the same capitalist system with the more developed Western countries. Consequently the less developed world finds tourism a political as well as a social, economic and moral dilemma; and actualizing community tourism an enormously difficult task. So community tourism and other related issues of the less developed world must be discussed in a broader perspective, across the theories of modernization and [under]development. Both theories are debated widely, of which Harrison (1992; 1998) and Oakes (1998) have offered some especially insightful views.

Modernization theory focuses on the process of industrialization, whereby the development pattern of the industrialized Western countries is proposed as an ideal model for constructing the internal structure of the less developed world. Economically, modernization is an evolutionary process by which societies shift from agriculture to industry and rural to urban, where money and money market play a central role. Parallel to this is the social aspect of the process whereby the influence of family and other collectives declines, institutions become more differentiated, and a pivotal role is played by 'modernizing' elites and other 'change agents' in introducing modern values and institutions to challenge the hostile or resistant tradition. In the process, societal changes occur at both the cultural and psychological levels, with the modern consciousness that allows greater autonomy for the individual.

The modernization theory has been challenged by the [under]development theory which considers development and underdevelopment (as opposed to a lack of development) to be linked elements in the same process. It is argued that development in one part of the world system occurs only at the expense of another part (Mandel, 1978). That is, 'centers or metropoles' exploit 'peripheries' or 'satellites' through the mechanism of unequal exchange, thus transferring value from the relatively underdeveloped to the relatively developed regions. Such an argument explains 'underdevelopment' by reference to the structurally subordinate position of the less developed societies within the world system, rather than by the dead hand of tradition, the lack of educated elite, or the absence of values conducive to capitalist development.

The two theories seem to be mutually exclusive paradigms, but they have much in common. Both are Eurocentric, embody the notion of transition from one state to another, and accommodate the idea of a world system—disagreeing, though, on how it is to be envisaged. Both virtually ignore the wants and ambitions of those about to be developed. Guided by either, the welcome of tourism development by the less developed world may appear ambivalent, consequently becoming, least unusually, a symptom rather than a cause of economic development. Such a symptom, in one way or another, can find expression in the idea about the paradoxes of modernity.

Modernity and the Chinese Perspective of Community Tourism

Modernity is a tense and paradoxical process through which people produce, confront, and negotiate a particular kind of socio-economic change (Giddens, 1990). As such, modernity has two meanings. One is the 'false modernity' constructed in the utopian, teleological modernity of nineteenth- and twentieth-century historicism, of the nation-state, and of the institutions of rationalism and scientific objectivity. The other is the so-called 'authentic modern' by which modernity is constructed in a process-oriented approach, one in which human subjectivity is ambivalently but irrevocably engaged in a struggle over the trajectory of socio-economic change. Modernity is thus understood as a condition of paradox, contradiction and basic anxiety that desperately demands, and yet simultaneously denies, constructions of meaning and identity.

Both modernization and [under]development theories would become rather problematic were they applied to examine the complexity of modernity in China—the development and change associated with the country's current modernization campaign. Although China is in the midst of 'modernizing' its norms and values, it still has no civil society to counterbalance the power of the state. Since the Chinese central government decided to open the country to the outside world in the late 1970s, China has enjoyed the benefits of a growing economy that is generally successful and gradually showing the global implications. But China is far from being regulated, as Choi and Zhou (2001) criticize, by the invisible hand of the market. There is intense social opposition, especially in the late 1980's when the Tiananmen Incident took place, but there have been no major social movements, led by the 'educated' elites, that will introduce modern values and institution to challenge the current regime. China's contemporary development and change are rather complex, and in many ways manifest the paradoxes of modernity.

In China's tourism development, for instance, Oakes (1998) observes both 'authentic' and 'false' qualities of modernity revealing along with the process of the country's modernization. The obsession with achieving an industrialized society, remains paramount in China's largely incomplete 'transition' into modernity. In this process, tourism offers an especially appropriate illustration of the paradoxical struggles between the objectifications of 'false modernity' and the promise of an 'authentic' modern subjectivity that is potentially liberating. The experience of the current Chinese modernity thus should be perceived as an on-going struggle for meaning within, along with a desire for repair of, the fragmentation, dislocation, and alienation inherent in the modernization process. Through that experience, the idea of 'false modernity' emerges as the seductive promise of a resolution to the struggle for meaning and desire for repair. Its primary agents are the nation-state and capital, and one of its principal vehicles is tourism, in which places saturated with tradition and authenticity are constructed and consumed. As such, tourism is marked by the 'misplaced search for authenticity' which, one would argue, is the basis for the Chinese perspective of community tourism to form.

Some Chinese tourism scholars (Li and Wang, 1988; Liu, 1992) begin to explore strategies for monitoring tourism impacts that become substantial along with the country's modernization process. Zhang's (1998) "Translation of Agenda 21 for the Travel and Tourism Industry: towards Environmentally Sustainable Development" (cf. World Travel and Tourism Council et. al., 1995) indicates the Chinese scholars realize tourism growth cannot be sustained by over exploiting the resources and sacrificing the environment. They begin to study tourism-community relationship in order to encourage sustainable development (Wu, 2000; Wu, 2001). Community involvement thus appears in the Chinese scholars' working agenda. They recommend planners enable community residents to appreciate both the positive and negative impacts of tourism (Liu, 2000; Liu, 2001). While trying to prove in theory that tourism need community support, they are proposing a 'stable' tourism-community relationship in line with the Chinese government's top concern of maintaining social stability. Their proposal is, obviously, to sustain tourism rather than the community, explicit in Liu's (1999: 29) view "when the community residents realize they can exercise influence and gain economic benefits, they will support tourism development". The essential difference between the perspectives of the Chinese and the Western scholars about community tourism, therefore, clearly hinges on the ultimate goal of the practice. For the Western scholars, community tourism should be considered a democratic process with the ultimate gaol to sustain the community rather than tourism or some specific aspects of tourism development. For the Chinese scholars, community tourism remains, predominantly, a planning strategy with an ultimate goal to sustain the tourism economy.

METHODOLOGY

The literature review helps develop a conceptual framework that the existing principles of community tourism promote a form of voluntary action by which individuals confront opportunities and responsibilities of citizenship. The ultimate goal of such is to achieve sustainable development by empowering the destination community. Guided by the principles, community participation in the tourism development process should be regarded as a political as well as a social, economic and moral issue associated with the modernization process. China, with its long history, sheer size, and political system, has experienced a distinct modernization and development process. To appropriately study a distinctly 'modern' issue such as community involvement in the tourism development process of China, we must examine the complexity of the Chinese modernity. In other words, the focus should be placed on the contradictions manifest in China's current modernization process in order to investigate the community tourism issues of the country. This process, suggested by Oakes (1998), reflects China's struggles over various contradictions for an 'authentic' modern subjectivity gradually revealing from the specific and distinct social realities of the country.

Based on the theoretical framework, a paradoxical perspective of the Chinese modernity is adopted to raise two focal questions for the investigation: 1) What are the major obstacles to actualizing community tourism in China? 2) What are the contradictions associated with China's modernization campaign which have caused the obstacles? Three testable hypotheses are formed for answering the questions. The first is individuals work co-operatively with stakeholder groups to deal with both political and economic issues of mutual concerns. It is tested by the first criterion of modernity: the relationship between politics and economy in the Chinese society. The second is the Chinese institution contains mechanisms for establishing and maintaining the cooperation between individuals and the powerful stakeholders—the state and the entrepreneurs. It is tested by the second criterion of modernity: the question of civil society and public sphere in the current Chinese society. The third hypothesis is individuals confront opportunities and responsibilities of citizenship by responding to authoritative decisions that impact on the community life. It is tested by the third criterion of modernity: China's development towards democracy. The investigation started, in 2001, with empirical field surveys including in-depth interview and on-site observation. The researcher's understanding of the phenomena in question is developed and grounded on personal data, experiences, and analyses (Li, 2002; 2003; 2004).

Table 1. List of Interviewees Involved in the In-depth Interviews

No	Hainan, Sanya, and NCTZ	Representing	Anhui, Huangshan, and Wan'an	No.
1	Planning director, tourism bureau (TB)	Government	Director, tourism bureau of a county	35
2	Vice-director, TB		Party secretary, a district of the city	36
3	Official, tourism information centre (TIC)		Executive head, a district of the city	37
4	Official, TIC		Director, tourism bureau of a county	38
5	Official, bureau of ethnic and religious matters		Officials #1,2and3, ACMHSDA	39-41
6	Vice executive manager, NCTZ*			
7	Human resources director, NCTZ*			
8	Professor and tourism researcher, local university	Academics	Professors #1and2, a university	42-43
9	Lecturer and tourism planner, local university			
10	Professor of social science research, local university		Postgraduate students #1,2 and3, a university	44-46
11	Director, SNIDL	Industry	Marketing director, a local resort	47
12	Executive general manager, SNIDL		Manager and consultant, a local tourism company	48
13	Head of human resources, SNIDL		Manager and consultant, a local tourism company	49
14	Chief executive officer, SNIDL		Front desk receptionist, a local hotel	50
15	Planner, SNIDL		Marketing representative, a local hotel	51
16	General manager assistant, SNIDL		Owner, a local souvenir shop	52
17	Vice-general manager, Buddhist Cultural Park (BCP)		President and general manager, a local tourism company	53
18	System manager, BCP		Porter, ACMHSDA	54
19	Vice-general manager, a local hotel		Housekeeper, a local hotel	55
20	Resident manager, a local hotel		Waiter, a local hotel restaurant	56
21	Village head	Community	Principal, a local secondary school	57
22	Village police officer		Teacher, a local secondary school	58
23-27	Pesants #1,2,3,4#5, village residents		Pesants #1,2,3,4and5, resident of Wan'an	59-63
28	Buddhist and chief executive officer, a local religious foundation			
29-32	Monks#1,2,3and4			
33	Waitress (a Buddhist) at a local vegetarian restaurant			
34	Shop assistant (a Buddhist) at a souvenir store			

* The Chinese central state designated the Nanshan area as a zone for developing cultural tourism, so NCTZ is a government institution

Face-to-face interviews were conducted to 63 respondents who had been chosen, by random sampling, to cover the major stakeholder groups (available in the Chinese society) of the community. They are representatives from the provincial and city tourism bureaus, the academic society, tourism project developers and tourism companies, as well as the community residents (see Table 1). In addition, reviews of official documents and statistics, printed tourism promotion and marketing materials as well as results of website search and media watch, all contributed to understanding the phenomena in question.

DISCUSSIONS

Findings at Nanshan of Sanya City

Located on the south coast of the sun-blessed Hainan Island, Sanya (see Figure 1) used to be a small fishing village. Recently selected to be China's first special zone for tourism, Hainan Island is historically and geographically on the periphery of the Chinese civilization, long reputed for rebelling against the central government and for lawlessness. China's 'SEZ fever' through the 1980s and 1990s encouraged the island to separate from Guangdong Province. It became China's largest SEZ in 1988, and the tourism industry has experienced fast growth ever since (see Table 2). This has transformed Sanya into a modern tourist city.

Table 2. Hainan Tourism Development Statistics

	1995	1996	1997	1998	1999	2000	2001	2002
Tourist arrival (10,000)	361	485.8	791	856	929.3	1007.6	1124.8	1254.96
Tourist income (billion RMB*)	52.4	57.23	61.67	66.96	72.46	78.56	87.89	95.38
Annual tourist arrival growth (%)	24.7	34.6	62.8	8.2	8.5	8.5	11.6	8.1%
Annual tourist income growth (%)	9.9	9.2	7.8	8.6	8.2	8.4	11.8	7.4%
Tourist income of GDP (%)	16.28	14.63	15.04	15.26	15.19	15.20	N/A	N/A

* 1 RMB = 0.12 US Dollars

Based on Hainan Tourism Bureau (1995-2002) statistics

Forty kilometers west to the city centre, Nanshan (South Mountain) area fifteen years ago was nothing but barren mountains and rugged coasts sparsely inhabited by Li ethnic minority peasants. During the 'SEZ fever', Hainan Provincial Government selected Nanshan for a cultural tourism zone development, on the basis of some legendary tales of Buddhism that describe Nanshan as a blessing land where the benevolent Guanyin (Goddess of Mercy) vowed twelve oaths to save all living things. To dwell permanently at South China Sea near Nanshan was her third oath. Master Jianzhen, a renowned monk in the Tang Dynast (A.D. 618-907), tried in vain five times to sail eastward to Japan for spreading Buddhism. On the fifth sail he was drifted to Nanshan where he stayed to preach Buddhism for a year, and successfully arrived in Japan. The legendary tales characterize the major themes of Nanshan, such as a 'blessing land of longevity' and 'Buddhist culture'. Currently under construction, Nanshan were partially opened to public in 1998, with two sites—Nanshan Temple and Buddhist Cultural Park, and has seen consecutive increase of tourism receipts.

This study finds, since the beginning of Nanshan, the Chinese state has been manipulating the development. Sanya Municipal Tourism Development Corporation, represented by Sanya City Government, has 40% shareholding of the development agency Sanya Nanshan Industry and Development Limited (hereafter "SNIDL") that involves two other domestic and overseas investors. In China, state owns the land, can designate a place to be a development zone as long as the residents are compensated. For instance, China's land law (cf. "Law of the People's Republic of China on Land Management" by China National State Council 1998) specifies that such compensation must include a land compensation fee, resettlement allowance, and compensation for attachments to the land and for young crops. But in the case of Nanshan, matters regarding land expropriation and the compensation issues were negotiated only between the developer—SNIDL—and the landowner—Sanya City Government. The residents were excluded. Sanya City Government – a shareholder of the development agency – should have shared the fees to compensate the relocated residents. However, the negotiation resulted in a deal that the developer would pay the government's share, while the government calculated the total to distribute to the residents. This encouraged corruption among state officials. Around 2002 the director on board and president of SNIDL was removed for a corruption scandal which, revealed by a few anonymous respondents, had dragged in some higher rank officials.

State manipulation of the tourism development also made some intellectuals corrupted either by power or by money. It is observed that 'experts' were invited from a few prestigious universities and institutions to deliver 'academic' speeches on the relationship between tourism and real estate development. At a real estate forum, the 'experts' popularised, in one voice, the theory of tourism-discretionary income relationship by predicting China's prospect for tourism development to be very bright as the country's memory-fresh commodity shortage was a bygone history and the Chinese people are ready to enjoy the 'luxury' of tourism. To a large audience, they speculated tourism estate to be a profitable investment, and suggested the best purchase should be the European-style villas built in Nanshan. On the contrary, it is found that the commercial estate is one of some serious problems that have emerged in the development of Nanshan.

During an interview, an official from Sanya city tourism bureau described these problems as including, firstly, unrealistic market anticipation led to over-expanding Nanshan from a planned size of 34.7 square kilometers to 50 square kilometers and, eventually to 60 square kilometers involving a total investment of RMB 70 billion (approximately US$820 million). Projects of neither market potential nor the cultural theme were developed, such as the commercial estate, laying financial burden on the developer. Secondly the developer was unaware that China's religious laws (cf. "Regulations regarding Management and Operation of Religious Sites and Temples" by China National State Council, 1981) had specified that religious sites should be owned, operated and managed by religious groups. The developer assumed the Buddhist community should be grateful for their investment, took it for granted that the community would let the developer operate the sites. Once Nanshan started to generate revenue the Buddhist community came to claim the ownership. Conflicts thus emerged to hinder Nanshan's further development. Thirdly the developer's misanalysis of the ecological environment encouraged imports of plants alien to Nanshan – a dry area with little source for irrigation. Consequently over a hundred workers must be hired to look after the man-made ecological environment, increasing the financial burden. Fourthly the representation of Buddhist culture concentrated only on tourism, reflecting the culture theme rather superficially through architecture arrangements such as Nanshan Temple and the giant statue of Guanyin. Nearby those sacred symbols were built European-style villas, resort hotels and even a golf course, which would distort the cultural theme and fail to offer tourists a cultural experience.

Besides corruption, state manipulation of development and its favourable policies towards capital investment encouraged the entrepreneur's superiority to the local community. The majority of the interviewed managerial staff of SNIDL assumed that the Buddhist community should be grateful for the investment in building the Buddhist sites. Some of them despised the local residents as "money-driven primitives who know nothing but money", the Buddhist monks "ignorant of business rules", "incapable of handling tourism business". They considered the local residents and the Buddhist monks either "uneducated and rustic" or "simple-minded and dumb", not suitable to participate in planning the development of Nanshan. They assumed any conflicts with the local community could be easily resolved by "paying them compensation money". When asked about the concept of community tourism, their answers would be, "I don't know about that sort of thing," or "it is too difficult and complicated to carry out in practice".

Nanshan is a remote district of Sanya City. The economy is poorly developed and the majority of the residents are poverty-driven, illiterate or semi illiterate Li ethnic minority peasants. In the Duck Pond Village where land was expropriated, it is found that the villagers would generally show apathy towards participating in Nanshan's development. They would regard tourism as the matter between the *lao ban men* (the entrepreneurs) and the government officials, having little to do with themselves. The *Cun Zhang* (Chief) of the village, from the interests of the community, initiated contacts with the developer in order to get involved. But many villagers thought he had an ulterior motive to gain more compensation money. This upset him, and he blamed the villagers' apathy towards participating in the development of Nanshan for their narrow vision that holds up to the "peasant livelihood and ideology".

It is also found that the Li ethnic minority villagers would rather try to gain benefits from tourism than develop a realistic understanding of the impacts. Responding to the interviews, the majority of the villagers would support the Nanshan project because the development needed their land and as the result they would get the compensation money. But few of them ever thought of how their lives would change once the land was gone, or considered investing the compensation money in other businesses to sustain their livelihood. It is observed, since 2001, the village gradually has lost half of its cultivated land for Nanshan. In the meantime the village population has increased from 680 to 730 people. Such an increase is a great challenge to the livelihood of the villagers. The land compensation fee paid to each household ranged from RMB100, 000 to RMB300, 000 (approximately US$12,000 to US$36,000)—a large sum of cash for the peasants whose average annual household income had never reached RMB3, 000 (approximately US$360). When asked about how they had spent or would spend the money, the responses suggested they would rather use the money to build new houses, buy motor vehicles, or even consume drugs. The 'good fortune' of the Duck Pond Village stimulated the jealousy of the peasants in nearby villages whose land was not to be expropriated. In order to get compensation, those peasants even lodged a complaint against the developer with the Provincial People's Congress and the Provincial People's Political Consultation Conference.

Findings at Wan'an of Huangshan City

Huangshan is a mountainous city that covers 154 square kilometres in the south corner of Anhui Province (see Figure 1). Its name originates from Mount Huang, a national mountain resort worldly renown for its natural beauty of extraordinarily rugged peaks, exotic pine forests, strange stone formations, hot springs and misty clouds. It extends across four agricultural counties of Yixian, Shexian, Xiuning and Taiping; and three urban districts including Tunxi City Centre, Huizhou Urban Area and Mount Huang Scenic Spot. Wan'an, an ancient street of two and half kilometres, is located in the agricultural county of Xiuning, and had been the administration base of the then prosperous Xiuning County through the period of Three States (around 258AD) to Sui Dynasty (around 589AD). This left a legacy of cultural and economic traditions visible today only in the poorly preserved rows of old stores, workshops and residences along the street, elegantly built in the style typical of south Anhui during the old days, reminiscing about a bygone era of glory. An official of Xiuning Tourism Bureau revealed, during the field survey, that the county leaders had made efforts for years to attract investment in order to preserve Wan'an for cultural tourism. So far no significant results have been produced.

Although the recorded number of domestic tourist arrivals of Huangshan is ranked the top among the major cities of Anhui (see Table 3), the tourism development has relied, solely, on Mount Huang Scenic Spot – a "World Natural and Cultural Heritage" listed by United Nations Educational, Scientific and Cultural Organization. The Administrative Committee of Mount Huang Scenery Development Area (hereafter ACMHSDA) takes a monopoly of running the scenic spot. Under the administration, Huangshan Tourism Group Corporation—represented by Huangshan City Government, and Huangshan Tourism Development Limited—represented by various local businesses and private shareholders, respectively hold 51% and 49% shares of the asset (cf. "A Brief Introduction to the Administrative Committee of Mount Huang Scenic Development Area" [hereafter "Introduction"] by ACMHSDA, 2003). The General Secretary of Huangshan City Communist Party Committee is the chief director. Authorized by the city government, ACMHSDA operates all fields of the tourism sector including chief managing departments like gardens, hotels, cableways, and travel agencies; has the sole right to prepare materials and allocate funds within the city to develop tourism. From 1997 to 2003, the number of subordinated units under Huangshan Tourism Group Corporation increased from 14 to 26. Its total asset increased from RMB 43.3 million (approximately US$ 5.1 million) to RMB107 million (approximately US$13 million). In a similar manner the number of subordinates under Huangshan Tourism Development Limited had increased from 12 at its incorporation in 1996 up to 23 by 2003 (cf. "Introduction").

The majority concentrates in the three urban districts, running hotel businesses, scenic spot cableways, travel services, florist and gardening as well as entertainment and catering. By 2003, tourist arrivals to Huangshan had reached 6.2 million. Direct income generated from tourism had reached RMB 21.2 billion (approximately US$2.5 billion). Based on the high rate of the tourist arrival increase (10-15 % annually), ACMHSDA predicts, by 2006 the tourist arrivals will reach 10 million per year (cf. "Introduction"). However, the state monopoly has resulted in unbalanced developments among the counties and districts.

Table 3. Ranking of industry performance (according to domestic tourist arrivals) among major cities of Anhui Province

Ranking	City	Domestic tourist arrival 10000 persons
1	Huangshan	346.28
2	Hefei	342.94
3	Anqing	333.08
4	Suzhou	235.61
5	Wuhu	227.02
6	Chizhou	203.80
7	Xuancheng	171.75
8	Fuyang	157.35
9	Bengbu	142.23
10	Caohu	137.82

Strategies for Huangshan Scenic Area Tourism Development (School of Geography and Planning, Sun Yat-Sen University 2004

During an interview, a government official from Wan'an revealed that a lot of heritage assets are neglected in the city's tourism development and an obvious case of such is Wan'an Ancient Street. Xiuning County leaders want to preserve the street for tourism, but cannot achieve it due to constraints in funding. Being a lower level state unit, the county has to wait for the city government to allocate the fund for carrying out the project. Besides, Xiuning is a predominately agricultural county in the city's development agenda, doomed to be poor, unattractive to investors. It is found that the residents in the scenic spot gain immediate benefits by participating in economic activities such as running family guest houses and souvenir stores. But those from other districts and counties are not even allowed to drive taxis into the scenic spot under the regulations of ACMHSDA. In 2003, the average annual household income of Tangkou—a village in the scenic spot district – was RMB 22,000 (approximately US$2600), while that of Wan'an remained below RMB 2500 (approximately US$294) (*cf.* "Basic Information about Xiuning and Wan'an" by Xiuning Tourism Bureau, 2004). Of the 11,000 residents currently registered in Wan'an, nearly half left to work in urban areas along China's coasts such as Shanghai and Guangdong because, "nowadays in China working on agriculture only produces poverty" (direct quotation from the respondents during the interviews). Those who left could have survived locally to benefit from tourism, but the unfair competition with the scenic spot residents only allows them to take the job such as a transport laborer. This job requires carrying tourism supplies of 100-150 kilograms to walk up and down the mountains (average height is above 1800 meters; a single return walk takes 10 hours), at the wage of RMB50 (approximately six US Dollars) *a* day. So the leaders of Wan'an are desperate to exploit their heritage resources for tourism development which, they believe, will help Wan'an gain a fair share of the city's tourism benefits. However, regarding the community residents' rights to participate in tourism for a fair share of the benefits, the majority of the leaders' attitudes are rather negative.

During an interview, an official from Xiuning county government addressed much the need of the county for capital investment which, he emphasized, to be vital to the survival of the county's economy. According to him, the working agenda of the county government is simple. That is, to ask whoever comes to Xiuning, from abroad or China's wealthier regions, to bring in investment capital that will help Wan'an transform itself into a popular tourist site. In order to attract outside investment, the county will guarantee good returns by offering labour thrice cheaper than coast provinces, and will let the investors decide how to preserve the street. In his point of view, the local people are not qualified to get involved in planning the development for Wan'an because "they have no sense of style...are only capable of towing down the old houses and replacing them with ugly new buildings". Contrary to the hunger for the development capital to revitalize Wan'an, the local leaders' 'generosity' about spending on 'public relation work' is enormous. During the first five-day field survey in Wan'an, the researcher was invited, by both Wan'an and Xiuning authorities, to attend ten 'working' lunches and dinners for 'exchanging ideas' about the future tourism development of both. Usually two banquet tables of delicacies would be served at each meal, and the cost should be around RMB2000 (approximately US$235). Although Xiuning is a poor agricultural county where the average annual household income remains below RMB2500 (approximately US$290), this type of 'public relation work' is necessary. An official of Xiuning County People's Congress upheld, "it is part of the Chinese culture that 'guanxi' [networks of personal connections] should be cultivated at banquet tables. 'Guanxi' is crucial to success of business". It is found that the local leaders' 'public relation work' was covered and promptly reported by the 'public' media. It made the headline news about one of the banquets, describing it as "good work of exercising efforts of both local and international wisdom to help the tourism industry take off", after its head had attended the banquet.

Wan'an residents, when interviewed, generally would be enthusiastic about joining in the tourism ventures of Huangshan in order to share the economic benefits. At present Wan'an cannot offer tourism business opportunities, but many of its residents have joined in tourism related economic activities at the popular tourist sites of the city. The activities include selling handicrafts to tourists or even working as transport labourers. The involvement, however, has been limited in the economic activities of tourism. Wan'an is famous for winning the gold prize by its locally made compass at Panama World Fair in 1915. Today it still produces compasses and sunshine guides as tourist souvenirs. During the field survey, the researcher had the chance to meet and interview Mr. A – a Wan'an resident and a successful compass producer. Wan'an authorities arranged the first meeting for a lunch at Mr. A's workshop. Among the poorly preserved old houses along the ancient street, Mr. A's workshop stands with newly renovated appearance, suggesting his good business. After being introduced, the researcher started to feel the workshop was owned by the leaders rather than Mr. A. He discharged soon to prepare lunch while the local leaders kept the researcher's company in the meeting room to 'discuss' the prospects of the tourism development. When the lunch was ready, Mr. A did not sit at the table to host the guests but rather stood by serving dishes. He seemed to be happy with the role, always smiling in silence. The leaders seemed to be satisfied by Mr A's hospitality. They praised his talent of doing good business and promised to be continually supportive. Before the meeting ended, one of the leaders picked up several compasses at the workshop as 'samples' to help Mr. A 'promote' the products; and he gave one to the researcher as a 'gift'. Was Mr.A happy about the meeting? To what degree was Mr. A involved in the tourism development? What were Mr. A's thoughts about involving himself in the tourism development process? Those questions remained to be answered therefore the researcher decided to return for a personal interview to Mr. A.

Mr. A was interviewed three months later. He admitted, "I probably am the only person in Wan'an who can make a good living on tourism". Making compasses and sunshine guides is a special gift of his family, and he will only pass it to his descendents. Currently Mr. A owns five stores in Huangshan to sell compasses and sunshine guides to tourists. He believes that he is making a much better living than other Wan'an residents. Apparently Mr. A is quite contented with his business success. When asked about his thoughts regarding community involvement in the tourism development of Wan'an, he showed high enthusiasm about participating in the economic activities on one hand. But on the other hand, he thought it should be up to the government and some specialized experts to plan for the tourism development. In his view, ordinary Wan'an residents cannot do anything about specific planning and management of the project. He would be happy as long as he was allowed to do business afterwards. He was reluctant to disclose the profit margin and scale of his business. But his positive attitude towards hosting the lunch three months before and his willingness to "do more of the public relation work" indicate that he had a profitable business. In his opinion, the cost of that lunch is nothing because good returns are assured along with the 'guanxi' being established and well maintained. He revealed that each year he would reserve a special budget just for 'treating' the local authorities and media representatives so as to gain their support. Otherwise, his business could not have been so successful.

Implications for Community Tourism Development

The findings reveal a series of contradictions in contemporary China. First and foremost, such contradictions manifest the dialectic relationship between 'centre' and 'periphery' under China's current regime of economy and politics. Hainan Island, being the country's first special zone for tourism and the largest SEZ, is playing an increasingly important role in the country's modernization process, despite its historical and geographical peripheral status. Huangshan region, an important civilisation centre in the past, is being increasingly marginalized now for its location in the country's relatively neglected inland Anhui Province. A latest report has ranked Anhui the 26th place among the 31 provinces and municipalities in terms of economic development potential, while Hainan has moved up to the 20th place (*cf.* "Comparison and Contrast of Economic Development Potentials among China's 31 Provinces and Municipalities" by Yang, 2003). It is clear that the two selected cases where manifests the tension between a 'centre' and a 'periphery' of China, either historical or contemporary; and the impetus for achieving 'modernization', have enabled a significant exploration of the various contradictions in the country today. Those contradictions, examined by the three criteria of modernity, help identify three major obstacles, at the political structural, business operational and socio-cultural levels, to actualizing the Western concept of community tourism in the Chinese society.

At the political structural level, the Chinese central state's reach is wide-ranging and varied into every economic sector, posing a major obstacle to community participation in the tourism development process. This lack of an autonomous economic sphere to counterbalance the state power creates such a problem that market forces and law cannot guarantee the rule of economic rationality, obvious in the making of Hainan's Nanshan project. Through the 1980s and 1990s, 'SEZ fever' characterized China's economic reform. When the Central Committee of the Communist Party formally proposed establishing 'experimental' SEZs on the south

China coasts in 1979 (*cf.* "Selected Works of Deng Xiaoping from 1975 to 1982" by Bureau for the Compilation and Translation of Works of Marx, Engels, Lenin, and Stalin, 1984), the state carved out large tracts of coast area for development. Hainan was designated as China's largest SEZ in 1988, because of its coast location and strategic proximity to Hong Kong, one of Asia's economic powerhouses. This transformed Hainan into a tourist island but the tourism success was not achieved by rational planning. Tourism was initially not a priority in Hainan's development agenda as the central government's goal of establishing a system of SEZs was to promote a foreign trade-oriented economy. Being the largest SEZ, Hainan in the late 1980s and early 1990s was characterized by a roaring economy based on smuggling, the sex trade and, above all, property speculation, which helped to fuel corruption.

Hainan provincial government had ignored Hainan's tourism development until its deep economic malaise a decade ago forced a radical rethinking of the island's development potential of being China's warmest and least polluted province. The 'SEZ fever' of the past two decades drew the whole nation's attention to Hainan. Waves of migrants came from the mainland to join the 'rush for modernization'. They found the island's mountain green; sky clear, ocean blue, and life simple. Being long time on the cultural and economic periphery, the island was far behind in the modern race for progress. This naturally evoked both nostalgia and fascination – the very driving elements behind 'the tourist gaze' (MacCannell 1989; Urry 1990) that stimulated the tourism industry to take off. The Chinese state politics redefined Hainan, placed it in the center of the new cultural and economic systems of China's modernization campaign, which encouraged numerous projects including Nanshan.

In contrast to the making of Nanshan, Wan'an is desperately begging tourism investment in order to survive. Facing such a cruel reality is rather contradictory to its legacy of a 1700-year cultural and economic tradition. Contemporary Chinese state politics have nearly left the heritage street abandoned, for its location at the increasingly marginalized inland Anhui Province. Although the outstanding Mount Huang Scenic Spot awards the city with great tourism appeal, state monopoly of tourism practice has not generated any positive effects on preserving and developing Wan'an. Since state monopoly of economy prevails in China, the government should take primary responsibility for resolving the issues regarding fair distribution of the economic benefits and generating the moral guidelines. But how can it be assured that the government is a guardian of justice, instead of the source of injustice? In order to guarantee each social group an equal access to opportunities, a civil society of political pluralism must be developed. Under the current political system, it is impossible for the Communist Party Government of China to act as a representative of all social groups. If government officials share the same human nature as ordinary people, they cannot simply be expected to behave in a more moral way. Based on this general scepticism about human nature, democratic political processes must be allowed to nurture a public sphere that provide channels for people from each social group to use legitimate means to protect themselves. Otherwise, they will retaliate against the whole society through illegal channels.

Consequently serious social problems occur due to China's contradictions between a rapidly modernizing economy and a largely old-fashioned institution that lacks of a public sphere and developed civil society. The problems lead to another major obstacle, at the business operational level, to actualising community tourism. Indicated by both cases, the business operation involves the settlement of social relationship on the exchange of resources among members of the society. Since means of production in China are still largely under the state control, there are basically two types of resources in the society – tangible and intangible resources. Tangible resources are land and materials under state central planning; intangible ones are permission for doing some businesses, certificates for importing and exporting, and other opportunities including using the knowledge and education one possesses. What kind of scarce resources people have and can offer to other people would determine their value in business (whatever it is) and in the society as well. The education and knowledge possessed by the 'experts' (who delivered the 'academic' speeches at the real estate forum) enabled them to offer information, skills, technology and advice—desirable and fungible resources still scarce in China. Their 'brainpower' placed them in the strategic position of the 'business' relationship of resources exchange. Dependent on one another, people with political influence, brainpower and business capital form a social elite group to exclude community involvement in the tourism development process.

China experienced a long period of shortage in the development capital due to its centrally planned economy. The current market-oriented reform of the economy intends, among other goals, to feed China's capital hunger by diversifying capital sources. In order to attract investment, all levels of state adopted various policies favourable to business developers. This has encouraged an elite business group to grow. The elite's superiority over the masses is obvious in the negative attitudes towards community tourism, shown by the managerial staff and the state officials of both Nanshan and Wan'an. Unwatched by a public sphere, the government can never be a guardian of justice, indicated by the explicit conflict of interests that shadowed the negotiation process concerning the compensation for the relocated residents of Nanshan. Instead, the government may easily be the source of injustice to fuel corruption, indicated by the Wan'an officials' philosophy about 'guanxi'.

'Guanxi', as a kind of networks of personal connections, is morally as well as economically bounding members of the Chinese society into exchange networks which produce themselves through an endless process of banquet holding and gift-giving. 'Guanxi', along with other 'traditions' in the Chinese 'culture', creates another major obstacle, at the socio-cultural level, to actualizing community tourism. Nicely put as 'public relation work', the Wan'an officials perceive of their 'guanxi' networks as the very foundation of the society in which they live. They cannot survive without it and must cultivate it at all costs regardless of the poverty the community is suffering. From bottom up through all levels of state, officials attempt to cultivate good relationships with their superiors in order to construct horizontal networks vitally important for exercising power and remaining in office. By giving gifts and holding banquets, at the public costs, government officials attempt to create their alliances through cultivating 'guanxi'. Such an exercise fuels the corruption joined rather than watched by the 'public' media, shown in the case of Wan'an. On one hand, the exercise of cultivating 'guanxi' symbolizes a legacy of the single party regime. On the other hand, it reveals China's contradiction that the strong social opposition is still incapable of forming a major social movement towards democracy. Consequently, addressing the issues of economic liberty, economic democracy, political liberty and political democracy is absolutely out of the question. This is a great obstacle to actualizing the Western concept of community tourism in China.

Besides the difficulties in China's development towards democracy, there are other social realities that make it hard to actualize community tourism. For instance, in Nanshan we see meeting the basic and felt needs are still the ethnic minority peasants' daily fight for survival. Participating in the tourism development process will demand time and energy, a luxury for them to afford. Being a small ethnic minority group they have been excluded, for centuries, from handling social, economic and political issues. It is impossible for them to develop the cultural and economic capacity to handle such as tourism development. Due to their peasant livelihood, their interest in participation is rather low, and they would rather try to gain benefits of tourism than attempt to determine, through democratic processes, what they can do to achieve the benefits from the development of Nanshan. Such a peasant livelihood, according to Zhang (1957), is a die-hard baggage from China's long history of feudalism. It characterizes a 'natural economy' conceptualised as peasant production for home consumption by the unity of farming and handicraft industry in peasant household. And it leads to peasants' lack of vision and attachment to a singularly tenacious form of production, resistant to the separating out of industry from farming into town workshops and hence to capitalist development.

In contrast to Nanshan residents' apathy and incapability of involving in tourism, Wan'an residents are enthusiastic about participating in the tourism development. Their participation, however, is limited to joining in the tourism ventures of Huangshan in order to share the economic benefits. The economic participation, within the 'guanxi' networks, can hardly contribute to the development of democracy. Given the primacy of interpersonal relations in contemporary China and the Chinese culture in general, 'guanxi' has become a great constraint that keeps China from moving towards democracy. The pragmatic functions of 'guanxi' networks and the heavy reliance of the Chinese people on these networks in daily life generate significant costs both in economic and socio-cultural terms. Since many resources are under the monopoly control of the central state, power remains one of the most important resources. It is chased by all social groups and highly fungible. Different privileges can be achieved as long as one can cultivate 'guanxi' to the right state levels. At the costs of democracy, the privileges can be circulated as currency that not only fuels corruption but also creates 'opportunities', which has every indication from the findings of both cases.

The aforementioned obstacles lead three main arguments to evolve from this research. The first is that the Chinese state politics exercise a supreme power from the top down to different state levels. It manipulates tourism economy and keeps the necessary information from being released to the concerned community residents about how tourism may impact on their lives. If the people concerned have no rights to define their own needs and make their own decisions regarding how tourism should impact on their lives, it will be impossible to establish the dynamic tourism-community relationship. The second is that the community tourism principles are to encourage the residents to question about the role of the state in protecting their interests. They must be regarded as a challenge, by the single party that rules contemporary China, to the foundation of the country's large and entrenched bureaucracy. Consequently, actualizing such principles can be politically risky, and will require relatively more bureaucratic formalities that demand more money, organizational skills, time and efforts. Applying the Western concept of community tourism in the current Chinese social reality is far from being cost effective in terms of business operation. The third is the lack of cultural and economic capacity, and the pragmatic norms and values cause the community residents' apathy towards participation and neglect of democracy. It is the major socio-cultural constraint for actualizing the community tourism principles in China.

In the findings of this study the supports of the three arguments are obvious and in variety, which must allow us to recognize such a reality. China is quite different from the industrialized and much more developed Western countries. There is still a long way to go in the country's largely incomplete transition to modernity: the rule of law is far from being in control, democracy is still not on the cards, market is still not the determining factor in economic life, and there still not seems to be intermediary space between society and state power. The consequences are a series of contradictions: market rules versus political irrationality, development of a modern economy versus construction of a modernized civil society and, traditional Chinese norms and values versus appreciation of a modern sense of democracy. They create three key settings—the political structural, business operational and socio-cultural—in which obstacles stand to actualizing the Western concept of community tourism in China.

CONCLUSION

These three key settings encourage the quality of 'false' modernity to prevail in contemporary China, thereby affecting the transformation of the Western ideas about community tourism to the Chinese context. Therefore, one would argue the current situation in China is still not suitable for a direct application of the Western concept of community tourism. Otherwise we may fall into the fallacy of comparing China with a somewhat hagiographic image of modernity. That is, in Oakes's view (1998), to see China not in the light of the modernity which actually arose, and continues to exit, in so-called modern societies. It is essential that we understand both 'false' and 'authentic' qualities exist in the Chinese modernity, just like the modernity elsewhere in human societies. Without such an understanding we will not be able to appreciate why the Chinese tourism scholars are currently holding a different perspective about community tourism. Furthermore, we may mistakenly set China against an ideal world where the market, democracy, law and liberty would reign supreme. To assess the applicability of community tourism in China, we must not take it for granted that in theory, through the processes of 'development' and 'modernization', the Chinese economy ought to be giving birth to a new social stratum wedded to principles of independent individualism. According to the modernization theory, this stratum should arise initially from within the economic sphere through a defence of private accumulation. And then it should achieve acceptance on the political levels, thanks to its reach into the power apparatus. In Turner's (1993) view, there out to be the gradual emergence of a private sphere within which the individual would be master of her/his fate, then a public sphere in which matters of common interest would be discussed, and finally democratic procedures would be established to formalise the decision-making process itself. So we must find out appropriate measures or criteria to compare China with the 'modernized' and much more developed Western countries. Such a comparison should permit us to focus on the possible reasons why China is not, or is not yet, completely 'modern'; or even why in some senses it never can be. No doubt such a comparison will be conducive to studying community tourism in China.

Being a typically modern phenomenon, community tourism requires a study that appreciates the complexity of modernity. To study community tourism issues of China, therefore, the correct approach must firstly recognize the distinct contradictions and the associated problems that characterize China's modernization process. And then it should determine the extent to which China conforms to the ordinary conditions of modernity. In addition, it is necessary to state the obvious fact that the Chinese state remains dominant by the single Communist Party. The feature is both a major characteristic of China and one of the stumbling blocks to actualising the Western concept of community tourism. But does that mean the regime should be held responsible for all the consequences of modernization? By this study, it is found what is being set up in China is capitalism, with its 'normal' swathe of shift between 'centre' and 'periphery'. The creation of Nanshan is aimed far more at accumulating capital and creating a tourist attraction, than at exercising the state control of development. Tourism and its impacts – irrational exploitation and waste of resources, relative transformation of 'centre' and 'periphery', over-exploitation by particular groups and exclusion of others – closely resemble what the more developed and modernized Western countries experienced in the past. These upheavals provoke reactions from those individual and groups who are adversely affected, at the same time as they create new relationships between society and the state. No-one can say for certain whether the twin processes of production of the state and of a corresponding modern society will reach completion, or what formations it will give rise to. All in all, to study community tourism in China it is imperative not to ignore the essential differences between China and the more developed and industrialized Western countries with regard to the overlap between their political and economic spheres (but rather to gauge its extent). It is similarly important to uncover the contradictions at work within the political processes of modernization itself. Otherwise such a study will let a significant part of the Chinese social reality pass unnoticed.

ACKNOWLEDGEMENT

This research is supported by Hui Oi Chow Trust Fund

REFERENCES

Administrative Committee of Mount Huang Scenery Development Area (2003) Huanshan fengjingqu guangli weiyuanhui jianjie [A brief introduction to the Administrative Committee of Mount Huang Scenery Development Area - Unpublished company document].

Bell, R.H. (1987) Conservation with a human face: Conflict and reconciliation in African land use planning. In D. Anderson and R. Grove (Eds), *Conservation in African: people, policies, and practice* (pp. 79-101). Cambridge: Cambridge University Press.

Body, S. and Singh, S. (2003) Destination communities: Structures, resources and types. In S. Singh, D.J. Timothy and R. K. Dowling (Eds), *Tourism in destination communities* (pp. 19-33). Oxford: CAB International.

Brohman, J. (1996) New directions in tourism for Third World development. *Annals of tourism research* 23, 48-70.

Bureau for the Compilation and Translation of Works of Marx, Engels, Lenin, and Stalin. (1984). *Selected works of Deng Xiaoping (1975-1982)*. Beijing: Foreign Languages Press.

Butler, R. W. (1980). The concept of a tourism area cycle of evolution: Implications for the management of resources. *Canadian geographer,* 24, 5-12.

Chamberlain, H. B. (1994). Coming to terms with civil society. *The Australian journal of Chinese affairs*, 31, 113-117.

China National State Council. (1981). *Zongjiao huodong changsuo guanli tiaoli [Regulations regarding management and operation of religious sites and temples]*. Beijing: China National State Council.

China National State Council. (1998*). Law of the People's Republic of China on land management, the National People's Congress (promulgated 29 August 1998 as Order No. 8 of the President of the People's Republic of China*. Beijing: China National State Council.

Choi, E. K and Zhou, K. X. (2001). Enterpreneurs and politics in the Chinese traditional economy: Political connections and rent-seeking. *The China review*, 1, 111-136.

Clarkson, (1995)

Donald, Heather and Wanda (2004)

Fallon, L.D., and Kriwoken, L. K. (2003). Community involvement in tourism infrastructure: The case of the Strahan Visitor Centre, Tasmania. *Tourism management*, 24, 289-308.

Fry, (1977)

Getz and Timur, (2004)

Giddens, A. (1990). *The consequences of modernity*. Stanford, USA: Stanford University Press.

Göymen, K. (2000). Tourism and governance in Turkey. *Annals of tourism research*, 27, 1025-1048.

Granovetter, M. (2001). Economic action and social structure: The problem of embeddedness. In Swedberg, R. and Granovetter, M. (Eds), *The sociology of economic life* (51-76). Boulder: Westview Press.

Hainan Tourism Bureau. (2003). *Tourism statistics 1995-2001 [Unpublished government documents]*. Kaikou, Hainan, China: Hainan Provincial Government.

Harrison, D. (1988). *The sociology of modernization and development*. London: Unwin Hyma.

Harrison, D. (1992). International tourism and the less developed countries: The background. In Harrison, D. (Ed.), *International tourism and the less developed countries* (1-17). Belhaven Press, London.

Harrison, D. (1994). Learning from the old South by the new South? The case of tourism. *Third world quarterly*, 15, 707-721.

Hatton, M. J. (1999). *Community-based tourism in the Asia-Pacific*. Vancouver: APEC Publication 99-to-01, 1.

Hollingworth, J. R. and Boyer, R. (Eds.). (1997). *Contemporary capitalism: the embeddedness of institutions*. Cambridge: Cambridge University Press. Horn and Simmons (2002).

Inskeep, E. (1991). *Tourism planning: an integrated and sustainable development approach*. New York: Van Nostrand Reinhold.

Keller, C. P. (1987). Stages of peripheral tourism development—Canada's Northwest Territories. *Tourism management*, 8, 20-32.

Keogh, B. (1990). Public participation in community tourism planning. *Annals of touris research,* 17, 449-465.

Li, T. Y., and Wang, L. Y. (1988). Luyou xue gailun [Of tourism studies]. Tianjing, China: Nankai University Press.

Li, Y (2002) The impact of tourism in China on local communities. *Asian studies review, 26,* 472-486.

Li, Y. (2003). Development of Nanshan Cultural Tourism Zone in Hainan, China: Achievements made and issues to be resolved. *Tourism geographies,* 5, 436-445.

Li, Y. (2004). Exploring community tourism in China: The case of Nanshan Cultural Tourism Zone. *Journal of sustainable tourism,* 12, 175-193.

Liu, M. (2001). Luyou di zhoubian xiangguan shequ de gongneng yu jiegou gengxin [Functional and structural renewal of rural communities surrounding tourism destinations]. *Huazhong shifan daxue xuebao [Academic journal of Central China Normal University]*, 35, 95-95.

Liu, W. H (2000). Guanyu shequ canyu luyou fazhan de yuogan sikao [Reflection on community participation in tourism development]. *Luyou xuekan [Tourism studies]*, 151, 47.

Liu, Z. L. (1992). Luyou dui jiedaidi de yingxiang [The impacts of tourism on a destination]. *Luyou xuekan [Tourism studies]*, 7, 52-55.

Liu, Z. P. (1999). Luyou dui zhoubiandi shehui wenhua yingxiang yanjiu jiegou kuangjia [A framework for studying the social and cultural impacts of tourism on destinations]. *Guilin luyou gaodeng zhuake xuexiao xuebao [Academic journal of Gui Lin Tourism Institute]*, 10, 29.

MacCannell, D. (1989). *The tourist: A new theory of the leisure class.* New York: Schocken.

Mandel, E. (1978). *Late capitalism.* London: Verso.

Mason and Mowforth, (1995)

Mitchell, R. E. (2001). Community integration: Island tourism in Peru. *Annals of tourism research,* 28, 113-139.

Murphy, P. E. (1985) 'Tourism: a Community Approach', Methuen, New York.

Oakes, T. (1998). *Tourism and modernity in China.* London: Routledge.

Ryan, C., and Montgomery, D. (1994). The attitudes of Bakewell residents to tourism and issues in community responsive tourism. *Tourism management,* 15, 358-369.

Sanya Nanshan Industry and Development Limited (2002). Feasible report of Sanya Nanshan Cultural Tourism Zone 1998-2001 [Unpublished company documents].

Sanya Tourism Bureau (2002). Tourism statistics 1998-2001 [Unpublished government documents].

School of Geography and Planning (2004). Strategies for Huangshan scenic area tourism development [Unpublished planning report]. Guangzhou, China: Sun Yat-sen University

Scheyvens, R. (1999). Case study: Ecotourism and the empowerment of local communities. *Tourism management,* 20, 245-249.

Scheyvens, R. (2003). Local involvement in managing tourism. In S. Singh, D. J. Timothy and R. K. Dowling (Eds), *Tourism in destination communities* (pp. 229-252). Oxford: CAB International.

Smith, V. L. (1989). Eskimo tourism: Micromodels and marginal men. In Smith, V. L. (Ed.), *Hosts and Guests: the Anthropology of Tourism* (55-82). Philadelphia: University of Philadelphia Press.

State Statistical Bureau, People's Republic of China (2001). *Zhong guo tong ji nian jian [China statistical yearbook].* Beijing: China Statistical Press.

Stone, L. (1989). Cultural cross-roads of community participation in development: A case from Nepal. *Human organization,* 48, 206-213.

Timothy, D. J. (1999). Participatory planning: A view of tourism in Indonesia. *Annals of tourism research*, 26, 371-391.

Tosun, C. and Jenkins, C. L. (1998) The evolution of tourism planning in Third-World countries: A critique. *Progress in tourism and hospitality research*, 4, 101-114.

Tosun, C. (2000). Limits to community participation in the tourism development process in developing countries. *Tourism management*, 2, 613-633.

Tosun, C., Timothy, D. J. and Öztürk, Y. (2003). Tourism growth, national development and regional inequality in Turkey. *Journal of sustainable tourism*, 11, 133-161.

Urry, J. (1990). The tourist gaze: Leisure and travel in contemporary societies. London: Sage Publications.

Whyte, M. K. (1992). Urban China: A civil society in the making? In Rosenbaum, A. (Ed.), *State and society in China: The consequences of reform* (pp - -) Boulder: Westview Press.

World Travel and Tourism Council, World Tourism Organization, and Earth Council (1995). *Agenda 21 for the travel and tourism industry: Towards environmentally sustainable development*. London: World Travel and Tourism Council.

Wu, B. H (.2001). *Quyu luyou guihua yuanli [Principles of regional tourism planning]*. Beijing: China Tourism Press.

Wu, R. W. (2000). Luyou guihua de fazhan licheng yu qushi. [Evolution and trend of tourism planning]. *Nongcun shengtai huanjing [Ecological environment of the countryside]*, 16, 38

Xiuning Tourism Bureau (2004). Basic information about Xiuning and Wan'an' [Faxed information—personal communications between the researcher and Xiuning Tourism Bureau]

Yang, K. Z. (2003). 31 shengshi jinji shili duibi [Comparison and contrast of economic development potentials among China's 31 provinces and municipalities]. http://finance.sina.com.cn/guest69.html

Zhang, G. R. (1998). Guanyu luyouye de 21 shiji yicheng: Shixian yu huanjing xiang shiyin de kechixu fazhen [Agenda 21 for the travel and tourism industry: Towards environmentally sustainable development]. *Luyou xuekan [Tourism studies]*, 13, (2), 3, (4), (5).

Zhang, Y. (1957). *Zhongguo jindai nongyeshi ziliao [Source materials on the agricultural history of modern China]*. Beijing: Sanlian Shudian [Joint Publications].

In: Tourism Management: New Research
Editor: Terry V. Liu, pp. 65-90

ISBN 1-60021-058-9
© 2006 Nova Science Publishers, Inc.

Chapter 3

REGIONAL TOURISM ATTITUDE MAPS: A SPATIAL APPROACH TO THE COMMUNITY ATTITUDES TOWARDS TOURISM IN REGIONAL VICTORIA, AUSTRALIA

Robert J. Inbakaran[1]*, *Mervyn S. Jackson*[2] *and Prem Chhetri*[3]

[1]Senior Lecturer in Tourism Management, School of Management
Portfolio of Business, RMIT University, Australia
[2]Undergraduate Program Leader, Division of Psychology
School of Health Sciences, RMIT University
[3]Research Fellow, Centre for Research into Sustainable Urban and
Regional Futures (CR-SURF), University of Queensland
St. Lucia Campus, Brisbane, QLD

ABSTRACT

Research into local community attitudes has been on the rise for the past two decades and variety attempts have been made to cluster the community segments on the basis of their expressed attitudes. More than 80 research articles have so far been published in various research outlets. The researchers of the current research have in the past were involved in segmenting the Victorian community groups in various regional tourism product regions of Victoria in order to identify the profiles of the community segments on the basis of demographic variables. A well structured five part resident attitude questionnaire comprising of 35 statements highlighting attitudes, tourism activities, intention toward tourism and community development was used to generate the data. The employment of multivari ate statistics to the overall sample of 812 residents has yielded four distinct community clusters and they difered from each other on gender ratio, age, lifecycle stage, education, migration status, occupation and current involvement with regional tourism. Further a five factor resident attitudes were extracted from the results of the previous

* Senior Lecturer in Tourism Management, School of Management, Portfolio of Business, RMIT University (Royal Melbourne Institute of Technology) GPO Box 2476V Melbourne 3001, Victoria , Australia; Email: robert.inbakaran@rmit.edu.au

research in terms of exploring the underlying causes of both positive and negative attitudes of community towards tourism. In this research, the researchers have surveyed 1425 residents and attempted the overlay of the clusters on Victorian product regions with reference to the postal code of the residents to find out the diferences in the spatial distribution of cluster profiles by using Map Info GIS. Also, the researchers have used the previously extracted attitude factors as a determining overlay on to the tourism product regions in order to measure their diferences right across the tourism regions. The researchers have developed a set of resident attitudinal maps for the state of Victoria as a result of this spatial analysis and the implications of this will be discussed in light of advising the local governments, local tourism associations and tourism industry bodies on future tourism planning, marketing and resource allocation.

Keywords: Clusters; Attitudes; Factors, Community; Map Info GIS; Tourism Product Region; Attitude Maps.

INTRODUCTION

For the past two decades regional tourism development has been given extraordinary importance in the state of Victoria (Australia). Tourism Victoria (formed in 1993) has focused tourism marketing with regional tourism development planning. Regional Victoria was divided into 13 tourism product regions *(They were reconstituted as 7 regions in 2004 after a change in the government)* and appropriate tourism product and services development strategies were identified through research and industry cooperation (Strategic Tourism Business Plan: Tourism Victoria, 1993). The vision and mission envisioned have once again been strengthened through a Strategic Business Plan developed for 1997-2001 with core objectives focused on to maintain and expand a commercially sustainable tourism industry; develop local industry leadership with positive vision with direction and institution of tourism cooperative partnerships between public and private tourism entrepreneurial organizations (Strategic Business Plan 1997-2001, Tourism Victoria, 1997). This Strategic Tourism Business plan set very ambitious performance indicators in order to keep the Victorian tourism industry clearly focused on outcomes. The other key features of the plan were to make progress in domestic tourism marketing by launching the next phase of *'you 'll love every piece of Victoria'* through constructive steps such as improving the signage around Victoria, upgrading the visitor information services, producing material to promote the regional experience and finally, continue to target the market segments approved and endorsed by the research endeavours.

ECONOMIC CONTRIBUTION OF TOURISM TO THE STATE ECONOMY

In the year 2003-2004, the overall contribution from the Victorian tourism industry to Victoria's state's economy was around AUD$ 10.9 billion or 5.3 % of the total Victorian Gross State Product (GSP) (Tourism Victoria, 2005). Whilst Victoria's share of Australia's tourism GDP increased from 18.9% in 1997-1998 to 21.3% in 2003-2004, its share of national tourism employment also increased from 19.7% to 21.4%. (ibid). In the year 2003-2004, tourism generated around AUD$ 10.9 billion and this was thanks to the interstate (AUD$2. 8 billion) overseas (AUD$3.1 billion) and intrastate (AUD$5.1 billion) visitation (ibid).

The number of persons employed was around 159,000 in the Victorian tourism industry in 2003-2004 -a 6.6 % representation of the total employment of the state's work force (ibid). This is considered to be a 19% increase from what the work force used to be in 1997-1998. It is estimated that for every AUD$ 99,000 tourist expenditure an additional job is created inside the Victorian economy. Accommodation, restaurants and cafes industry, the retail trade industry and the transport and storage industry accounted 31%, 29% and 11% of jobs created on account of tourism respectively in side the state of Victoria in 2003-2004 (ibid). The following table illustrates the supply side of the tourism industry with regard to its percentage share in every other industry sector.

Table 1. Sector Wise Distribution of Tourism Related Employment in Victoria (2002-2003)

Supply Side Industry	Industry Share of Tourism Employment (%)
Accommodation, Cafes and Restaurants	31%
Retail trade	29%
Transport and Storage	11%
Education	7%
Manufacturing	6%
Health and Community Services	5%
Cultural and Recreational Services	4%
Wholesale Trade	2%
Personal and Other Services	2%
Agriculture , Forestry and Fishing	1%
Communication Services	1%
Property and Business Services	1%
Finance and Insurance	0%
Mining	0%
Electricity, Gas and Water Supply	0%
Construction	0%
Government Administration and Defence	0%
Total Direct Tourism Employment	100%

Source: Tourism Victoria, 2005

TOURISM'S CONTRIBUTION TO REGIONAL VICTORIA

Undoubtedly, tourism plays a vital role in reinvigorating the regional Victorian economy in recent years and in many tourism product regions the communities are finding tourism as an alternative to the established traditional primary industry occupations. While salinity and its associated diminishing agricultural returns threaten the regional economy, tourism could be considered as an effective alternative to the falling land based incomes (Inbakaran, 2005)

According to Tourism Transport Forum (TTF, 2005) the tourism related employment has grown in all the reconstituted 11 product regions of Victoria and the following table demonstrates its claims.

Table 2. Percentage Change of Tourism Employment in Regional Victoria (1997-98 to 2002-03)

Tourism Product Regions	Direct Tourism Employment			
	1997-1998	2002-2003	% Change (97-98 to 02-03)	% Share of Total Employment
Gippsland	4,249	4552	7.1%	4.8%
Goldfields	4642	5301	14.2%	5.4%
Grampians	1833	1841	0.4%	4.4%
Great Ocean Road	7399	8966	21.5%	5.7%
Legends, Wine and High Country	2,501	2,840	13.6%	9.9%
Macedon Ranges and Spa Country	1882	2215	17.7%	6.0%
Melbourne	69,063	74,085	7.3%	5.0%
Mornington Peninsula	4,610	5731	24.1%	4.0%
Murray	6,768	7,059	4.3%	5.0%
Phillip Island	689	792	14.9%	8.2%
Yarra Valley , Dandenongs and The Ranges	6,964	7,954	14.2%	4.5%

Source: Tourism Victoria, 2005

It was also estimated that during this period the regional Victorian tourism industry had employed 61,000 people and contributed $3.4 billion to the regional economy a 31% increase from the AUD$ 2.6 billion in 1997-98 (Tourism Victoria, 2005). This makes it abundantly clear about the importance of regional tourism growth in the state of Victoria. As per one estimate, 72% of the domestic visitors to the state of Victoria travel to regional Victoria and for the year ending December 2003, nearly 18 million visitors have visited Victoria and out of that 11.5 million visitors have made to the regional Victoria.

As per one of the monthly bulletins of Tourism Victoria (2005) tourism is considered to be a driving force for the economic revival of many regional centres hitherto languishing thanks to marginal agricultural returns. Regional tourism partnerships are emerging in various centres such as Beechworth, Grampians, Gippsland and Great Ocean Road with in regional Victoria where opportunities are abound concerning community based institutional employment and diverse economic development (Inbakaran, 2005) .Regional tourism centres such as Beechworth has focused on heritage preservation, hosting of special events, showcasing arts and crafts and investing in bed and breakfast in order to be successful in the competitive regional tourism market (Tourism Victoria, 2005)

REGIONAL TOURISM POLICY

Changes in government have not made any gross deviation from these and the release of Strategic Tourism Plan 2002-2006 has once again strengthened the resolve to project regional Victoria as a most attractive destination in whole of Australia (Strategic Business Plan 2002-

2006). The theme of this plan *'Advantage Victoria'* makes the most of the intended 2006 Commonwealth Games by consolidating regional tourism. The new regional tourism perspectives and initiatives envisioned in the 2002-2006 plan are as follows:

- Implement a dedicated strategy for the development of regional Victoria
- Shift from marketing product regions to marketing key destinations and attractions
- Increased focus on product development and visitor services.

The 2002-2006 Strategic Business Plan has identified the following tourist market segments for regional Victoria based on the Roy Morgan's Value Segments in particular and they are: *Visible Achievement, Socially Aware and Young Optimism.* However, the plan envisages that it is more important to market its products and services to yet another Roy Morgan segment namely, the *'Traditional Family Life* since the latest research findings shown the high propensity of this segment to undertake tourism holidays (ibid). Hence, the new plan gives prominence to this particular market segment which has more opportunities to mix with the local residents while on vacation.

According to the latest Tourism Victoria's regional tourism market profile study (2005) domestic overnight visitors will come from the age group of 25-44 years (38%) and 45-66 years (33%) age groups and they are likely to belong to the following lifecycle groups such as single , no kids, couple , no kids, parent, older working and older non-working categories.. The earlier projection made in the 2002-2006 Strategic Business Plan once again validated in 2005 as most of the domestic visitors to regional Victoria hailed from the values segments such as Visible Achievement (22%) Socially Aware (18%) and Traditional Family Life (18%) (Tourism Victoria, 2005). The following table explains the comparative tourist patronization of the Roy Morgan Values Segments within Victoria as against the whole of Australia.

Table 3. Roy Morgan Values Segments

Values Segments	Victoria	Australia
Fairer Deal	3%	3%
Traditional Family Life	18%	19%
Conventional Family Life	8%	8%
Look At Me	10%	10%
Something Better	7%	7%
Real Conservatism	4%	4%
Young Optimism	9%	8%
Visible Achievement	22%	21%
Socially Aware	18%	17%

Source: Victoria Market Profile, Tourism Victoria, June 2005

This particular aspect makes it mandatory for the planning agencies to have an unbiased view of the existing resident perceptions and attitudes of the overall tourism development in all the tourism campaign regions of regional Victoria (Inbakaran and Jackson, 2004). To have a cursory understanding of the business plan, it is necessary to take note of the latest regional Victorian tourism market profiles pertaining to the regional Victoria year ending June 2005. The projection of domestic visitor nights by Tourism Victoria for 2003-2013 based on the

Tourism Forecasting Council's projection in May 2004 is also crucial since it has predicted an overall 1 to 1.2 average annual growth rate from 2003-2013 in Business, Holiday, VFR and other market segments (Tourism Victoria , 2004).

Although the plan has proposed several strategies in its *phase 7 of the Jigsaw campaign to counter these issues* (such as low interstate awareness of regional Victoria), there were hardly any strategies to fathom the regional Victorian community's perception and attitude towards the overall tourism development. Despite several tourism promotional efforts in which the local tourism industry has the opportunity to develop cooperative partnership with public tourism promotional agencies, the thought of embracing the larger community has not been emphasized. This paper particularly focuses on this issue as an understanding of the overall resident attitudes towards the tourism promotional efforts would seem to be crucial to the success of any promotion of tourism in Victoria. While, the apex body (Tourism Victoria) intends to convert most of the day trips into an overnight stay in regional Victoria, it is essential understand to what degree the prevailing hospitality and friendliness would make that a reality. Campaign regions that are much sought after by the day trippers as well as the over night visitors, should have positive resident attitude toward tourism development. In the absence of such goodwill, it may be impractical for tourism organizations and local governments to get involved in the regional tourism promotional efforts (Inbakaran and Jackson, 2003).

REVIEW OF LITERATURE

The Australian Tourist Commission (ATC) in 2001 published the results of a representative sample of 1451 Australian residents and found 93% perceived some advantage that overseas tourists brought to Australia. The four major perceived advantages were: economic benefits (8 1%); opportunity to showcase Australia (24%); visitors stimulate the culture / life of the Australian community (17%); and, tourism boosts Australia's image overseas (14%). While 46% of respondents mentioned a disadvantage, 39% stated there were no disadvantages and a further 15% could not say if there were any disadvantages. The major disadvantages that were cited included: threats to safety or security (health risks; tourists attract crime) (12%); growth pressures and increased demands on facilities (6%); crowds and queues (6%); and, environmental damage / impact (5%). While this survey indicates Australian residents as a whole are overwhelmingly positive toward tourism, it does not segment the population in terms of perceptions, attitudes and opinions regarding current tourism levels and future growth. This research attempts to determine if mapping residential location will assist in understanding tourism development attitudes of the community.

Jafari (1986) reported systematic shifts in the focus of tourism research in terms of impacts. Tourism research focused on the positive aspects of tourism development in the 1960s; the negative impacts throughout the decade of the 1970s; and, achieved a balanced view of cost / benefits in the 1980s and early 1990s (Lankford, 1994). Researchers in the early years of the 21st century list an impressive range of both positive and negative impacts on the host community as a result of tourism development (Besculides, Lee and McCormick, 2002; Fredline and Faulkner, 2000; Gursoy, Jurowski and Uysal, 2002; Upchurch and Teivane, 2000). The major positive contributions of tourism include: creation of jobs and business opportunities (including employment of minorities); increased availability for recreation, shopping and entertainment; increased demand for preservation of historical and architectural monuments; increased knowledge by locals of own culture; and, promotion of community pride, tolerance and a stronger sense of ethnic / cultural identity within the host community.

The possible negative impacts of tourism development include: lack of economic diversification (tourism replaces other industries including fishing, mining, forestry, agriculture); economic strain due to inflation of prices of goods and services, emergence of crowding, congestion (including traffic), all forms of modern day pollution and the extra demands on limited resources (especially water); increase in undesirable behaviours such as prostitution, crime, gambling, alcohol and drug abuse, and, modification of cultural practices with a threat to authenticity by staging festivals / events entirely for tourists and the artificial reconstruction of sacred buildings and objects. This research paper investigates whether these impacts differentially affect attitudes toward tourism development depending upon residential location.

Past research has identified the following factors that may influence attitudes toward tourism development: demographics; person factors; social factors; and, tourism-related factors. Demographic factors associated with attitudes of residents toward tourism have been extensively studied. While some researchers (Davis et al, 1988; Liu and Var, 1986; Williams and Lawson, 2001) concluded that demographics do not have a causal influence, other investigators have reported significant relationships between resident demographics and host attitudes. In summary, a more positive attitude toward tourism is related to the following profile: being female; being employed (in general); higher income; high education attainment; higher political / demographic position in society; and, living in an urban environment. Working in the industry (and being economically dependent on tourism) leads to a strong positive attitude toward tourism. However, a number of researchers (Brunt and Courtney, 1999; Pizam, 1978; Williams and Lawson, 2001) concluded that residents with an economic reliance on tourism not only had a strong positive attitude toward tourism, but were quick to identify negatives associated with tourism that lead to the expression of strong negative attitudes as well.

While there appears to be no published research linking personality type of residents and their attitudes toward tourism development, there have been findings that increasing perceived control the host community members have over community decisions regarding tourism development increases pro-tourism attitudes (Ap, 1992; Gursoy et al, 2002; Lankford, 1994). Related to this, Davis et al (1988) found a positive correlation between increased knowledge of the industry and positive attitudes toward tourism. These findings seem linked to demographic data that indicates positive tourism attitudes are related to residents with high incomes, higher education levels, and high social/political status in the local community.

The major research focus regarding social factors has been length of residence. Again, inconsistent findings have been reported. While some researchers reported no relationship between length of residence and attitude toward tourism (Allen et al, 1993; Clements et al, 1993), others have reported a negative relationship. That is, the longer people have lived in the community, the more likely they are to have negative attitudes toward tourism development (Mansfeld, 1992; Stynes and Stewart, 1993; Ryan and Montgomery, 1994; Brunt and Courtney, 1999). Research into other social factors indicates the state of the local economy (poverty), home ownership and different geographical regions in a country can all influence resident attitudes toward tourism.

The final category of variables that seem to influence attitudes toward tourism development factors related to the tourism industry. Increasing the level of contact by residents with tourists increases the degree of negative attitudes toward further tourism development. If residents in their daily lives have frequent contact with tourists, they are likely to report negative attitudes. Two measures of this interaction are resident proximity to major tourism zones (Belisle and Hoy, 1980; Besculides et al, 2002; Fredline and Faulkner, 2000; Weaver and Lawton, 2001; Williams and Lawson, 2001) and the concentration of tourists in a given region (Madrigal, 1995; Williams and Lawson, 2001). Finally, Fredline and Faulkner (2000) reported that the longer the tourism facility had been in the community, the more positive the residents' attitude was to that product.

This research will attempt to use a map of the residential location (from urban fringe to rural/remote) and compare cluster profiles and positive and negative attitudes toward future tourism development in the local community.

Geographical Information Systems (GIS) and Their Efficiency in Spatially Highlighting the Resident Attitudes Inside the Tourism Product Regions

GIS has been found to be a powerful tool for data analyses, particularly when the data are attributed with spatial information (Grimshaw, 2000). In most of the geographical and environmental research GIS techniques are liberally applied to study the impact of several natural and man made impacts on the landscape features such as land cover , soil, vegetation also to a greater extent understanding the changing nature of plant and animal distributions, conflicting land uses and dangers to the ecological balance (Bridgewater, 1993) . It has been the practice of the GIS techniques to make use of the spatial data to produce multi-layered visual depictions normally called maps to study the gradual as well as sudden changes in the ecosystems. The fascinating capacities of many of the GIS techniques are such that they can readily be advocated for area planning, park planning and management of protected areas (Lopez, 1998).

Hitherto GIS have made a positive contribution to various facets of recreational resource management. This contribution ranges from a simple resource inventory to building a spatial-support system. Geographic information systems enable decision-makers and planners to assess environmental impact from developments, resolve recreational resource conflicts, and provide operational tools for modelling and predicting risks and impacts. GIS functionalities provide procedures for acquiring spatial information as well as making data more accessible, repeatable and useable. Also, there are a number of studies that have used GIS in tourism planning. Gunn (1990) has developed a 'tourism planning model' using natural and cultural resources for the State of South Carolina in USA. Three different maps of tourism potential were developed for natural, cultural and total potential for the region using an overlay function. The study assigns different weights to each input attribute layer; for example, a water resource layer was weighted as twice as significant as topographic attraction in the natural resource map. The study concluded that the counties of Oconee, Pickens and Anderson show the greatest potential for 'natural resource tourism' due to the presence of mountains, lakes and scenic rivers in the area. In contrast, two major metropolitan areas in Greenville and

Spartanburg in the eastern section of the region show high cultural resource tourism potential. However, the final map of total tourism potential shows that natural resources were not weighted as favourably as cultural resources in the region.

Boyd and Butler (1996) developed a method to identify ecotourism sites within Northern Ontario, Canada. Their study demonstrated the use of GIS techniques such as inventory mapping, buffering for human intrusion and overlay mapping for modelling appropriate spatial units for ecotourism. Williams *et al.* (1996) have developed a tourism resource inventory for British Columbia by integrating both biophysical and human parameters. Their study measured heritage and scenic values by creating three different types of information layers using several attributes. The information layers included tourism resource maps, tourism use maps and tourism capability maps. The attribute layers of each landscape unit include alteration, scenic layering, terrain height, scenic features and slope. Site type, themes, accessibility, level of interpretation and level of development are some of the attribute layers for heritage sites.

More recently Lawson *et al.* (2002) have used a simulation model that has estimated a numerical value for social carrying capacity (for hiking and vehicles) for Delicate Arch and Arches National Park, Utah, USA. Arrowsmith and Inbakaran (2001) have taken an approach of sustainability to modelling tourism potential for the Grampians National Park by combining environmental resiliency and tourist attractiveness. Their study has identified several alternative locations that not only offer potential recreational opportunities in environmentally resilient locations but also provide a diverse range of attractions that could be feasibly explored in a half to a whole day. There are also several attempts to integrate GIS generated data into agent based modelling for the asset planning in tourist destinations. Arrowsmith and Chhetri (2003) have used global positioning systems to collect data of tourist movements in Loc Ard Gorge at the Port Campbell National Park, Australia. Using the spatial data, coupled with a brief socio-demographic survey, four tourist typologies were identified in cluster analysis.

In recent times GIS modeling is attempted in the regulation of human movements during bushwalking within recreational areas in order to advocate suitable options to minimize the impact and lessen the undesirable environmental conflicts that generally plague most of the loved to death touristic and recreational sites (Bishop and Gimblett, 2000). As GIS measures are easily applicable to study any spatial phenomenon, (Bishop and Inbakaran, 1995) advocate the use of several spatial information methodologies to study issues concerning ecotourism development. Tremblay (2004) very lucidly argues the several difficult challenges that he had to encounter while attempting to fuse the tourism as well the ecological data in a Geographical Information System in his Australia's Top End study. Although he describes his adapted methodology in detail and the obtained preliminary results, the paper actually provides very a deep insight into the difficulties and limitations associated with the studies concerning wildlife resources and tourism planning. Few studies have gone that deep the way this study has gone into the issues pertaining to the methodological issues pertain to the application of GIS to tourism planning. Tremblay (2004) also questions some of the alleged capabilities of the GIS measures when suitable data are not available while wanting to research issues concerning tourism management, planning and decision making. Tremblay (ibid) is of the view that the above limitations constrain most of the GIS applications in tourism research to making inventories and case illustrations rather than detailed impact assessment studies as they require the combining temporal and spatial perspectives to develop reliable correlations between cause and effects.

Kliskey's (1994) study in New Zealand to map the multiple perceptions of wilderness from the users' perspective is yet another interesting contribution in the area where the GIS is being combined with multivariate methodology to study the individual perceptions of wilderness with regard to recreational usage. It is an in-depth study in the field of Wilderness perception Mapping (WPM) so essential for the preservation of the attractiveness of the wilderness for the user per se and suggests suitable measures to minimize the user impacts through suitability mapping.

Dickey and Higham (2005) have made use of the Arc GIS to study the spatial development of ecotourism in New Zealand and the study focuses on the commercial operators of ecotourism –a data base hitherto hardly existed in the study area- and the connection between commercial tourism operation and coastal ecotourism and related marine environments. Despite the major purpose of the study to develop an inventory, the study attempts to pave way for the development of suitable strategies, policies and systems for sustainably managing ecotourism in New Zealand. In general this study is very comprehensive as it covers national, regional and district spatial analysis of ecotourism.

McAdam (1999) strongly argues for the experimentation of GIS in tourism related development research and advocates that its intrinsic qualities such as data retrieval, manipulation, modeling and forecasting would comfortably meet the challenges required of several tourism related development issues especially with a planning focus. He further laments about the lukewarm reception GIS was getting from the tourism consultants and professionals in the UK in the late nineties. McAdam's findings that 45% of UK based tourism consultants were not familiar with GIS, and 90% never used GIS for any worthwhile planning projects and 85% did not have the skills to develop GIS applications seems to be slowly fading into a thing of the past as the new brand of researchers such as (Elliot White and Finn, 1998) have strongly advocate the use of GIS in tourism marketing and planning. Even several well managed urban and regional local governments with in Australia have well developed GIS systems at their disposals and increasingly making use of them for tourism development matters. However, it is true that although several researchers are quick to apply the GIS measures to study nature based tourism and ecotourism related issues, very few have attempted to show the same fervor towards social issues that concern the sustainable development of tourism in growing tourism regions. This particular research is aiming to fill up this gap and explore the avenues for employing and suitably modified GIS measures to make use of the difficult social data.

As a part of the study in this research, postcode information of residents' residing in several parts of regional Victoria was collected. The primary aim of this initiative was to attempt a map overlay at the end of the analysis with the results obtained. It was therefore possible to map out the spatial distribution of identified resident perceived attitudinal clusters using the location information (postcodes) tagged to every survey participant. GIS are more frequently used for the environmental mapping or lately for socio-demographic analyses. However, not much thought has been given to the employment of GIS to map the behavioral or attitudinal aspects of a population in a given geographical area or region. It has been found that the use of GIS in tourism and recreation is still in its infancy Boyd and Butler (1996). This study demonstrates the use of GIS technology to illustrate spatial variations of resident attitudes towards tourism development across the tourism product regions of regional Victoria.

This review indicates a widespread use of GIS in recreation planning. GIS has successfully resolved some of the complex contemporary problems underpinning our parks and tourist destinations in several tourist destinations. It has been found that GIS is still commonly used as a spatial data management tool, nonetheless recent trend reveals the emergence of GIS as a vital decision-support tool for tourism planning and marketing.

Research Aim

The primary aim of the present research is to explore the application of GIS to regional tourism. Using previous multivariate statistical measures, researchers found that residents from regional Victoria could be analyzed in terms of four dominate community segments (Cluster analysis) who variously expressed four (both positive and negative) attitudes toward future tourism development. The secondary aim is to spatially represent the derived attitudinal clusters and the factors on to the modified boundaries of the regional tourism campaign regions to see where the favorable and unfavorable attitudes prevail and what market implications they might have for the agencies that promote tourism in these regions.

METHOD

Procedure

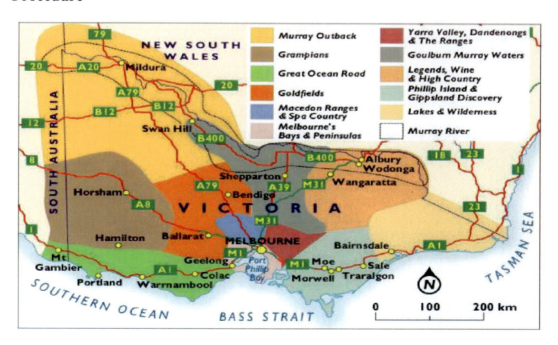

Map 1. Tourism Product Regions (1994-2004)

This research is an outcome of three consecutive field studies undertaken from 2002 to 2004. Although data was collected from all the Tourism Victoria's erstwhile delineated thirteen campaign regions (Map-1), it was decided for the final analysis to amalgamate contiguous product regions for the purpose of meaningful mapping. This has resulted in the modified map to resemble that of the Tourism Victoria's reconstituted product regions map released to the public some time in November 2004 whereas most of this research was carried well before end of August 2004. Adequate care was taken to include all the product regions in the survey so as to get a glimpse of the overall resident attitudes and perceptions.

The following flow diagram will summarise the entire study process involved to map the community attitudes towards tourism in Victorian tourism campaign regions.

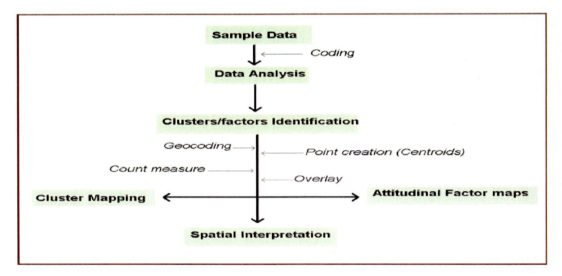

Figure 1. Flow Diagram Illustrating the Research Process

Participants

For this study a stratified purposive sampling framework was undertaken in order to get the balanced view. Residents were selected from all walks of life, age, gender, educational background, lifestyle nativity, location (postcode), volunteerism and involvement with tourism industry. A sample of 1425 residents was collected in all tourism campaign regions (see Map 2)

Although the over all sample for this study consisted of 1425 people, only 812 were used for the cluster analysis (resident segmentation) and factor analyses (resident attitudes toward tourism development) The salient features of the sample are: male: female ratio was around 48: 52; the mean age of the sample was 36.8 years (range 19-69 years); 47.5% were tertiary educated ; 39% were not married ; 46% had dependent children living at home ; and mean length of residence was 15.7 years with 39% of residents living in the region for more than 20 years.

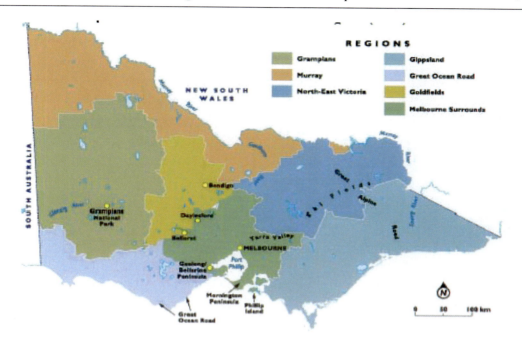

Map 2. Tourism Campaign (Product) Regions of Victoria (Tourism Victoria-2004)

Table 4. Victorian Tourism Product Regions: Attributes, Target Markets and Resident Samples

Name of the Product Region	Tourism Resource Potential	Target Markets (using Roy Morgan lifestyles for domestic tourists)	Current Sample (# of residents)
The Murray	• Encompassing Australia's greatest river • Region offers River Red Gum forests, extensive wetlands, semi-arid plains and rich Aboriginal and European heritage	Domestic: *Conventional Family Life; traditional Family Life.* Overseas: *free independent travelers*	32
Lakes and Wilderness.	• Nature based with world class touring routes • Suited for adventure activities • Comprises lakes, forests and rivers	Domestic: *Conventional Family Life.*	76
Phillip Island Gippsland Discovery	• Marine ecosystem, rolling hills and pristine promontory • Weekend destination –considered as Melbourne's recreation/adventure playground	Domestic: *Visible Achievement, Traditional Family Life, Socially Aware and Young Optimism.* Overseas: *Asia, Japan Europe and UK.*	158
YarraValley, Dandenongs and the Ranges	• Premier day trip destination with majestic national parks, wineries and public gardens	Domestic: *Socially Aware, Visible Achievement and Traditional Family Life* Overseas: *USA/ Canada, UK/Ireland and New Zealand*	112

Table 4. Victorian Tourism Product Regions: Attributes, Target Markets and Resident Samples (Continued)

Name of the Product Region	Tourism Resource Potential	Target Markets (using Roy Morgan lifestyles for domestic tourists)	Current Sample (# of residents)
Gold Fields	• Strong heritage product region • Comprises gold rush centres with heritage architecture, wineries and food production	Domestic: *Visible Achievement, Traditional Family Life, Socially Aware and Young Optimist* Overseas: *Europe, USA and Japan.*	*149*
The Great Ocean Road	• Long coastline in South West • Costal Karst topography, strong maritime heritage with scenic volcanic hinterland	Domestic: *Socially Aware, Visible Achievement, Young Optimism and Traditional Family Life.* Overseas: *Europe, USA, Asia and Japan.*	60
The Grampians	• Nature based tourism • Scenic mountain walks, wildlife and lookouts with Aboriginal heritage	Domestic: *Socially Aware, Conventional Family Life and Young Optimism* Overseas: Germany, Scandinavia and North America.	100
Bays and Peninsulas.	• Rich diversity of rugged coastlines, exotic maritime history and marine wildlife	Domestic: *Visible Achievement, Socially Aware and Traditional Family life* Overseas: *North America, New Zealand and Europe*	460
Murray Outback	• North western part of the state • Kaleidoscope of attractions and experiences with rich Aboriginal culture of national significance, abundant wildlife and water-based recreational activities	Domestic: *Conventional Family Life and Traditional Family Life* Overseas: *Germany, UK and North America*	83
Macedon Ranges and Spa Country	• Famous for its mineral springs, wineries health resorts and wealth of cultural and heritage attributes	Domestic: *Socially Aware, Visible Achievement and Traditional Family Life* Overseas: *New Zealand, UK/Ireland and Europe*	66
Goulburn Murray Waters.	• A riverine region contains lakes and rivers with abundant exotic vegetation, wineries and orchards.	Domestic: *Traditional Family Life and Conventional Family Life* Overseas: *UK and North America*	109
Legends and high country	• Victoria's Alpine regions and famous wine regions.	Domestic: *Socially Aware, Visible Achievement and Traditional Family Life* Overseas: Germany, Scandinavia and North America.	80

(Based on Tourism Victoria's Regional Tourism Plan, 2001)

Materials

Questionnaire

The administered questionnaire consisted of five well separated sections. The first section consists of *ten tourism positive and ten negative attitude statements* based on a five point Likert scale for the sample to choose. Examples of the positive statements are:

- International tourism in my place has helped the local population to have a better perspective of the world
- My region would be dull place if tourism did not develop to this extent
- Overseas investment through tourism is good for my region

Examples of the negative attitude statements are:

- The general quality of life has deteriorated thanks to tourism in my region
- The tourism development in general has alienated our local communities to a greater extent.
- Local indigenous culture has not been promoted in a true sense.

The second section contained 10 *tourism preference statements* based on a five point Likert scale for the sample to choose. Some of the examples are:

- I would like to see more tourists outside my culture.
- I would like to see more tourists from USA/Canada. UK to visit my region.
- I would like to see more families visit my region /town for tourism.

The third section consists of *four residents' own attitude (positive) towards tourism questions* structured on a yes or no direct questions basis. The examples of some of them are:

- Volunteer to help in festivals, plays etc that attract tourists
- Recommend local tourist sites to friends and relatives
- Interact/talk to visitors/tourists

The fourth section contained four residents' own attitude negative) questions with a yes or no option only and the examples are:

- During the tourist peak season, do you avoid visiting shopping centres?
- Does it annoy you should visitors stop and ask for directions?

The final section five contained demographic and behavioural questions and included the following :gender; age; highest level of education; life-style categories; nativity; occupation; business or occupational connectional with local tourism industry; distance of residence from a major tourist attraction/destination; length of residence in the region; voluntary association with tourism; and over all involvement with the tourism industry.

Generation of Community Cluster Groups (for More Details, See Inbakaran and Jackson, 2003)

The final section five contained demographic and behavioural questions and included the following :gender; age; highest level of education; life-style categories; nativity; occupation; business or occupational connectional with local tourism industry; distance of residence from a major tourist attraction/destination; length of residence in the region; voluntary association with tourism; and over all involvement with the tourism industry.

Results

The following four resident clusters were derived after seven demographic and four behaviors related to interactions with tourists were subjected to a K-means Cluster analysis (Coakes and Steed, 1999). Nominal names were provided with the assistance of main attributes of each cluster. The following is the concise description of each cluster characteristics. They are:

-   *Cluster #1 (High tourism industry connection; negative attitudes)* Cluster 1 is the largest cluster and includes a high percentage of females. Members of the cluster are significantly younger and better educated than members of the other clusters. They are typically single or a young couple with no children and live relatively near a major tourist attraction. Their length of residence in this community has a bimodal distribution of either less than five years or between 10 to 20 years. The cluster has the highest percentage of people born in Australia, have the highest business connection to tourism, but have the lowest rates of volunteerism. Overall, they have the greatest involvement with the tourist industry and they hold positive and strong negative attitudes toward tourism.
-   *Cluster #2 (Low tourism connection; negative attitudes)* This cluster is the second largest group, has the highest percentage of females; have an average age in the mid-30s, are well-educated, and are married with young to pre-adolescent dependent children. A high percentage live near a major tourist attraction, have lived in this community from five to 20 years, have a low voluntary connection to tourism and a low business / occupation link with tourism. Living near a major tourist attraction but with the second lowest involvement with the tourism industry, it was correctly predicted these group members will have strong negative attitudes toward tourism development.
-   *Cluster #3 (Neutral tourism development; limited connection, neutral attitudes)* Cluster 3 is demographically dissimilar compared to the other three clusters. The cluster is principally made up of males (6 1%), the average age is around retirement (64 years), and the cluster members are not well-educated and have lived in the area for more than 20 years. This cluster has the highest ratio of people born overseas. They belong to a mature family with adult children either still living at home or visiting regularly. They reside a far distance from any major tourist attraction, they have few occupational connections to the tourist industry and have the lowest

involvement with the industry. This group had neither strong positive nor strong negative attitudes to tourism development in the community.

-   *Cluster #4 (High tourism connection; positive attitudes)* This cluster is gender-balanced, have an average age in middle to late forties, not well-educated and have a bimodal distribution in terms of life cycle: either mature family or mature single status. They appear average in terms of ethnic representation, length of residence in this community, and, residential distance from any major tourist attraction. They have the second highest business connection with the tourist industry, the highest rate of volunteerism to the industry and the second highest overall involvement with the tourist industry. It was correctly predicted that this cluster will have strong positive attitudes toward tourist development in their community.

Generation of Five Tourism Attitudinal Factors (More Details, See Inbakaran and Jackson, 2004)

The factor analysis of attitude survey resulted in a five factor 20 item scale which has been named the *Inbakaran Community Attitudes toward Tourism Scale* (ICATT scale) Inbakaran and Jackson, 2004). The researchers independently read the items on each scale and indicated provisional labels for each of the five factors.

Factor 1-Tourism: Negative impact (Tourism development has negatively impacted on the quality of life of the local community)
Examples of items on the final scale are:
17   General quality of life has deteriorated thanks to tourism in my region
19   Tourism development has interfered with our cultural and heritage properties
20   Tourism development has depreciated the true value of the community festival in my region.

Factor 2-Tourism: Positive impacts (Tourism has benefited the community and promoted it overseas)
7   Through tourism our local culture gets international respect
6   Overseas investment through tourism is good for my region
3   International tourism in my place has helped the local population have a better perspective of the world

Factor 3-Tourism: Positive change (Tourism has promoted local infrastructure)
10   The retail activities have changed for the better thanks to tourism in my region
5   Thanks to tourism the regional recreational facilities have got a facelift
9   My region would be a dull place if tourism did not develop to this extent

Factor 4-Tourism: Negative change (Tourism industry is perceived as insular and self-serving)
Tourism benefits those who are promoting it for profits
Tourism has increased the cost of living in my region
Local indigenous culture has not be promoted in a true sense

Factor 5-Tourism: Local community role (Tourism has a positive role in the local community)
14   The tourism traffic should be regulated so as to safeguard the interests of the local population

2   I think tourism has contributed to the welfare of the local population

Generation of Attitudinal Maps

To generate the first map representing the residents' perceived attitudinal clusters in side the tourism product regions of regional Victoria the following methodology has been adopted.

The actual boundaries of the tourism product regions of regional Victoria had to be modified in order to make the mapping easier and meaningful (See map 1). Since it was not the aim of the researchers to make use of the actual Statistical (SLA) or Local Government Areas (LGA) as the research was primarily focused on the tourism campaign regions and the sample points were solely selected from within these boundaries. Hence, the authors have combined the contiguous product regions to show a meaningful spatial spread of the resident attitudes with in most of the product regions where the sample was taken.

However, care was taken to maintain the actual boundaries wherever necessary. No new product region was created and within the existing product region boundaries the mapping has been done.

The modified product region map consists of the following six combined product regions. They are:

- The Murray and The Oasis Country;
- The Great Ocean Road and the Grampians;
- Melbourne and Surrounds (Bays and Peninsulas, Yarra Valley, Dandenongs and The Ranges);
- Gippsland and Lakes and Wilderness;
- North East Victoria (Legends, Wine and High Country and Goulburn Murray Waters); and the
- Goldfields

As mentioned earlier, as a part of the data collection, postcode information of the resident participants was collected. A total of XXX points (X and Y Coordinates) representing the centroids of postcodes were imported onto Map Info GIS (Version 7.5). The Survey participants sharing the same postcode are represented by multiple graphics, though they are all located at the same point. These graphics were therefore randomly dispersed within the postcode area.

The postcodes of the each cluster residents were transferred in to the respective product regions in order to see the spatial spread as well the intensity of their individual representation. The map thus derived (Map-2) was aptly titled 'Resident Clusters in Tourism Campaign Regions of Victoria'. The actual number of residents taken in from the survey has been depicted inside the respective product regions as proportional circle diagrams as well as in the legend provided. While mapping the perceived resident clusters, care was taken to depict the cluster characteristics as true as possible inside the product regions.

The derived factors showing the residents attitudes towards tourism development contextually transferred to the amalgamated tourism product regions with reference to the individual postcodes derived from the collected sample. The factors for the purpose of more clarity and precision depicted in different strong colours and named as: *Strong Negative Impact, Strong Positive Impact, Strong Negative Change and Strong Positive Change respectively*. The researchers for the sake of minimizing the space and as well as reducing the number of GIS maps, decided to depict all the four factors inside a single map and ignoring the last attitude factor as it failed to reach statistical significance.

The entire process is briefed through the following figure 2.

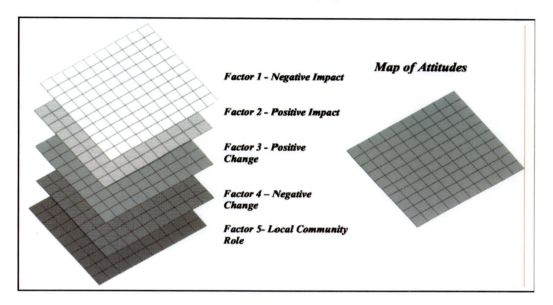

Figure 2. The Overlay Function in GIS

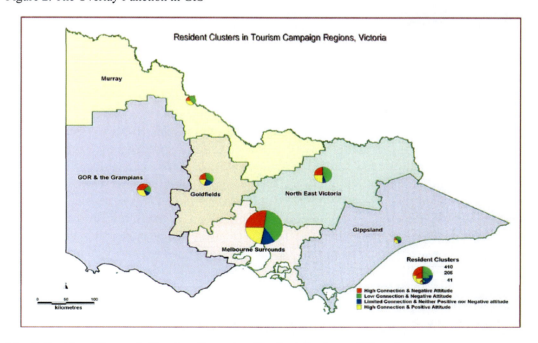

Map 3. Resident Clusters in Tourism Campaign (Product) Regions of Victoria

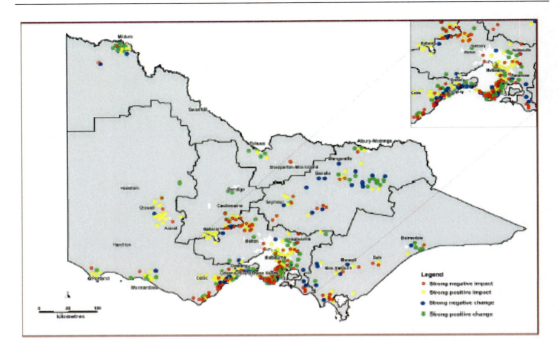

Map 4. Distribution of Resident Attitude Factors in Tourism product Regions of Victoria

RESULTS AND DISCUSSION

The primary aim of this paper was to compile traditional community data (cluster group membership and attitudes toward tourism development) on maps generated using the GIS. While the GIS has been traditionally used for studying the human impacts on the fragile natural environments .and managing the environment sustainably while allowing the development of industries including tourism related recreational pursuits (Bishop and Inbakaran, 1995; Bahaire and Elliot White, 1999; Grimshaw, 2000; Bishop and Gimblett, 2000, .a number of key researchers are now exploring the use of this technology in tourism (Gunn, 1990; Williams et al., 1996; Elliot White and Fin, 1998; Mc Adam, 1999; Arrowsmith and Inbakaran, 2001; Lawson et al., 2002; Arrowsmith and Chhetri, 2003 Tremblay, 2004;).

This research produced two maps. The first map illustrated the distribution of community groups in terms of location within Victorian tourism product regions. The second map illustrated the regional distribution of attitudes toward future tourism development. The conceptualization of such maps formed around the notion that while tourism planners had failed to widely consult with general community members living in regional Victoria, the communities in these tourism campaign regions will vary in their composition and their attitudes toward future tourism development. A survey of such maps allows tourism planners to effortlessly determine the residential location of types of community members and their positive and negative attitudes toward tourism development. By overlaying proposed future tourism developments (as listed in the 2002 – 2006 Strategic Business Plan), planners (tourism industry and local / state governments) can readily identify the acceptance (residents with positive attitudes) or social impacts (residents with negative attitudes) on the related community.

It is argued in the previous research that the people living in the less patronized areas tend to develop a positive image of tourism. Contrary the people from more matured areas acknowledged both the positive and negative impacts of tourism development. This thought has emerged well in map 2, wherein more peripheral regions such as Murray and Gippsland indicate pro-tourism opinion and therefore express the positive side of the tourism. Whilst the more connected communities with tourism trade and industry encounter negative and positive impacts of tourist on natural environment, culture and economy. Residents living in Melbourne and Surrounds have expressed mixed opinions, as the trades pursued by these communities varied and over commoditization and over utilization of attractions are readily perceivable by host communities.

Using the Map 4 as a tool, distributional characteristics of attitudes can be discerned. This map clearly shows that respondents within Melbourne metropolitan and surrounding day trip tourist destinations have varied views about the impact of tourism on economy and lifestyle. These respondents acknowledged the significance to tourism, though they are also cautious and skeptic about its impact on culture and economy. Factor 1, labelled "high connection and positive attitude" indicated that the host communities, which are more connected with tourism, have more appreciation of tourism as an economic development instrument.

The researchers have selected only two among the combined six product regions for discussion to high light the tourism planning and development implications. They are *Melbourne and Surrounds* (located close to the Melbourne Urban fringe-a non-destination product region) and *Murray /Oasis* product region (located far from the tourism generating region can be classified as rural and remote-a destination tourism product region). Please refer map-1.

It can be seen from the cluster map that in *Melbourne and surrounds* the resident clusters with *low industry connection but with a strong negative attitude and high industry connection but with a negative attitude score over other two clusters.* Similarly, the factor distribution inside this region reveals the dominance of the factors *strong negative impact strong positive change* and the *strong positive impact.*

This particular product region enjoys being proximity to the biggest tourism generating region –Melbourne and hence has received the second highest number of domestic tourists next only to the Melbourne city-the gate way to the Victorian tourism hinterland. The tourism development strategies envisaged for this region by Tourism Victoria are to increase the yield by converting the predominant day trips into overnight stays and develop products that appeal to the regular and VFR markets. It also cautions about the increased urban encroachment in these product regions and lobbies for the development of appropriate tourism products to the increasing international markets of USA/ Canada and UK/Ireland.

To combat the high summer season oriented tourism in this product region, the public agencies of tourism development have plans to encourage year long restaurant, educational or interpretive facilities and increase the commercial sustainability of the product region (Bays and Peninsula-Regional Development Plan, 1997). The plan also mentions about the issues underpinning the tourism development such as the use of foreshore land, licensing and complex management arrangements and hoped these would be resolved before the new regional focus takes off. Many of the projected developmental initiatives have already been carried out till 2003 and there are ongoing developments throughout the length and breadth of the product region.

However, it looks as though the summer season overcrowding, dense tourism related real estate growth, wanton incursion of natural reserves and the recent community disapproval for the commercialization of the Point Nepean Marine Reserve have a profound impact on the resident community. A closer look at the cluster's demographic composition and the high factor loadings on the attitudinal statements would support this interpretation. Perhaps, some of the urgent infrastructure issues such as sewerage treatment and clean water supply through the Mornington Peninsula could be more important to the residents than the ever increasing visitor demand on these necessities. The public agencies and the concerned local councils need to show more pragmatic approach with regard to the implementation of the envisaged developments since the overall resident attitude does not seem to be heartening.Tourism planners need to take stock of the entire product region's social and environmental carrying capacity since the tourist towns inside the Mornington and Bellarine peninsulas wear a look of a destinations' in decline. Local government initiated tourism plans and endeavours need to be friendly towards the cluster which has strong negative attitudes with very low industry connection. This cluster has large number of well educated females, married with pre-adolescent children, live close to the major tourist attractions for five to twenty years. By involving and listening to this cluster local tourism associations could increase the product strength of the region in the future.

In the combined Murray and Oasis product regions, the attitudinal cluster dispersal shows a dominance of *low connection negative attitude* followed by *high connection positive attitudes* over other two clusters. The factor scattering shows a combination of the dominance of *strong positive change and strong positive impact* factors over other factors. This combined region was visited by 2823000 tourists in 2003 and mostly frequented by visitors from within the region. As per the Murray Outback Regional Tourism Development Plan (1996-2000) the target markets for the region are: *Conventional Family Life, Traditional Family Life, Socially Aware and Visible Achievement.* Since this region resident attitude is very much mixed, there is a strong possibility to convert the low connection negative attitudes into modest positive attitudes. Perhaps, at the completion of the designed three phase regional tourism plan, with the expected economic upturn, the resident attitude might change for the better. The strategies proposed towards developing the region's infrastructure, product diversification, accommodation and touring should open the avenues for those who hold a *Strong Positive Impact* and *Strong Positive Change* attitudes.

CONCLUSION AND FUTURE RESEARCH

As local governments in most of the developed countries use GIS for land use planning and mapping of attributional data into series of convenient maps will not be a daunting task. Further the cost involved to generate these maps is negligible as the cost of desk top GIS has become competitive these days. With the availability of data sets generated through primary surveys and the existing secondary data on statistical divisions, the task of generating maps of this nature will be a worthwhile exercise since it will create a mosaic of existing phenomenon and in this case the community attitude in an entire state. In a single snap shot this can be captured and presented for future developmental activities.

The authors are of the view that despite a small sample, they were able to extract the required clusters and the factors for the residents and successfully transformed the same into a spatial dimension. Although there could be several other ways to depict this attitude phenomenon spatially, with out the employment of the powerful GIS tools, it would have been cumbersome and tedious. By way of depicting the resident attitudes with reference to their postcodes, it helps us to generalize the prevailing resident attitudes towards the nature and structure of the tourism industry development perceived for the region concerned. This would in turn be compared against the already implemented tourism or intended promotional endeavours by the local councils, regional tourism development organizations, federal and state tourism promotional bodies.To an extent, it is logical to assume that the local tourism industry entrepreneuer are also part of the resident community and should reflect the majority perception and attitudes in their product development and marketing so as to establish a sustainableindustry that is owned and nurtured by all the sections of the community in residence.

The future research will be loking into the possibility of enlarging the sampling frame on the basis of local government areas in order to be more precise and test someof the hypotheses developed through these three years of research and developm workable community based tourism developmental planning models for the study region.

REFERENCES

Allen, L., Hafer, H., Long, R., and Kieselbach, S. (1988). "The impact of tourism development onresidents' perception of community life." *Journal of Travel Research 27:* 16 - 21.

Ap, J. (1992). "Residenst perception of research on the social impacts of tourism" *Annals of Tourism Research 19:* 665 - 690.

Arrowsmith, C. and P. Chhetri (2003). *Port Campbell National Park: Patterns of Use.* Final report to the Parks Victoria, 2003.

Arrowsmith, C.A. and R. Inbakaran (2002). "Estimating environmental resiliency for the Grampians National Park." *Tourism Management* 23 (3): pp.295-309.

Ausrealian Tourist Commission (2001). *Community Attitude to international Tourism.* Canberra, Australian Tourism Commission.

Belisle, F., and Hoy, D. (1980). "The perceived impact of tourism by residents: A case study in Santa Marta. Columbia." *Annals of Tourism Research* 7: 83 - 101.

Besculides, A., Lee, M., and McCormick, P. (2002). "Residents' perceptions of the cultural benefits of tourism." *Annals of Tourism Research* 29: 303 - 319.

Bishop, B., and Drew, N. (1999). Multiple Discriminant Analysis. SPSS: Analysis without anguish (Version 7.0). S. Coakes, and Steed, L. Brisbane, John Wiley and Sons.

Bishop, I.D., and Gimblett, H.R. (2000). Management of recreational areas: GIS, autonomous agents, and virtual reality. *Environment and Planning B:Planning and Design*, 27 (3), 423-435.

Bishop, I.D., and Inbakaran, R.J. (1995) *"Relevance of Spatial Information Technologies to Eco-based Tourism Development."* Working paper presented at the University of Madras Geographical Information Systems symposium, Feb 22-24, 1995 in Madras, India

Boyd, S.W and R.W. Butler (1996). " Seeing the Forest through the trees: Identifying potential ecotourism sites in Northern Ontario" in L.C. Harrison and W. Husbands (Eds) *Practicing Responsible Tourism: International Case Studies in Tourism Planning, Policy and development,* Wiley and Sons, New York, pp. 3 80-403.

Brunt, P., and Courtney, P. (1999). "Host perceptions of sociocultural impacts." *Annals of Tourism Research* 26: 493 - 515.

Clements, C., Schultz, J., and Lime, D. (1993). "Recreation, tourism, and the local residents: Partnership or co-existence?" *Journal of Park and Recreation Administration 11:* 78 - 91.Coakes, S., and Steed, L. (1999). SPSS: Analysis without anguish (Version 10). Brisbane, John Wiley and Sons Australia.

Davis, D., Allen, J., and Cosenza, A. (1988). "Segmenting local residents by their attitudes, interests, and opinions toward tourism." *Journal of Travel Research* 27: 2 - 8.

Diaz-Martin, A., Iglesias, V., Vazquez, R. and Ruiz, A. (2000). "The use of quality expectations to segment a service market." *The Journal of Services Marketing* 14: 132 - 146.

Dickey, A., and Higham, J.E.S. (2005) A Spatial Analysis of Commercial Ecotourism Business in New Zealand: Ac 1999 Benchmarking Exercise Using GIS. *'Tourism Geographies,* Vol.7, No4, 373-388.

Edgell, D. (1990). *International tourism policy.* New York, Van Nostrand Reinhold. Elliott-White, M.P., and Finn. M. (1998) Growing in Sophistication: The application of geographical information systems in post-modern tourism marketing. *Journal ofTravel and Tourism Marketing,* 7 (1), 65-84.

Fishbein, M., and Ajzen, I. (1975). *Belief, attitude, intention, and behaviour: An introduction to theory and research.* Reading: MA, Addison-Wesley.

Fredline, E., and Faulkner, B. (2000). "Host community reactions: A cluster analysis." *Annals of Tourism Research* 27: 763 - 784.

Grimshaw, D.J. (2000). *Bringing geographical information systems into business* (2 edn) .Chichester, New York: John Wiley and Sons.

Gunn, C.A. (1990). *Upcountry South Carolina Guidelines for Tourism Development.* College Station, TX.

Gursoy, D., Jurowski, C., and Uysal, M. (2001). "Resident attitudes: A structural modeling approach." *Annals of Tourism Research 29:* 79 - 105.

Haralambopoulos, N., and Pizam, A (1996). "Perceived impacts of tourism: The case of Somoa." *Annals of Tourism Research* 23: 503 - 526.

Hernandez, S., Cohen, J., and Garcia, H (1996). "Residents' attitudes towards an instant resort enclave." *Annals of Tourism Research* 23: 755 - 779.

Inbakaran, R.J (2005) Government and Community Partnerships: A Perspective of the Regional Tourism Development in Victoria, Australia. In Jacob, R (Eds) *New Facets of Tourism Management.* Abhijeet Publications, Delhi, India. Pages 34-65.

Inbakaran, R.J., and Jackson, M. (2003). Segmenting the host community: An empirical analysis of attitudes toward increasing tourism in Victoria, Australia. In M. Aicken and C. Ryan (Eds.). *Taking Tourism to the Limits Refereed Research Papers.* University of

Waikato Management School, University of Waikato, Hamilton, New Zealand. Pages 315 – 337.

Inbakaran, R.J., and Jackson, M. (2004). A multivariate analysis of resident attitudes towards tourism development in regional Victoria. In Cooper, C., Arcodia, C., Solnet, D., and Whitford, M. (Eds.). *CAUTHE 2004: Creating tourism knowledge. Proceedings of the CA UTHE Conference.* CD-ROM, The University of Queensland, Brisbane.

Jafari, J. (1986). Systematic view of sociocultural dimensions of tourism, *Presidents commission of Americans outdoors:* 33 - 50.

Kliskey, A.D. (1994) mapping multiple perceptions of wilderness in southern New Zealand, II: an alternative multivariate approach. Applied Geography, 14, 308-326.Krippendorf, J. (1987). *The holiday makers: Understanding the impact of leisure and travel.* Oxford, Butterworth Heinemann.

Lankford, S. (1994). "Attitudes and perceptions toward tourism and rural regional development." *Journal of Travel Research* 32: 35 - 43.

Lawson, S., R. Manning, W. Valliere, B Wang and M. Budtruk (2002). "Using simulating modelling to facilitate proactive monitoring and adaptive management of social carrying capacity in Arches National Park, Utah, USA" in Arnberger A., C. Brandenburg and A. Muhar (Eds) *Monitoring and Management of Visitor Flows in Recreational and Protected Areas,* Conference Proceedings, pp. 205-2 10.

Liu, J., and Var, T. (1986). "Residents attitudes toward tourism impacts in Hawaii." *Annals of Tourism Research* 13: 193 - 214.

Lopez, W.S. (1998) Application of the HEP methodology and use of GIS to identify priority sites for the management of white –tailed deer. In B.G. Savitsky and T.E. Lacher (Eds), *GIS Methodologies for developing conservation strategies-tropical forest recovery and wildlife management in Costa Rica* (pp. 127-137). New York: Columbia University Press.

Madrigal, R. (1995). "Residents' perceptions and the role of government." *Annals of Tourism Research 22:* 86 - 102.

Mansfeld, Y. (1992). "Group-differentiated perceptions of social impacts related to tourism development." *Professional Geographer* 44: 377 - 392.

Mc Adam, D. (1999). The value and scope of geographical information systems in tourism management. *Journal of Sustainable Tourism,* 7 (1), 77-92.

Mill, R. and Morrison, A. (1998). *The Tourism System* (3rd ed.), Kendall/Hunt Publishing.

Pizam, A. (1978). "Tourism's impacts: The social costs to the destination community as perceived by its residents." *Journal of Travel Research* 16(4): 8 - 12.

Ryan, C., and Montgomery, D. (1994). "The attitudes of Bakewell residents to tourism and issues in community responsive tourism." *Tourism Management* 15: 358 - 369.

Sadava, S., and McCreary, D. (1997). *Applied social psychology.* Upper Saddle River, New Jersey, Prentice Hall.

Sharpley, R. (1994). *Tourism, tourists and society.* Huntingdon, ELM.

Stynes, D., and Stewart, S. (1993). "Tourism development and recreation: Some findings from a case study." *Journal of Parks and Recreation Administration* 11(4): 30 - 44.

Tourism Transport Forum Australia (2005) Victorian Tourism Employment Atlas, 2005. Tourism Victoria (1997) *Strategic Business Plan* 1997-2001.

Tourism Victoria (2002) *Strategic Business Plan* 2002-2006.

Tourism Victoria (2005) *Economic Contribution of Tourism to Victoria* 2003-2004

Tremblay, P (2004) Integrating Tourism and Environmental Knowledge in Space and Time: Challenges for GIS and Sustainable Management in the Top End of Australia. In Cooper et all (Eds) *Creating Tourism Knowledge: A Selection of Papers from CAUTHE 2004*, Council for Australian University Tourism and Hospitality Education Inc, Brisbane, Queensland, Australia, Pages, 3 8-57.

Upchurch, R., and Teivane, U. (2000). "Resident perceptions of tourism development in Riga, Lativa."*Tourism Management 21:* 499 - 507.

Weaver, D., and Lawton, L. (2001). "Resident perceptions in the urban-rural fringe." *Annals of Tourism Research* 28: 439 - 458.

Williams P. W., J. Paul and D. Hainsworth (1996). "Keeping track of what really counts: tourism resource inventory systems in British Columbia" in L.C. Harrison and W. Husbands (eds.) *Practicing Responsible Tourism: International Case Studies in Tourism Planning, Policy and development.* New York. Wiley and Sons, pp. 404-42 1.

Williams, J., and Lawson, R. (2001). "Community issues and resident opinions of tourism." *Annals of Tourism Research* 28: 269 - 290.

In: Tourism Management: New Research
Editor: Terry V. Liu, pp. 91-122

ISBN 1-60021-058-9
© 2006 Nova Science Publishers, Inc.

Chapter 4

MICRO SEGMENTATION BY INDIVIDUAL TASTES ON ATTRIBUTES OF TOURIST DESTINATIONS

Juan L. Nicolau[1] and Francisco J. Más*
Dpt. de Economía Financiera, Contabilidad and Marketing
Facultad de Económicas and Empresariales, Universidad of Alicante, Alicante

ABSTRACT

The existence of strong heterogeneous tourism demand looking for service provision adapted to its specific needs, along with the recent intensification of competition in the tourism market, has led to segmentation becoming fundamental to the marketing strategies of tourism organizations. This study presents the innovation of identifying decision processes individual by individual, tourist by tourist. To achieve this, we propose a segmentation of the tourism market based on revealed preferences towards a destination at an individual tourist level; in other words, the real destination choices made by a tourist. These real choices reveal preferences in tourist destinations; the method has the twofold implication that it allows us to form groups of tourists with similar preferences or to treat them individually. Moreover, this analysis is based on *real choices* made by individuals, which avoids the measurement errors of segmentation criteria that use subjective variables, based on evaluations or declarations of intent. With this objective, the subsequent sections of this study are arranged as follows: The second section reviews the analysis of choice in tourism, in which we state the importance of studying the choice behavior of tourists, we examine the fundamentals of choice through *revealed preferences* and compare them to *stated preferences*, we study how to introduce heterogeneity into the modelization of tourist choice and we review the literature of destination choice in order to propose its determinant attributes. The third section presents the research design, in which we detail the methodology applied and the sample and data used. The fourth section shows the results obtained, both from the estimation of the utility function for each tourist and from the segmentation analysis. In the fifth and

[1] This study has benefited from a "Turismo de España" grant from the Secretary of State for Commerce and Tourism of the Ministry of Economy for the realisation of the Doctoral thesis of the first author.
* Dpt. de Economía Financiera, Contabilidad y Marketing. Facultad de Económicas and Empresariales, University of Alicante, Ap. Correos 99 E-03080 Alicante, Phone and Fax: +34 965.90.36.21; e-mail: JL.Nicolau@ua.es; Francisco.Mas@ua.es

final section we summarise the main conclusions reached, the implications for management and future lines of research.

1. INTRODUCTION

The existence of strong heterogeneous tourism demand looking for service provision adapted to its specific needs, along with the recent intensification of competition in the tourism market, has led to segmentation becoming fundamental to the marketing strategies of tourism organizations (Díaz and Iglesias, 2000; Blomm, 2003; Chen, 2003).

Basically, the heterogeneity of the tourism market reflects the existence of a diversity of needs and desires and, therefore, of differentiated consumer behaviour among tourists. Because of this, tourism companies, in order to identify their target customer types and accurately find their characteristics, use market segmentation strategies that form and select typologies or groups of tourists in the market to develop marketing products and programmes adapted to each group (Kotler, 2003). However, despite the fact that segmentation allows the definition of different market segments that group tourists with shared behaviour and needs and with a well defined reaction to the availability of different products (Sánchez, 2000), nowadays there is more and more importance attached to personalised service for each tourist. More pro-active tourists and an intense competition increase the demand for better service, better adapted to their individual needs and, therefore, personalised. Customers expect to be treated as individual clients. This situation leads to the appearance of one-by-one marketing, which entails individual consideration of tourists and a one-by-one service. This approach is the basic pillar of relationship marketing –and, therefore, the application of CRM (*Customer Relationship Management*)-, which is designed to create, strengthen and maintain relationships between companies and their customers, in order to maximise income per customer (Vázquez, 2000). With this relationship marketing approach, the application of the segmentation strategy entails the identification of the most profitable customers to establish a close relationship with them, bearing in mind their needs and adapting products accordingly. In summary, mass marketing has been transformed into fragmented or micro-segmented marketing to satisfy the demands of smaller and smaller segments, even down to the level of the individual customer (see Figure 1).

The maintenance of a continuous long-term relationship with tourists requires knowledge of their behaviour; and this implies observation of their purchase decisions. Underlying this matter is the concept that knowing how tourists make their purchase choices allows us to identify the factors that lead them to opt for particular alternatives (e.g. choosing a destination, a certain hotel or a specific type of holiday); i.e. the choice process that reveals their preferences. In this sense, Bronner and De Hoog (1985) show that the manner in which individuals make decisions is an appropriate aspect to use as a base for market segmentation. Following this proposal, some studies use tourist decision making process to identify market segments. Chief among them are Woodside and Carr (1988), Hsieh et al. (1997) or more recently, Decrop and Snelders (2005). However, these decision making processes are analysed at a segment level, with no identification of the decision process at an individual level.

Alternatively, this study presents the innovation of identifying decision processes individual by individual, tourist by tourist. To achieve this, we propose a segmentation of the tourism market based on revealed preferences towards a destination at an individual tourist level; in other words, the real destination choices made by a tourist. These real choices reveal preferences in tourist destinations; the method has the twofold implication that it allows us to form groups of tourists with similar preferences or to treat them individually[2]. Moreover, this analysis is based on *real choices* made by individuals, which avoids the measurement errors of segmentation criteria that use subjective variables, based on evaluations or declarations of intent.

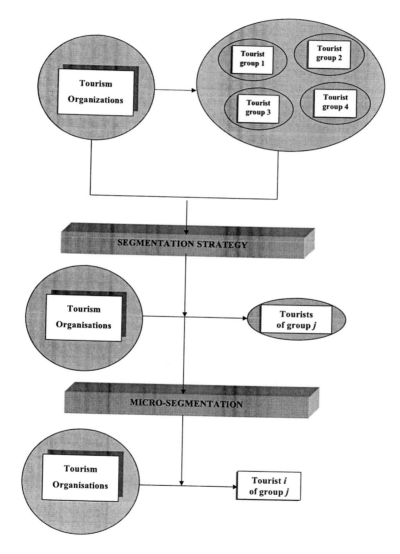

Source: Own work
Figure 1. From mass marketing to micro-segmentation

---

[2] Note that the use of individual data allows us to either treat tourists one by one or to form segments from the individual data. In sections 4.1 and 4.2 we exemplify these options.

With this objective, the subsequent sections of this study are arranged as follows: The second section reviews the analysis of choice in tourism, in which we state the importance of studying the choice behavior of tourists, we examine the fundamentals of choice through *revealed preferences* and compare them to *stated preferences*, we study how to introduce heterogeneity into the modelization of tourist choice and we review the literature of destination choice in order to propose its determinant attributes. The third section presents the research design, in which we detail the methodology applied and the sample and data used. The fourth section shows the results obtained, both from the estimation of the utility function for each tourist and from the segmentation analysis. In the fifth and final section we summarise the main conclusions reached, the implications for management and future lines of research.

2. CHOICE IN TOURISM AND MICRO-SEGMENTATION OF THE MARKET

Tourist decision making processes are often examined at a segment level, with no identification of individual level processes. Drawing upon the literature, we argue that the way in which individuals make decisions is an important aspect for the segmentation of the tourism market. In this sense, we discuss the importance of analysing tourist choice and its implications to management; and we review revealed as opposed to stated preferences, as well as the introduction of heterogeneity in the modelization and the determinants of tourist choice.

2.1. Choice in Tourism

The analysis of choice in the field of tourism entails the study of one of the fundamental processes of the tourism system (Monfort et al., 1996). We should not forget that choice is a crucial phase in the buying process, from the perspectives of both the tourist and the tourism service provider organizations. For the tourist, the choice of a purchase option represents the end of a process in which s/he has invested effort and time in the search for information and subsequent comparison, in order to satisfy a previously identified need. Therefore, a final decision is of great importance, not only because the tourist has been implicated in a buying process to make the most of the energy and financial outlay involved, but also because the chosen alternative will determine his/her future satisfaction.

From the point of view of tourism organizations -public and private-, the choice made by a tourist to buy their services, is the moment at which their investment is materialised, from the most intrinsic such as R+D, to the most visible such as promotion campaigns. Evidently, when resources are designated for a tourism product or service, from their conception to their commercialisation, the objective is for them to be selected from among the various alternatives available to consumers. However, in the current competitive environment, the reaching of this is complicated, as tourism organizations not only have to adequately meet their customers' needs, but they also have to do so at higher standards than the competition. This is of more importance if we consider that the consumer culture is more and more prevalent in society, so that individuals are not prepared to choose a service that they could obtain with better conditions from a rival destination or company. Hence, success will only be found by organizations that are valued by the market; in other words, those that provide products and services that individuals are willing to buy (Kotler, 2003). In this regard, the concept of differentiation with respect to rivals reaches its maximum importance (Anderson et al., 1992), being a vital factor for assuring market survival. Therefore, tourism organizations should know the valuation that tourists give to their products and note the aspects that lead to their selection.

In virtue of the above, the analysis of individual choice behavior and its determinants is fundamental for organizations in order to explain the success of tourism marketing actions, identify the aspects most valued by customers and estimate demand changes resulting from modifications to these aspects. Moreover, by recognising the way in which tourists optimise their actions and the circumstances under which they reach this optimum situation, tourism organizations can reproduce them for as many people as possible. In fact, De Rus and León (1997) show that the analysis of holiday choice is of vital importance for both tourism companies and public institutions, insofar as individual tourist decisions act as a guide to their actions. Additionally, tourism companies use the tourist decision making process as a starting point when analysing demand behavior and, in this way, adjust their supply. Therefore, the success of marketing actions is determined by knowledge of the factors that affect tourist choice. In addition, public bodies are interested in this analysis in order to attain better organization and implementation of their tourism policies, whether they are aimed at revitalising already consolidated areas or at identifying new opportunities, which ultimately allows them to foment sustainable tourism development and increase social wellbeing through financial income. The literature of choice in tourism develops various theories and micro-economic models to formally represent tourist decisions; most of which follow the proposals of Rugg (1973) and Morley (1992) from the extension of the Neoclassical Economic Theory of Lancaster (1966), in which they suggest that the attributes of the available choices are key elements of the decision; and the proposals of Morey (1984, 1985) and Eymann (1995) based on the household production function of Becker (1965), in virtue of which they propose that tourists *produce* their own satisfaction through the products they acquire.

One aspect of these theories to be highlighted is that they are based on the calculation of utility functions, which links them to the Theory of Random Utility. Moreover, the fact that they are not capable of collecting interpersonal and intrapersonal differences among tourists leads the majority of authors to apply discrete choice models (Jen and Fesenmaier, 1996). Discrete choice models distinguish revealed and stated preferences, which we will discuss below.

2.2. Revealed Preferences vs. Stated Preferences

Basically, the tourist processes and integrates information to choose an alternative (e.g. destination, type of accommodation or method of transport) that maximises utility. The objective or subjective character with which the researcher examines the result of this choice process determines the different approximations of analysis of choice.

The study of tourist behaviour and, therefore, of the way in which they process, evaluate and integrate the information used to make a decision, is traditionally made in two ways. The first approximation is centred on the analysis of the *real choices* made by individuals (Ben-Akiva and Lerman, 1985). This approach is based on the Neoclassical Economic Theory and the Theory of Discrete Choice, and assumes the existence of *preferences* that are unobservable to the analyst but that tourists implicitly consider when ranking alternatives, and which are only *revealed* through the real purchase choice. Therefore, this approximation is known as the *Revealed Preferences* approach.

The second approach examines the ranking or scoring according to *preferences,* given by individuals to hypothetical choice alternatives. This approximation is based on the Information Integration Theory and the Social Judgement Theory, and assumes that the decision maker is capable of ranking alternatives according to his/her preferences (Timmermans and Golledge, 1989; Batsell and Louviere, 1991). In contrast to the previous case, the analyst does not observe the real purchase choice, given that the individual only makes a *declaration of intent* based on his/her preferences (i.e. which alternative would be chosen if he/she had to choose from the given possibilities). This approximation, therefore, is known as the *Stated Preferences* approach.

To give an example, an individual declares that Hawaii is the destination he/she would like to go to on his/her next holiday. In other words, the individual selects Hawaii from a series of destinations and, through this *declaration,* preferences are analysed. However, this aspect has been widely criticized, due the fact that this approach does not reflect reality in the sense that the declaration of the preferred alternative of an individual does not necessarily coincide with his/her real behaviour, i.e. with the alternative that is really chosen (Kroes and Sheldon, 1988). The fact that an individual *declares* that he/she would like to go to Hawaii on his/her next summer holiday does not necessarily mean that he/she will go there in the end.

Conversely, the *Revealed Preferences Approach* analyses the real choices made by tourists in order to obtain their preferences. In the example above, the individual *reveals* his/her preferences when, from a group of destination choices, he/she chooses and goes to Hawaii.

Tables 1 and 2 respectively summarise the main empirical evidence found through each approach (revealed and stated preferences) in terms of tourist destinations.

2.2.1. Individual Revealed Preferences

One of the weak points of the *Revealed Preferences Approach* derives from the fact that the estimation of preferences is made at a global sample level, which does not allow representation of individual level preferences. If U_{in} is the utility of alternative i for tourist n, explained through the personal characteristic x_n of individual n and through attribute z_i of the same alternative i. The utility function is expressed as

$$U_{in} = \alpha_i + x_n \beta_i + z_i \gamma_i + \varepsilon_{in}$$

where α_i is the utility constant, β_i and γ_i are the parameters that measure (respectively) the effects of characteristic x_n of the individual and attribute z_i on the utility of alternative i and ε_{in} is the error term.

Table 1. Empirical evidence of destination choice with *revealed preference* probabilistic models

Authors	Destination	Model	Explicative Dimensions	Operative Variables
Wennergren and Nielsen (1968)	Natural parks	Probabilistic based on the Luce model	Destination attributes	- Surface area of recreational area - Distance
Perdue (1986)	Nature parks	Multinomial Logit	Destination attributes	- Attraction - Distance
Borgers, Van deir Heijden and Timmermans (1988)	Nature parks	Multinomial Logit	Destination attributes	- Surface area - Distance - Type of recreation area - Existence of specific installations
Fesenmaier (1988)	Nature parks	Multinomial Logit	Destination attributes	- Type of vegetation - Distance - Infrastructure
Morey, Shaw and Rowe (1991)	Nature parks	Multinomial Logit	Personal characteristics Destination attributes	- Motivations - Price (Cost of travel)
Dubin (1998)	Nature parks	Multinomial Logit	Destination attributes	- Activities at the destination - Price (travel costs)
Train (1998)	Nature parks	Multinomial Logit y Multinomial Logit with Random Coefficients	Destination attributes	- Size of each area - Price (Travel costs) - Naturals attributes (Number of species, aesthetics number of camping sites number of access points) - Number of protected species - Ranking in tourist guides

Table 1. Empirical evidence of destination choice with *revealed preference* probabilistic models (Continued)

Authors	Destination	Model	Explicative Dimensions	Operative Variables
Riera (2000)	Nature parks	Multinomial Logit	Destination attributes	- Surface area - Price (Travel costs) - Natural attributes - Infrastructure - Accessibility - Programmed Activities
			Personal characteristics	- Income - Age - Sex - Studies - Nationality - Occupation
Eymann and Ronning (1992)	Administrative Units (Countries)	Nested Multinomial Logit	Destination attributes	- Price (Purchase parity differential) - Repetition of destination - Organization of the trip - Fragmentation of holidays
			Personal characteristics	- Price (Specific cost index) - Motivations
Eymann and Ronning (1997)	Macro-destinations formed by perceptions of similitude of countries.	Nested Multinomial Logit	Destination attributes Personal characteristics	- Repetition of the destination - Members < 18 years old - Age - Marital status - Education - Size of city of residence - Residence
Siderelis and Moore (1998)	Macro-destinations formed by the analyst by geographical proximity	Nested Multinomial Logit	Destination attributes	- Surface area - Price (Travel cost) - Attributes related to natural attractions, quality and services.

Table 2. Empirical evidences of destination choice with *stated preferences* probabilistic models

Authors	Destinations	Model	Explicative Dimensions	Operative Variables
Adamowicz, Louviere and Williams (1994)	Nature parks	Multinomial Logit	Destination attributes	- Distance - Natural characteristics (beach, water quality, land type, size, quantity and type of species)
Adamowicz, Boxall, Williams and Louviere (1998)	Nature parks	Multinomial Logit applied to Experimental Discrete Choice	Destination attributes	- Restrictions to navigation - Surface area - Population of species - Restrictions of use
Schroeder and Louviere (1999)	Nature parks	Multinomial Logit applied to Experimental Discrete Choice	Destination attributes	- Distance and time of journey - Entry Prices
Haider and Ewing (1990)	Administrative Units (Countries)	Multinomial Logit applied to Experimental Discrete Choice	Destination attributes	- Attributes related to parks - Global price - Hotel size - Hotel services - Proximity to beach - Proximity to the city - Distance to the airport - Proximity to other accommodation
Morley (1994a)	Administrative Units (Countries)	Binomial Logit and Probit applied to Experimental Discrete Choice	Destination attributes Personal characteristics	- Shops - Price (Air tickets, Hotel prices and exchange rates) - Income - Age
Morley (1994b)	Administrative Units (Countries)	Multinomial Logit applied to Experimental Discrete Choice	Destination attributes Personal characteristics	- Sex - Price (Air tickets, Hotel prices and exchange rates)- - Income - Age - Sex

Specifically, β_i and γ_i represent the marginal utilities of individuals of alternative i; and these parameters allow us to answer questions such as "If a destination improves one of its attributes (for example, the quality and cleanliness of its water), to what extent would preferences for this destination increase?". The value of this instrument for the decision making of tourism organisations is indubitable, as it allows them to know the responses of a series of people to this improvement. However, note that the estimations of parameters β_i and γ_i are made at the global sample level (similar to the parameters obtained through regression analysis) (see Figure 2).

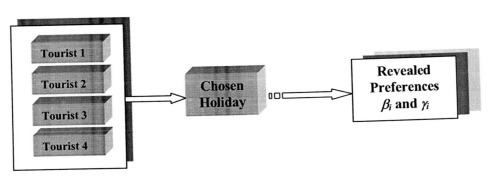

Source: Own work
Figure 2. Obtaining the *sample revealed preferences* through the observation of the choices made

This is where the study takes tourist choice a step forward by proposing the estimation of these parameters tourist by tourist, so that

$$U_{in} = \alpha_i + x_n \beta_{in} + z_i \gamma_{in} + \varepsilon_{in}$$

where, in this case, β_{in} and γ_{in} represent the preferences of tourist n around alternative i. Note that now we obtain a parameter for each tourist (and not for the whole sample) (see Figure 3).

Source: Own work
Figure 3. Obtaining *individual revealed preferences through the* observation of choices made

The main implication of knowing the tourist by tourist preference structure is that it allows the adaptation of each product to each individual, as well as the formation of groups of individuals with similar preferences.

In the next section, we review the different ways that the literature deals with this diversity of individual preferences in the choice models, stressing the advantages of our proposal.

2.2.1.1. Introduction of Heterogeneity into Choice Models

The introduction of the heterogeneity of individual preferences into the analysis of the choice process has awoken growing interest in recent years (Sorensen, 2003). This is due to the fact that the presence of heterogeneous preferences could provoke biased and inconsistent estimations in the choice models that do not explicitly consider it (Hsiao, 1986).

One of the procedures proposed in the literature to avoid this problem incorporates heterogeneity of preferences by estimating choice models that assume the existence of differentiated response parameters for each individual[1]. The most used models in this approach are the random effects models[2], which model heterogeneity with the assumption that the coefficients of the utility functions of each individual vary according to the probability distribution, either continuous -which gives rise to the Random Coefficients Logit Model- or discrete -which leads to the Latent Class Logit Model-. Initially, the Latent Class Logit Model has been widely accepted in the literature of segmentation due to the fact that the estimation of the *mass probabilities* -or points where the distribution reaches the greatest *probability masses* (Jain et al., 1994) allows identification of *latent segments* in the market, which are represented by groups of individuals with similar response profiles. Moreover, in order to segment the market, discrete distribution has an advantage over continuous distribution in that there is no need to assume a concrete probability distribution, as the segments are obtained through empirical data[3] (Cavero and Cebollada, 1999). However, the discrete approach has two important limitations (Allenby et al., 1998; Allenby and Rossi, 1999): i) the estimation becomes complex with six or more *mass probabilities*, which hinders the capture of the complete sample heterogeneity; and ii) the impossibility of identifying the preferences of individuals situated beyond a certain threshold of the distribution function (e.g. in the distribution tails).

Because of this, some authors consider that the optimum method of capturing market heterogeneity is to estimate the parameters of each individual, as this allows the capture of any individual preference structure (Allenby and Rossi, 1999). Following this approach, Revelt and Train (2002) suggest a two-stage market segmentation technique. The first stage is the estimation of the individual utility functions of a Random Coefficients Logit Model with simulation methods (based on the Bayesian estimation of Rossi and Allenby (1993)); this is

---

[1] Alternatively, heterogeneity has been collected as follows (González Benito, 2000): i) applying discrete choice models to different market segments, defined a priori through the similitude of certain characteristics of the individuals (Currim, 1981). This implies a priori definition of the segments through certain common personal characteristics in order to estimate a choice model for each group, and finally testing the differences of the parameters of each specification; and ii) directly incorporating the characteristics of the individuals into the models (Ben-Akiva and Lerman, 1985). The personal characteristics are used as covariates, thus allowing prediction of the choice of any individual, independently of his/her socio-demographic profile.

[2] For their part, the fixed effect models entail the application of discrete choice modelization to a single individual through a longitudinal sample of his/her choices (purchase history), which allows one to obtain individual estimations of the coefficients (Chintagunta et al, 1991). However, the use of these models has important restrictions derived from the available information; because the number of observations for each individual is usually low, and the choices made are limited to the available options, which leads to the apparition of parameter identification problems (Rossi and Allenby, 1993).

followed by a second stage application of a cluster analysis to the individual parameters of the attributes of the utility function in order to form segments of individuals. This approach is based on the application of the Random Coefficients Logit as Greene and Hensher (2002) suggest that, although the two approximations (Random Coefficients Logit and Latent Class Logit) offer alternative methods of capturing unobserved heterogeneity, the Random Coefficients Logit Model (even though it is fully parametric) has enough flexibility to provide a tremendous range within which to specify individual unobserved heterogeneity. This flexibility can even offset the specificity of the distributional assumptions.

With the advantages of operating with individual utility functions and the fact that we can find no previous application of this procedure in Tourism Marketing, the objective of this study is to segment the tourism market through the individual revealed preferences of tourists.

In order to place the study within the framework of tourist destination choice, the following section reviews the tourism literature on this subject, in order to propose the determinant attributes to be used as segmentation criteria.

2.3. Tourist Destination Choice

The analysis of tourist destination choice represents one of the most fruitful lines of investigation in Tourism studies (Fesenmaier et al., 2002), and distinguishes various approaches to the definition of tourist destination (see Tables 1 and 2 of section 2.2). One thread bases itself on destination type (discrete nature), such as regional or national natural parks (Wennergren and Nielsen, 1968; Perdue, 1986; Borgers et al., 1989; Fesenmaier, 1988; Morey et al., 1991; Dubin, 1998; Train, 1998; Riera, 2000; Adamowicz et al., 1994; Adamowicz et al. 1998; Schroeder and Louviere, 1999). Another approach defines choice alternatives (destinations) through the aggregation of geographical areas according to administrative units, geographical proximity and individual perceptions of similarity. The first criterion correlates the alternatives with countries as administrative areas (Haider and Ewing, 1990), which implies a consideration within one alternative of all the destinations found in a country. This approach allows for analysis of the global attraction of an administrative unit, which facilitates tourism decision making by public administrators as, in the final instance, it is the administrative division which determines lines of action. However, this partition can present problems in geographical areas which are shared between administrative frontiers. If two neighbouring regions have similar attraction to tourists, their degree of substitution will be higher than that of others, which could violate the assumption of Independence of Irrelevant Alternatives of the Multinomial Logit Model.

The second criterion aggregates the alternatives by their geographical proximity (independently of their administrative partition), defining the so called "macro-destinations" or "macro-site" (Siderelis and Moore, 1998). However, this procedure presents inconveniences (Fotheringham and O'Kelly, 1989): i) this destination grouping by the dimension of *space* is not direct due to its continuous nature, meaning that the delimitation of macro-destinations cannot always be made with clarity with the position of the divisionary lines being left to the discretion of the analyst. Moreover, incoherent situations can arise, such

---

[3] Heckman and Singer (1984) show that discrete distributions have enough flexibility to approximate any distribution function with a sufficient number of supports.

as the case of two neighbouring destinations which belong to different macro-destinations and are not treated as substitutes when they should be. ii) Among the destinations of a macro-destination there can be a hierarchical order based on spatial separation, which implies that these destinations are not equally substitutable, thus violating the axiom of transitivity. iii) The composition of two groups of alternatives is not constant for all individuals, as people situated in different places have different perceptions of space and, therefore, of macro-destinations.

The third criterion aggregates tourist destinations by similitude of tourist perceptions (Eymann and Ronning, 1997). In essence, it tests whether parameters referring to these individual perceptions vary significantly among the alternatives of different groups, applying the test of Cramer and Ridder (1991).

With this second approach (with three criteria), we avoid an overly-high number of alternatives (e.g. if a tourist wishes to take a holiday on the Mediterranean coast, this option would cover any point in the whole area); which is a consequence of the continuous nature of the spatial dimension (Fotheringham and O'Kelly, 1989). The studies of Eymann and Ronning (1992), Haider and Ewing (1990) and Morley (1994a; 1994b) define destinations in terms of administrative units (countries), whereas Siderelis and Moore (1998) and Eymann and Ronning (1997) resort to the use of macro-destinations through the aggregation of geographical areas and tourist perceptions, respectively.

Within this line of research, it is important to stress that the probabilistic analysis of intra-country destinations defined by administrative units has had little coverage in literature; despite the fact that the majority of national tourism in many countries is domestic, as in the case of Spain (Bote et al., 1991; Martínez, 2002); and that the territorial examination of tourism demand is a valuable element of regional economic planning (Usach, 1998), as it can characterize the tourist flow behaviour of nationals within their own country from the point of view of geographical distribution.

Our study is based upon this destination definition (intra-country administrative units) in order to define the attributes which determine the choice of tourist destinations.

2.3.1. Influence of Attributes on the Choice of Destination

Literature distinguishes the dimensions of "attributes of the destination" and "personal characteristics" in order to explain destination choice (Mak and Moncur, 1980; Borocz, 1990; Gartner, 1993; Sirakaya et al., 1996; Seddighi and Theocharous, 2002). Focusing on the attributes of the destination, we see that they represent dimensions which can contribute to the formation of perceived attraction among tourists; they are also known as pull factors (Mak and Moncur, 1980; Borocz, 1990; Gartner, 1993; Kim and Lee, 2002). Chief among them, due to their greater utilization, are distance (Wennergren and Nielsen, 1968; Stopher and Ergün, 1979; Moutinho and Trimble, 1981; Perdue, 1986; Borgers et al., 1989; Fesenmaier, 1988; Adamowicz et al., 1994; Schroeder and Louviere, 1999; Riera, 2000); and prices (Walsh et al., 1992; Siderelis and Moore, 1998; Schroeder and Louviere, 1999; Riera, 2000). However, there is no consensus among authors on their impact on destination choice, since for each individual the distance and prices of destinations can act as attraction or deterrent factors. Clearly, this fact increases heterogeneity among tourists:

i) Literature does not reach a consensus on the influence of distance on destination choice. One train of thought holds that distance -or the geographical position of the tourist relative to destinations- is considered a restriction or a dissuasive dimension of destination choice, as the displacement of an individual to the destination entails physical, temporal and monetary cost (Taylor and Knudson, 1976). This is the result reached by the studies of Wennergren and Nielsen (1968), Perdue (1985), Borgers et al., (1988), Fesenmaier (1988), Adamowicz et al. (1994) and Schroeder and Louviere (1999). Alternatively, another line of research proposes that distance can lend positive utility. Baxter (1980) shows that the journey itself, as a component of the tourism product, can give satisfaction in its own right so that, on occasions, longer distances are preferred. Similarly, Wolfe (1970; 1972) indicates that distance does not always act as a dissuasive factor, as the friction derived from it disappears after passing a certain threshold and it becomes a favourable attribute of the utility of a destination. Beaman (1974; 1976) explains this behaviour through a marginal analysis of distance, by observing the reaction of individuals to each unit of distance and concluding that each additional unit travelled offers less resistance than the previous.

ii) Literature does not reach a consensus on the influence of prices on destination choice. One line of thought holds that demand for tourism products is that of an *ordinary good*, in such a way that price increments diminish consumption (Smith, 1995; Lanquar, 2001; Serra, 2002), meaning that price is considered as a factor which reduces the utility of a destination. At an empirical level, a negative relationship between price and destination choice is found by Morey et al. (1991), Dubin (1998), Train (1998), Riera (2000) and Siderelis and Moore (1998) in the case of natural parks; by Haider and Ewing (1990), Morley (1994a; 1994b) and Eymann and Ronning (1992) for countries (administrative units) and by Siderelis and Morre (1998) for macro-destinations. Conversely, another line of thought proposes that price does not have a dissuasive effect on destination choice, but that it is an attraction factor. Morrison (1996) indicates that the underlying hedonistic character often found in the consumption of tourism products implies that high prices do not always act against demand; rather that the concept of value for money, which compares the amount spent with the quality of installations and service, takes over (Morrison, 1996). This implies an association of price increase with demand increase.

In summary, these opposite effects of distance and prices are the reason why we base our segmentation on these dimensions, since heterogeneity among tourists is more evident in these attributes.

3. RESEARCH DESIGN

3.1. Methodology

The proposed methodology to segment the tourism market by individual observed choices is based on the *Bayesian segmentation* procedure suggested by Revelt and Train (2002), which allows capture of any individual preference structure and operates with specific information for each individual. This methodology is developed through the following two-stage process (Revelt and Train, 2002): i) Bayesian estimation of individual parameters through a Logit Model with Random Coefficients; and ii) application of a cluster analysis on the individual coefficients estimated.

3.1.1. Estimation of the Individual Parameters

To estimate the individual parameters of a Random Coefficients Logit Model we apply Bayesian estimation methods[4]. We use the Multinomial Logit Model with random coefficients (RCL) because of: i) its ability to deal with the unobserved heterogeneity of tourists, by assuming that the coefficients of the variables vary among tourists; and ii) its flexibility, which allows representation of different correlation patterns among alternatives.

Following the formal approach of Train (2003), the utility function is defined as

$$U_{in} = \sum_{h=1}^{H} \beta_{nh} z_{ih} + \varepsilon_{in}$$

where z_{ih} is a vector that represents attribute h of destination i; β_n is the vector of coefficients of these attributes for each individual n which represent personal tastes; and ε_{in} is a random term that is iid extreme value. The likelihood of the observed choice y_n for individual n conditioned to parameters b and W (mean and variance of β_n, respectively) is expressed as

$$L(y_n / b, W) = \frac{\exp\left\{\sum_{h=1}^{H} \beta_{nh} z_{ih}\right\}}{\sum_{j=1}^{J} \exp\left\{\sum_{h=1}^{H} \beta_{nh} z_{jh}\right\}} \phi(\beta_n / b, W)$$

where ϕ is the function of Normal distribution.

Let $k(b,W)$ be the prior distribution of parameters b and W[5]. Bayes' rule allows the analyst to obtain the posterior distribution $K(b,W,\beta_n/Y)$ for the group of choices and of the sample individuals (n=1,..., N) as:

$$K(b, W, \beta_n / Y) \propto \prod_{n=1}^{N} L(y_n / b, W) k(b, W)$$

---

[4] Train (2001b) points out the following advantages of Bayesian procedures over classical procedures: i) they avoid the usual problems of global and local maximums, given that they are not based on the maximisation of any likelihood function; and ii) they obtain consistent and efficient estimations under more flexible conditions. The advantages of Bayesian estimation have been little used by choice researchers, and only through the work of Albert and Chib (1993) have different techniques been developed for their application (Allenby and Ginter, 1995; Lenk et al., 1996).

[5] In general, it is assumed that b has a Normal distribution and W an Inverted Gamma distribution (or Inverted Wishart distribution in the case of multi-variation) of type f(W)=W^{-(v+1)/2}e^{-vs/2W} with v being the degrees of freedom and s a parameter of scale to be estimated.

The posterior distribution has three parameter types to estimate $\theta=\{b,W,\beta_n\}$: the average b, the variance W, and the parameters of each individual β_n, from which we obtain the utility functions of each individual and, therefore, the preference structure. The estimation of the parameters is obtained through the following expression

$$\hat{\theta} = \int_{\theta} \theta \cdot K(\theta/Y)d\theta$$

This integral has no closed solution, which leads the researcher to use a procedure of estimation by simulation. Therefore, θ is estimated as the average of the simulated drawings. However, the posterior distribution $K(\theta/Y)$ does not always take the form of a known distribution from which one could immediately take draws. Train (2001a), in the case of choice models, suggests the use of Monte Carlo Markov Chains; specifically, the sample simulation algorithms of Gibbs and Metropolis-Hasting for the draws of the density function. Train (2001b) also demonstrates that the estimator of the simulated average of the posterior distribution is consistent, asymptomatically normal and equivalent to the estimator of maximum likelihood.

3.1.2. Segment Formation

Once we obtain the estimations of the parameters for each individual, we proceed to construct the segments with similar preferences. To this end, we apply cluster analysis (Ward's minimum variance hierarchical algorithm) to the matrix of the parameters of each individual. The final number of segments is reached when the segments observed explain at least 65% of the global variance, and when another segment is added, the increase in the total variance is less than 5% (Lewis and Thomas, 1990). In the opinion of Grande and Abascal (2000) and Gené (2002), this is the most appropriate method when using variables derived from previous statistical procedures; and Sorensen (2003) indicates that this method is regarded as very efficient. Additionally, we apply a Variance Analysis, both univariant (ANOVA) and multivariante (MANOVA), to confirm the segments obtained; i.e. to validate the existence of differences in the preference structures of the individuals.

3.2. Sample, Data and Variables

To reach our proposed objectives, we have used information on tourist choice behaviour obtained from the national survey "Spanish Holidaying Behaviour (III)", which was carried out by the Spanish Centre for Sociological Research. This is due to the following reasons: i) The availability of information on individual tourist destination choice behaviour in terms of intra-country administrative units; and ii) The survey is directed at a sample (over 18 years old) obtained in origin (at home), which avoids the characteristic selection bias of destination collected samples, leading to a more precise analysis of tourist demand. The sample is taken by using multistage sampling, stratified by conglomerations, with proportional selection of primary units -cities- and of secondary units –censorial sections-. The information was collected through personal, at home, interviews with a structured questionnaire. Of the initial sample of 3,781 individuals, we are left with 2,127 that take holidays. This final sample represents a sample error of ±2.16% for a confidence level of 95.5%.

In order to make the choice models operative, we will define the variables used and identify the dependent and independent variables.

(1) *Dependent variables.* To represent the set of intra-country destinations (administrative units) available to the tourist, we use 50 dummy variables for the 50 Spanish provinces.

(2) *Independent Variables*:

a) **Distance to the destination.** In general, studies use different indicators of real distance[6], such as the Euclidean distance -in kilometres or miles- (Wennergren and Nielsen, 1968; Stopher and Ergün, 1979; Moutinho and Trimble, 1981; Peterson et al., 1983; Perdue, 1986; Borgers et al., 1988; Fesenmaier, 1988; Adamowicz et al., 1994; Dellaert et al., 1997; Schroeder and Louviere, 1999), and displacement time (Louviere and Hensher, 1983; Dellaert et al., 1997; Schroeder and Louviere, 1999; Kemperman et al., 2000).

Following these authors, we measure distance in kilometres (DKm) and in time invested in displacement (Dtime), which facilitates a comparison of the results with those of other international studies. The use of both variables implies the construction of two origin-destination matrices of a 50x50 order, in which we include kilometres and time between each origin and destination for the provinces. This information on distances and displacement times between origins and destinations is found in the Campsa Interactive Guide (taking the provincial capitals as reference points).

b) **Destination prices.** Literature measures the prices of a destination with different indicators. For example, costs at the destination in absolute quantities or in terms relative to individual tourist income. However, the difficulties tourists have in knowing, a priori, all costs (e.g. goods bought at destination) and the exact cost of each component, oblige researchers to make simplifications in their empirical applications. Consequently, various authors propose the use of widely available proxies (as opposed to finding detailed price lists of products and services in each destination) to reflect the prices of a destination.

Morey et al. (1991), Dubin (1998), Train (1998), Riera (2000), Siderelis and Moore (1998) and Morley (1994a,b) employ travel costs as a proxy of total price, as it is one of the highest costs to the tourist. However, the measurement of travel costs is not without problems. Travel costs are made up of the following

---

[6] Psychology and Geography of Behaviour show the existence of discrepancies among perceived distance by individuals -or subjective- and the real distance -objective or geographical-. Ewing (1980) argues the incidence of factors such as the familiarity or monotony of a route. Baxter and Ewing (1981) propose the "perceptual barrier effect", by which a distance is perceived to increase due to a perceived rather than real barrier (e.g. a mountain pass). Moreover, with the lack of "perceptual barriers", tourists perceive destinations closer than they physically are (Mayo and Jarvis, 1986). Finally, Baxter and Ewing (1979) propose the so called "intervening opportunities effect", which considers the flow of people between two destinations a and b with similar characteristics and equidistant from an origin o are influenced by intermediary destinations. Thus, a destination c situated between o and a produces a greater reduction on flows between o and a than between o and b, independently of the fact that c competes indistinctly with a and b. In other words, these intermediary opportunities act as "distance amplifiers" between two destinations. The lack of information in our study on the perceptions of individuals prevents us from using subjective measurements of distance.

three elements (Ewing, 1980): i) the effective cost of travelling, measurable by the price paid on public transport (Dellaert et al., 1997; Morley 1994a; 1994b) or in a private vehicle; whether by unit of distance (e.g., 24 ptas/km (Riera, 2000) or 0.16$/mile (Siderelis and Moore, 1998)) or by total fuel costs (Train, 1998); ii) the physical and psychological effort of realising the journey, which, to date, has not been modelled given the impossibility of representing it in monetary terms and by unit of time (Ewing, 1980); and iii) the opportunity costs of the time given to the journey (what an individual would earn if s/he spent the travelling time on money earning activities) whose measurement has been very limited in literature; using estimations from other fields (value of time spent travelling to work (Cesario, 1976; Edward and Dennis, 1976) - untrustworthy for tourism (Goodwin, 1976; Ewing, 1980); the result of regressing the number of journeys in a period on travelling time, salary and cost of transport (Hof and Rosenthal, 1987); or arbitrarily fixing a value of 1/3 of salary per hour (Train, 1998)).

Another indicator is the exchange rate of the destination country (Witt and Martin, 1987; Morley, 1994a, 1994b). However, authors such as Eymann and Ronning (1992) and Usach (1999) consider that the correct method of reflecting the prices of a certain tourist market is to compare destination prices with those of the home market and those of competing destinations. Along this line, Eymann and Ronning (1992) use purchase parity differentials between the origin and respective destinations, obtained from the corresponding consumer price indexes[7]. In line with these authors, our study measures destination prices of intra-country administrative units through consumer price index differentials among origins and destinations, which are published in the National Institute of Statistics (INE), which represent the cost of living of each origin/destination.

c) *Descriptive variables of the segments.* i) *Organization.* The way of organizing the vacation is collected with a dummy variable which takes a value of 1 if the tourist uses a travel agent and 0 if he/she organizes his/her own vacation. ii) *Children.* The number of children under sixteen who go on vacation (Moutinho 1987). iii) *Length of stay.* To represent the temporal demand for holidays, we obtain information on the length of stay with a quantitative variable of the number of days that a tourist spends outside the usual place of residence. iv) *Transport mode.* The study considers, by dummy variables, the following: car, train, coach, plane and ship. v) *Accommodation type.* By using dummy variables, the types of accommodation are: hotel, camping site, own apartment, rented apartment, staying with friends or family and wild camping. And vi) *Tourist expenditures.* The variable relative to tourism expenditures is found by a quantitative variable which represents costs incurred during the holiday.

---

[7] Morley (1994c) demonstrates that the Consumer Price Index of a geographical region is a good indicator of tourist prices, by showing high correlation between the two.

4. RESULTS OBTAINED AND DISCUSSION

4.1. Estimation of the Individual Parameters

First, we use Bayesian procedures to estimate the coefficients for each individual of the variables -distance and prices-, which are determinants of destination choice, using Random Coefficients Logit Models. We also propose two distinct specifications: i) *Segmentation PDK*, which includes prices at the destination and distance in kilometres; and ii) *Segmentation PDT*, which considers prices and distance measured as the time spent on the journey. Table 3 presents the aggregated estimation for the whole sample.

With regard to the impact of distance, we find that this dimension (in kilometres and in travelling time), is significant at a level below 0.1% in all the equations and presents a negative sign, which leads us to characterize distance as a dissuasive factor in the choice of destination province, in line with Taylor and Knudson (1976). In other words, the displacement of an individual to the intra-country destination supposes physical, temporal and monetary investment. Apart from this, the significance of its standard deviation (SD(β)) at 0.1% in all cases, suggests that distance has a differentiated effect among the individuals of the sample in that longer distances do not suppose less utility for all the sample tourists.

Table 3. Influence of prices and distance on destination choice
(Standard errors in brackets)

Independent Variables	Equation 1		Equation 2	
	b	SD (β)	b	SD (β)
Price	-0.222^a	0.056^a	-0.210^a	0.081^a
	(0.021)	(0.012)	(0.021)	(0.020)
Distance (Kilometres)	-0.398^a	0.146^a		
	(0.014)	(0.012)		
Distance (Time)			-0.508^a	0.535^a
			(0.023)	(0.044)

a=prob<0,1%; b=prob<1%; c=prob<5%; d=prob<10%

Regarding the impact of prices, we find that this dimension is significant at a level below 0.1% in all the equations, and presents a negative sign, which suggests that tourists tend to choose destinations with lower prices, in line with Smith (1995) and Lanquar (2001). This result allows us to support the idea that tourism products are *ordinary goods*. It is important to stress that, like the variable of distance, the standard deviation parameter of the coefficient (SD(β)) is significant in all equations, which implies a differentiated effect among the individuals of the sample. The differentiated effect found for both distance and prices suggests that they are good dimensions for segmenting the market.

Evidently, these are global results that represent the preferences of an average tourist. To illustrate the utility of obtaining estimations of individual preferences we select two tourists from the sample (for example, sample observations 328 and 1802 for segmentation PDK and sample observations 619 and 1276 for segmentation PDT) to compare their preference structures with the average tourist (Table 4).

Table 4. Illustration of the individual preferences

	Segmentation PDK		Segmentation PDT	
	Distance Km	Price	Distance Time	Price
Tourist 328	-0.3901	-0.3369		
Tourist 1802	0.3319	-0.1166		
Tourist 619			-1.0113	-0.0226
Tourist 1276			0.3549	-0.1213
Average Tourist	-0.398	-0.222	-0.508	-0.21

Source: Own work

For segmentation PDK, both tourists, 328 and 1802, show a negative marginal utility in relation to prices, although the first in this case has a greater price effect than the average tourist; the opposite is the case for the second tourist as there is a lower price effect than the average tourist. With regard to distance in kilometres, tourist 328 is clearly adverse to long distances, whereas tourist 1802 has a marginally positive utility for long distances (Graph 1).

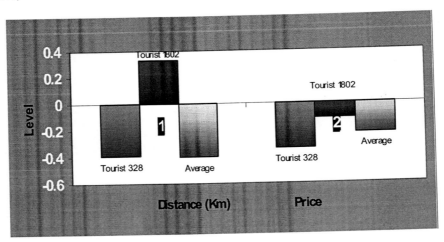

Graph 1. Individual Preferences PDK

For segmentation PDT, both tourists, 619 and 1276, show a lesser negative price effect in comparison with the average. Distance in time has a negative impact on the first tourist and a positive effect on the second (Graph 2).

This illustration with two observations shows the importance of knowing the individual preferences of each tourist, as in this way, tailor made tourist products can be offered, giving rise to a one by one or tourist by tourist segmentation.

4.2. Formation and Characterization of Segments

Secondly, we apply Ward's cluster method to the matrix of the estimations of the individual parameters. Applying the double explanation criteria of a minimum of 65% of the total variance, and of least 5% increase in variance when adding a new segment, we select three segments for segmentation PDK and four for segmentation PDT. Table 5 summarises the results of the application of both criteria; the shaded area represents the number of segments selected in each criterion.

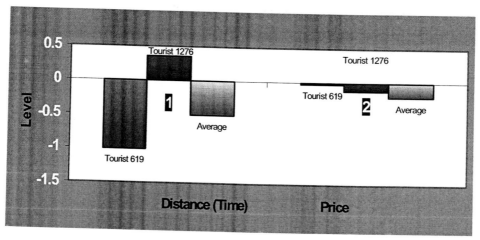

Graph 2. Individual Preferences PDK

Table 5. Determination of the number of segments

N. of Segments	Prices and distance in kilometres			N. of Segments	Prices and distance in time		
	σ^{2*}	$\sigma^2(\%)^*$	$\Delta\sigma^{2*}$		σ^{2*}	$\sigma^2(\%)^*$	$\Delta\sigma^{2*}$
10	6.028	4.286	0.616	10	17.489	2.853	0.295
9	6.895	4.902	0.687	9	19.301	3.149	0.325
8	7.862	5.590	0.925	8	21.298	3.475	0.459
7	9.164	6.516	1.581	7	24.115	3.934	0.524
6	11.388	8.097	2.094	6	27.328	4.459	1.413
5	14.333	10.191	3.566	5	35.989	5.872	1.527
4	19.348	13.757	4.649	4	45.349	7.399	7.841
3	25.887	18.407	11.195	3	93.404	15.241	8.347
2	41.631	29.603	70.396	2	144.563	23.589	76.410
1	140.631	100	0	1	612.835	100	0

*Intra-group variance

The segments identified are significantly distinct at a level of 0.1% with regard to the values obtained from the F tests for the variables considered separately (ANOVA) and simultaneously MANOVA), in the variance analyses applied to the average values of these variables (see Table 6). This confirms the existence of differences in the preference structures of the individuals.

Once we identify the segments according to the proposed criteria, we proceed to characterize them according to the dimensions of distance and prices, and various variables that represent tourist behaviour.

Table 6. ANOVA and MANOVA of the segments

Variable	Prices and distance in km		Prices and distance in time	
	F	Prob.	F	Prob.
Prices	27.288	0.000	13.445	0.000
Distance in kilometres	5,889.442	0.000		
Distance in time			11,843.08	0.000
MANOVA	1,689.40	0.000	2,300.83	0.000

4.2.1. Characterization of the Segments Obtained through Preferences on Distance in Kilometres and Prices

Table 7 characterizes the segments detected according to the criteria of "distance in kilometres" and "prices", showing the averages for each segment and the global averages for the whole sample. It also indicates the distinct or similar segments according to the Scheffé Test. This test allows us to show that the three identified segments have distinct preferences for the two dimensions considered (distance in kilometres and prices). In Graph 3 (with inverted axis values) we observe the position and dispersion of the segments in these dimensions. For each segment we obtain the following: Segment I has 811 individuals, clearly adverse to high prices and with a "moderate" position towards distance (-0.234>-0.398=average sample value). Segment II is the largest (1112 people) with the strongest adversity to long distances and an intermediate reaction to prices. Finally, segment III is the smallest group (204), with a positive preference towards long distances and is the least affected by price rises.

Table 7. Characterization of the segments through the marginal effect of prices and distance in kilometres

Segmentation: Prices and Distance in Kilometres				
Segments	Size	Proportion	Prices	Distance in Km
I	811	38.1	-0.232	-0.234
II	1112	52.3	-0.219	-0.603
III	204	9.6	-0.206	0.074
Average Values			-0.222	-0.398
Distinct Segments (Scheffé Test)			I, II, III	I, II, III
Similar Segments (Scheffé Test)			None	None

Table 8 presents the average values -of each segment and the whole sample- for the variables "self-organised holiday", "number of children under 16 going on the holiday", "number of days stay", "means of transport", "accommodation type" and "costs incurred on the holiday". It also indicates the segments with distinct values according to the Scheffé Test (Additionally, for the categorical variables, the results are corroborated with the Ji-square Test of the Contingency Tables).

Segment I, which is adverse to high prices and has a "moderate" response to distance, presents intermediate values in the variables that describe its tourist behaviour. To be precise, 83.1% organize their own holiday, they travel with 0.714 children under 16, they take an average holiday of 19 days, they mainly use their own cars or coaches, and they mainly stay in chalets or apartments (33.3%), with friends or family (32.8%) and in hotels (29%). Their spending is at an intermediate level of 727.45€.

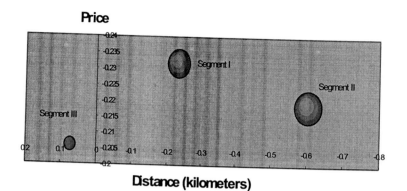

Graph 3. Segmentation PDK

Table 8. Characterization of the PDK segments by tourist behaviour

	Mean	Segment I	Segment II	Segment III	Anova	Different Segments
Self-organised holiday	0,874	0,831	0,934	0,714	49,75[a]	I, II, III
Children under16	0,821	0,714	0,928	0,646	7,314[b]	(I-III, (I-III)
Lenght of stay (days)	21,188	19,008	23,279	18,411	16,562[a]	(I-III), II
Transport mode 1 Car	0,748	0,700	0,831	0,490	64,855[a]	I, II, III
Transport mode 2 Train	0,068	0,094	0,038	0,132	19,182[a]	(I-III), II
Transport mode 3 Coach	0,114	0,153	0,085	0,123	11,005[a]	(I-III), (II-III)
Transport mode 4 Plane	0,053	0,043	0,027	0,230	77,898[a]	(I-II), III
Transport mode 5 Ship	0,009	0,002	0,014	0,010	3,587[c]	Ninguno
Accommodation type 1 Hotel	0,216	0,290	0,135	0,367	49,303[a]	I, II, III
Accommodation type 2 Camping site	0,064	0,042	0,087	0,031	9,89[a]	(I-III), II
Accommodation type 3 Own apartment	0,261	0,184	0,342	0,122	41,78[a]	(I-III), II
Accommodation type 4 Rented apartment	0,133	0,149	0,132	0,071	4,117[c]	(I-II), III
Accommodation type 5 Friends and relatives	0,316	0,328	0,290	0,408	5,818[b]	(I-II), III
Accommodation type 6 Wild camping	0,010	0,006	0,014	0,000	2,42[d]	Ninguno
Tourist expenditures €	645,48	727.45	563.37	753.17	6,606[b]	(I-II), (I-III)

Segment II, which is clearly adverse to long distances and has an intermediate price response, presents the greatest proportion of people who organise their own holidays (93.4%) and they travel with an average of 0.928 children under 16. This group also takes the longest holidays (23.27 days), is more likely to travel by car (83.1%), has the highest use of chalets or apartments (47.4%) and tends to spend less at the destination (563.37€).

Finally, segment III, which manifests a positive preference towards long distances and is the least affected by price rises, is characterised by having the largest proportion of individuals that use travel agents, travelling with fewer children under 16 and spending fewer days on holiday (18.41 days). Of the three segments, it is the one that uses air travel the most (23%), as well as hotels and the houses of family and friends. This group are also the biggest spenders (753.17€)

4.2.2. Characterization of the Segments Obtained Through Preferences on Distance in Time and Prices

Tables 9 characterizes the segments formed according to "distance in time" and "prices", showing the averages of each segment and the global values for the whole sample. We also indicate distinct or similar segments according to the Scheffé Test. This test shows that the four segments have different preferences for the dimension of "distance measured in time spent on the journey", but not with regard to prices. In the case of prices, only segment D presents a clearly higher negative effect than A, B and C. In Graph 4, we show the position and dispersion of the segments in these dimensions (with inverted axis values).

Table 9. Characterization of the segments through the marginal effect of prices and distance in time

Segmentation: Prices and Distance in Time				
Segments	Size	Proportion	Prices	Distance in Time
A	518	24.4	-0.210	0.209
B	496	23.3	-0.205	-0.698
C	654	30.7	-0.200	-1.124
D	459	21.6	-0.228	-0.234
Average Values			-0.210	-0.508
Distinct Segments (Scheffé Test)			D	A, B, C, D
Similar Segments (Scheffé Test)			(A- B-C)	None

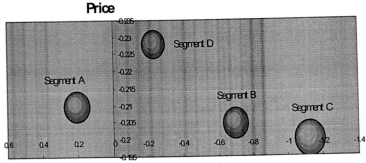

Graph 4. Segmentation PDT

In general, segments A, B and C present a relatively negative posture towards prices. Segment A derives positive utility from long journeys (0.209>-0.508=average sample value), whereas segments B and C are clearly adverse to long journeys (-0.698 and -1.124, respectively). With regard to price, segment D shows the highest negative effect, with a moderately negative reaction to long journeys.

Table 10 presents the average values -for each segment and the whole sample- for the variables "organizing own holiday", "number of children under 16 on the holiday", "length of holiday", "means of transport", "type of accommodation" and "holiday spending". We also indicate the segments with distinct values according to the Scheffé Test (Additionally, for the categorical variables, the results are corroborated with the Ji-square Test of the Contingency Tables).

Segment A, with a relatively negative posture towards high prices and deriving positive utility from long journeys, is made up of people that use travel agents more than the other groups (the lowest percentage of self-organisation of the holiday (78.5%)), travel with 0.727 children under 16 and take the shortest holidays. This segment makes the least use of the car (60.8%) and the most use of the train (12.5%), coach (15.6%) and aeroplane (10%). They also use hotels more (33.8%) and stay with friends and family more than the other groups (35.8%). Finally, it is one of the groups that spends the most on holiday (719.79€).

Table 10. Characterization of the PDT segments through tourist behaviour

	Mean	Segment A	Segment B	Segment C	Segment D	Anova	Different Segments
Self-organised holiday	0,874	0,785	0,903	0,960	0,819	33,116[a]	(A-D), B, C
Children under16	0,821	0,727	0,942	0,917	0,656	5,242[b]	(A-D), (A-B-C)
Lenght of stay (days)	21,188	18,414	20,217	25,576	19,097	20,701[a]	(A-B-D), C
Transport mode 1 Car	0,748	0,608	0,784	0,881	0,680	46,02[a]	(A-D), B, C
Transport mode 2 Train	0,068	0,125	0,054	0,024	0,081	16,702[a]	A, (B-C), (B-D)
Transport mode 3 Coach	0,114	0,156	0,117	0,058	0,144	11,306[a]	(A-B-D), C
Transport mode 4 Plane	0,053	0,100	0,020	0,021	0,078	18,109[a]	(A-D), (B-C)
Transport mode 5 Ship	0,009	0,004	0,018	0,011	0,004	2,387[d]	Ninguno
Accommodation type 1 Hotel	0,216	0,338	0,184	0,096	0,284	39,735[a]	(A-D), B, C
Accommodation type 2 Camping site	0,064	0,036	0,076	0,096	0,038	8,106[a]	(A-B-D), (B-C)
Accommodation type 3 Own apartment	0,261	0,143	0,256	0,408	0,191	41,717[a]	(A-D), (B-D), C
Accommodation type 4 Rented apartment	0,133	0,123	0,132	0,134	0,142	0,252	Ninguno
Accommodation type 5 Friends and relatives	0,316	0,358	0,333	0,253	0,340	5,908[b]	(A-B-D), (B-C)
Accommodation type 6 Wild camping	0,010	0,002	0,019	0,013	0,004	3,007[c]	Ninguno
Tourist expenditures €	645,48	719.79	506.66	594.32	771.68	6,167[a]	(B-C), (A-C-D)

Segment C, with a relatively negative attitude towards high prices and the most adverse to long distances, is made up of people that organise their own holidays in 96% of cases, travel with children under 16 and take the longest holidays. This is the segment that makes the most use of their own cars and of chalets and apartments (54.2%); and they spend a moderate 594.32€.

Finally, segment D with a moderately negative reaction to long journeys and the largest negative price effect of the four segments, contains a significant percentage of people that use travel agents (28.1%), a lower number of children under 16 and they take average holidays of 19.09 days. They are the group that most use air travel and coaches and least use their own cars. Also, they stay with family and friends (34%), in chalets and apartments (33.3%) and in hotels (28.4%); and have an average holiday spending of 771.68€.

In summary, of the two dimensions analyzed -distance and prices-, distance shows greater dispersion among the segments with regard to the sample average of either of the two measures used. Also, some segments obtain more utility from a destination from the fact that it is distant, which is in line with the proposals of Wolfe (1970; 1972), Beaman (1974; 1976) and Baxter (1980) that the journey itself can provide satisfaction. The negative posture towards prices has differing degrees of sensitivity according to the segment, although the differences are not as marked as those of distances (especially in the PDT segmentation), as the values are very similar and negative in all cases.

5. CONCLUSIONS

The implication that individual revealed preferences can be a starting point for market segmentation leads us to examine this phenomenon in the case of tourists with a sample of 2,127 individuals. The operative formalization is developed through a two-stage process, which firstly uses Bayesian procedures to estimate the individual parameters of a Random Coefficient Logit Model and secondly applies cluster analysis to the individual coefficients estimated.

Through the idea that certain attributes can have an impact on destination choice, with differentiated effects for different segments of the population, the empirical analysis carried out on the sample reveals the existence of tourist groups with distinct sensitivities to the dimensions of distance and prices. In short, the use of the attributes of "distance in kilometres" and "prices" detects three market segments with differing preferences towards these two dimensions: Segment I is made up of individuals clearly adverse to high prices and a moderate posture towards distance; segment II presents the greatest adversity towards long distances and adopts an intermediate posture towards prices; and segment III has a positive preference towards long distances and is less affected by price rises.

The use of the attributes of "distance in time" and "prices" finds four segments with distinct preferences towards the dimension of "distance measured by journey time", but not with regard to prices (with the exception of segment D, which has a higher negative effect than segments A, B and C). In general, segments A, B and C present a relatively negative and similar posture towards prices, and among the three, segment A obtains positive utility from long journeys, whereas segments B and especially C are adverse.

As implications for management, we would like to mention the following: i) Segmentation through *individual revealed preferences* is demonstrated to be useful insofar as it can identify individually differentiated behaviour patterns. This segmentation is particularly important in that it is based on the preferences of individual people. The application in the study deals with aspects that lead a tourist to choose a certain tourism product type. In other words, it is a segmentation based on the key elements that explain why a tourist goes to a destination. Moreover, the estimation of the individual parameters of the utility function of each individual reveals his/her preference structure and allows us to operate with precise information on each individual. At a time when tourists are increasingly demanding and insist on service provision adapted to their specific needs, knowledge of the profile of each tourist allows tourism organizations to offer the most suitable products. ii) The analysis is based on *real purchase choices* made by individuals (and not on *declarations of intent*), which allows a more accurate representation of the behaviour of each tourist. And iii) The heterogeneity of the preferences detected implies differentiated behaviour among the distinct tourist segments, which reveals the clear need to apply segmentation strategies to the tourism market.

Among the limitations of this study are the following: i) its static character, as it is only based on the main annual holiday of an individual. Alternatively, an analysis of all holidays taken (main holiday, weekend trips etc.) in a year or over various years with panel data would allow us a better understanding of the determinants of the choice; ii) the field of study is Spain. It would be useful if the results were reinforced by applications on other geographical areas in order to be able to generalise the conclusions; iii) the lack of available information on certain variables, such as psychological distance and individual perceptions of the attributes of the destinations; and iv) we do not consider a specific destination, rather any of the destinations chosen by Spanish tourists. This could impede knowledge of the impact of the characteristic factors of a particular destination. However, this way of working allows us to find the influence of different dimensions in a general manner.

Possible future lines of research are that the results of this study should be supported by research on other geographical areas in order to make comparisons. Similarly, it would be interesting to carry out the analysis from a longitudinal perspective, which would allow us to observe the temporal evolution of the effects of the proposed dimensions.

REFERENCES

Adamowicz, W., Bocal, P., Williams, M. y Louviere, J. (1998), "Stated Preference Approaches for Measuring Passive Use Values: Choice Experiments and Contingent Valuation", *American Journal of Agricultural Economics*, 80, febrero, 64-75.

Adamowicz, W., Louviere, J. y Williams, M. (1994) "Combining Revealed and Stated Preference Methods for Valuing Environmental Amenities", *Journal of Environmental Economics and Management*, 26, 271-292.

Albert, J. and Chib, S. (1993) "Bayesian Analysis of Binary and Polychotomous Response Data", *Journal of the American Statistical Association*, 88, 669-679.

Albert, J. and Chib, S. (1993) "Bayesian Analysis of Binary and Polychotomous Response Data", *Journal of the American Statistical Association*, 88, 669-679.

Allenby, G. M. and Ginter, J.L. (1995) "Using Extremes to Design Products and Segment Marketis", *Journal of Marketing Research*, 32, 392-403.

Allenby, G.M. y Rossi, P.E. (1999) "Marketing Models of Consumer Heterogeneity", *Journal of Econometrics*, 89, 57-78.

Allenby, G.M., Arora, N. y Ginter, J.L. (1998) "On the Heterogeneity of Demand", *Journal of Markeging Research*, 35, agosto, 384-389.

Anderson, S.P., de Palma, A. y Thisse, J-F. (1992). *Discrete Choice Theory of Product Differentiation*. Cambridge: MIT Press.

Batsell, R.R. y Louviere, J.J. (1991), "Experimental Choice Analysis", *Marketing Letters*, 2, 199-214.

Baxter, M. y Ewing, G. (1981), "Models of Recreational Trip Distribution", *Regional Studies*, vol. 15, 5, p. 327-344.

Baxter, M.J. (1980) "The Interpretation of the Distance and Attractiveness Components in Models of Recreational Trips", *Geographical Analysis*, 11 (3), p.311-315.

Baxter, M.J. y Ewing, G.O. (1979) "Calibration of Production-Constrained Trip Distributon Models and the Effect of Intervening Opportunities", *Journal of Regional Science*

Beaman, J. (1974) "Distance and the 'Reaction' to Distance as a Function of Distance", *Journal of Leisure Research*, 6, verano, 220-231.

Beaman, J. (1976) "Corrections Regarding the Impedance of Distance Functions for Several g(d) Functions", *Journal of Leisure Research*, 49-52.

Becker, G. (1965). "A Theory of the Allocation of Time" *Economical Journal*, 75, 493-517.

Ben-Akiva, M. y Lerman, S.R. (1985) *Discrete Choice Models:Theory and Application to Travel Demand*. Cambridge: MIT Press.

Bloom, J. Z. (2004) "Tourism Market Segmentation with Linear and Non-linear Techniques", *Tourism Management*.

Borgers, A.W. J., Van Der Heijden, R.E.C.M. y Timmermans, H.J.P. (1989) "A Variety Seeking Model of Spatial Choice-behaviour", *Environment and Planning A*, 21, 1037-1048.

Borocz, J. (1990) "Hungary as a Destination 1960-1984", *Annals of Tourism Research*, 17, 1, 19-35.

Bote, V., Huescar, A. y vogeler, C. (1991) "Concetración e Integración de las Agencias de Viajes Españolas ante el Acta Única Europea", *Papers de Turisme*, 5, 5-43.

Bronner, F. Y Hoog, R. (1985) "A Recipe for Mixing Decision Ingredients", *European Research*, 13, p. 109-115.

Cavero, S. y Cebollada, J. (1999) "Buscando Segmentos Latentes en el Mercado. Una Aplicación Empírica con Datos de Elección de Marca", *XI Encuentro de Profesores Universitarios de Marketing*, Valladolid.

Cesario, F.J. (1976), "Value of Time in Recreation Benefit Studies", *Land Economics*, 52, 32-41.

Chen, J. S. (2003) "Market Segmentation by Tourists' sentiments", *Annals of Tourism Research*, 30, 1, p. 178-193.

Chintagunta, P.K., Jain, D.C. y Vilcassim, N.J. (1991) "Investigating Heterogeneity in Brand Preferences in Logit Models for Panel Data", *Journal of Marketing Research*, 28, 4, 417-428.

Cramer, J.S. y Ridder, G. (1991) "Pooling States in the Multinomial Logit Model", *Journal of Econometrics*, 47, 267-272.

Currim, I.S. (1981) "Using Segmentation Approaches for Better Prediction and Understanding from Consumer Mode Choice Models", *Journal of Marketing Research*, 18, agosto, 301-309.

De Rus, G. y León, C. (1997) "Economía del Turismo. Un Panorama", *Revista de Economía Aplicada*, 15, 5, 71-109.

Decrop, A. y Snelders, D. (2005) "A Grounded Typology of Vacation Desision-making", *Tourism Management*, 26, 2, 131-132.

Dellaert, B.G.C., Borgers, A.W.J. y Timmermans, H. J.P. (1997) "Conjoint Models of Tourist Portfolio Choice: Theory and Illustration", *Leisure Sciences*, 19, 31-58.

Díaz, A. e Iglesias, V. (2000) "El Uso de las Expectativas de los Clientes como Criterio de Segmentación en los Mercados Turísiticos", en Blanquer, D., ed., *Turismo: Comercialización de Productso, Gestión de Organizaciones, Aeropuertos y Protección de la Naturaleza*, Valencia: Tirant lo Balnc.

Dubin, J.A. (1998) "The Demand for Recreations Fishing in Montana" en Dubin, J.A., ed., *Studies in Consumer Demand-Econometric Methods Applied to Market Data*, Boston: Kluwer Academic Publishers.

Edwards, S.L. y Dennis, S.J. (1976) "Long Distance Day-tripping in Great Britain", *Journal of Transport Economics and Policy*, 10, 237-256.

Eymann, A. (1995) Consumers' Spatial Choice Behavior, Heidelberg: Physica-Verlag.

Eymann, A. y Ronning, G. (1992) "Discrete Choice Analysis of Foreign Travel Demand" en Vosgerau, H.J., ed., *European Integration in the World Economy. Studies in International Economics and Institutions*, Berlin: Springer.

Eymann, A. y Ronning, G. (1997) "Microeconometric Models of Tourists' Destination Choice", *Regional Science and Urban Economics*, 27, 735-761.

Fesenmaier, D.R. (1988) "Integrating Activity Patterns into Destination Choice Models", *Journal of Leisure Resesarch*, 20, 3, 175-191.

Fesenmaier, D.R., Yeong, H., Pan, B. y Gretzel, U. (2002) "Behavioral Foundations for Travel Destination Recommendation Systems", Working Draft, National Laboratory for Tourism and e-Commerce, Universidad de Illinois (Urbana-Champaign).

Fotheringham, A.S. y O'Kelly, M.E. (1989), *Spatial Interaction Models: Formulations and Applications*, Dordrecht (The Nederlands): Kluwer Academic Publishers.

Gartner, W.C. (1993) "Image Formation Process", en *Communication and Channel Systems in Tourism Marketing*, Uysal, M. y Fesenmaier, D.R., eds., Nueva York: The Harworth Press.

Gené, J. (2002) "Construcción de una Tipología y Caracterización. Aplicación a los Turistas de la Costa Dorada", *Investigación y Marketing*, 74, 50-55.

González Benito, O. y Santos, L. (2000) "Buscando Segmentos Latentes en el Mercado: Aplicación en el Contexto de Selección de Establecimiento Minorista", *XII Encuentro de Profesores Universitarios de Marketing*, Santiago de Compostela.

Goodwin, P.B. (1976) "Human Effort and the Value of Travel Time", *Journal of Transport Economics and Policy*, 10, 3-15.

Grande, I. y Abascal, E. (2000) Fundamentos y Técnicas de Investigación Comercial, Madrid: Esic.

Greene, W.H. and Hensher, D.A. (2002) "A Latent Class Model for Discrete Choice Analysis: Contrasts with Mixed Logit", Working paper ITS-WP-02-08, Institute of Transport Studies, The Australian Key Centre in Transport Management.

Haider, W. Y Ewing, G.O. (1990) "A Model of Tourist Choices of Hypothetical Caribbean Destinations", *Leisure Sciences*, 12, 33-47.

Heckman, J. y Singer, B. (1984) "A Method for Minimizing the Impact of Distributional Assumptions in Econometric Models for Duration Data", *Econometrica*, 52, 271-320.

Hof, J.G. y Rosenthal, D.H. (1987) "Valuing Opportunity Cost of Travel Time in Recreation Demand Models: An Application to Aggregate Data", *Journal of Leisure Research*, 19, 3, 174-188.

Hsiao, C. (1986) "Analysis of Panel Data", Cambridge, Cambridge University Press.

Hsieh, S., O'Learly, J.T., Morrison, A.M. y Chiang, D. (1997) "Travel Decision Pattern Segmentation of Pleasure Travel", *Journal of Vacation Marketing*, 3, 289-302.

Jain, D.C., Vilcassim, N.J. y Chintagunta, P.K., (1994) "A Random-Coefficients Logit Brand-Choice Model Applied to Panel Data", *Journal of Business and Economics Statistics*, 12, 3, 317-328.

Jeng, J-M. y Fesenmaier, D.R. (1996) "A Neural Network Approach to Discrete Choice Modeling", *Journal of Travel and Tourism Marketing*, 5, 1/2, 119-144.

Kemperman, A.D.A.M., Borgers, A.W.J., Oppewal, H. y Timmermans, H.J.P. (2000) "Consumer Choice of Theme Parks: A Conjoint Choice Model of Seasonality Effects and Variety Seeking Behavior", *Leisure Sciences*, 22, 1-18.

Kim, S. y Lee, Ch. (2002) "Push and Pull Relationships", *Annals of Tourism Research*, 29, 1, 257-260.

Kotler, P. (2003) *Marketing Management*, New Jersey: Prentice-Hall.

Kroes, E.P. y Sheldon, R.J. (1988). "Stated Preference Methods: An Introduction", *Journal of Transport Economics and Policy*, 20, 11-25.

Lancaster, K.J. (1966), "A New Approach to Consumer Theory", *Journal of Political Economy*, 14, 132-157.

Lanquar, R. (2001) *Marketing Turístico*, Barcelona: Ariel Turismo.

Lenk, P.J., DeSarbo, W.S., Green, P.E. and Young M.R. (1996) "Hirerachical Bayes Conjoint Analysis: Recovery of Partworh Heterogeneity from Reduced Experimental Designs", *Marketing Science*, 15 (2), 173-191.

Lewis, P. y Thomas, H. (1990) "The Linkage between Strategy, Strategic Groups, and Performance in the UK Retail Grocery Industry", *Strategic Management Journal*, 11, 1990, 385-397.

Louviere, J.J. y Hensher, D.A. (1983). "Using Discrete Choice Models with Experimental Design Data to Forecast Consumer Demand for a Unique Cultural Event", *Journal of Consumer Research*, 10, diciembre, 348-361.

Mak, J. y Moncur, J.E.T. (1980) "The Demand for Travel Agents", *Journal of Transport Economics and Policy*, mayo, 221-231.

Martínez, E. (2002) "Flujos Regionales del Turismo Doméstico en España", Documento de Trabajo, Universidad de Genrona.

Mayo, E.J. y Jarvis, L.P. (1981) *The Psychology of Leisure Travel*, Boston: CBI Publishing Co.

Monfort, V.M., Morant, A. e Ivars, J. (1996) "LA Demanda Turística", en Pedreño, A., ed., *Introducción a la Economia del Turismo en España*, Madrid: Civitas.

Morey, E.R. (1984) "The Choice of Ski Areas: Estimation of a Generalized CES Preferencie Ordering with Characteristics", *Review of Economics and Statistics*, 66, 584-590.

Morey, E.R. (1985) "Characteristics, Consumer Surplus and New Activities", *Journal of Public Economics*, 26, 221-236.

Morey, E.R., Shaw, W.D. y Rowe, R.D. (1991) "A Discrete Choice Model of Recreational Participation Site Choice, and Activity Valuation when Complete Trip Data are not Available", *Journal of Environmental Economics and Management*, 20, 181-201.

Morley, C.L. (1992) "A Microeconomic Theory of International Tourism Demand", *Annals of Tourism Research*, 19, 250-267.

Morley, C.L. (1994a). "Experimental Destination Choice Anaylsis", *Annals of Tourism Research*, 21, 4, 780-791.

Morley, C.L. (1994b) "Discrete Choice analysis of the Impact of Tourism Prices", *Journal of Travel Research*, otoño, 8-14.

Morley, C.L. (1994c) "The Use of CPI for Tourism Prices in Demand Modelling", *Tourism Management*, 15, 5, 342-346.

Morley, C.L. (1995) "Tourism Demand: Characteristics, Segmentation and Aggregation", *Tourism Economics*, 1, 4, 315-328.

Morrison, A.M. (1996) *Hospitality and Travel Marketing*, Nueva York: Delmar Publishers.

Moutinho, L. (1987) "Consumer Behaviour in Tourism", *European Journal of Marketing*, 21, 10, 1-44.

Moutinho, L. y Trimble, J. (1991) "A Probability of Revisitation Model: The Case of Winter Visits to the Grand Canyon", *The Service Industries Journal*, 11, 4, 439-457.

Perdue, R.R. (1986) "Traders and Nontraders in Recreational Destination Choice", *Journal of Leisure Research*, 18, 1, 12-25.

Peterson, G. L., Dwyer, J.F. y Darragh, a. J. (1983) "A Behavioral Urban Recreation Site Choice Model", *Leisure Sciences*, 6, 1, 61-81.

Revelt, D. y Train, K.E. (2002) "Customer-Specific Taste Parameters and Mixed Logit: Houshold' Choice of electricity Supplier", Working Paper, Universidad de California, Berkeley.

Riera, A. (2000) "Modelos de Elección Discreta y Coste del Viaje. Los Espacios Naturales Protegidos en Mallorca", *Revista de Economía Aplicada*, 8, 24, 181-201.

Rossi, P.E. y Allenby, G.M. (1993) "A Bayesian Approach to Estimating Household Parameters", *Journal of Marketing Research*, 30, mayo, 171-182.

Rugg, D. (1973) "The Choice of Journey Destination: A Theoretical and Empirical Analysis", *The Review of Economics and Statistics*, 55, 1, 64-72.

Sánchez, M. (2000) "El Análisis de Clases Latentes como Técnica de Segmentación de Mercados: El Caso de la Demanda Turística Nacional", en Blanquer, D., ed., *Turismo: Comercialización de Productos, Gestión de Organizaciones, Aeropuertos y Protección de la Naturaleza*, Tirant lo Balnc, Valencia.

Schroeder, H.W. y Louviere, J. (1999) "Stated Choice Models for Predicting the Impact of User Fees at Public Recreation Sites", *Journal of Leisure Research*, 31, 3, 300-324.

Seddighi, H.R. y Theocharous, A.L.(2002), "A Model of Toursim Destination Choice: A Theoretical and Empirical analysis", *Tourism Management*.

Serra, A. (2002) *Marketing Turístico*, Madrid: Ed. Pirámide.

Siderelis, Ch. y Moore, R.L. (1998) "Recreation Demand and the Influence of Site Preference Variables", *Journal of Leisure Research*, 30, 3, 301-318.

Sirakaya, E., McLellan, R.W. y Uysal, M. (1996) "Modeling Vacation Destinations Decisions: A Behavioural Approach", *Journal fo Travel and Toursim Marketing*, 5, 1/2, 57-75.

Smith, S.L.J. (1995). *Tourism Analysis: A Handbook*, Reino Unido: Longman Group Limited.

Sorensen, H. (2003) The Science of Shopping, *Marketing Research*, 15(3), 30-35.

Stopher, P.R. y Ergün, G. (1979) "Population Segmentation in Urban Recreation Choices", *Transportation Research*, 59-65.

Taylor, Ch. E. y Knudson, D.M. (1976) "Area Preferences of Midwestern Campers", *Journal of Leisure Research*, primavera, 39-48.

Timmermans, H. y Golledge, R.G. (1989), "Application of Behavioral Research on Spatial Problems II: Preference and Choice". *Progress in Human Geography*, 14, 311-354.

Train, K.E. (1998) "Recreation Demand Models with Taste Differences over People", *Land Economics*, 74, 2.

Train, K.E. (2001a) "Halton Sequences for Mixed Logit", Documento de Trabajo, Universidad de California, Berkeley.

Train, K.E. (2001b) "A Comparison of Hierarchical Bayes and Maximum Simulated Likelehood for Mixed Logit", Documento de Trabajo, Universidad de California, Berkeley.

Train, K.E. (2003) *Discrete Choice Methods with Simulation*, Nueva York: Cambridge University Press.

Usach, J. (1999) "Un Modelo de Demanda Turística Interna para la Economía Española", *Papers de Turisme,* 25, 59-100.

Vázquez Casielles, R. (2000) "Estrategias de Marketing de Relaciones para el Desarrollo de la Oferta y Distribución de Productos Turísticos", en Blanquer, D., ed., *Turismo: Comercialización de Productos, Gestión de Organizaciones, Aeropuertos y Protección de la Naturaleza*, Valencia: Tirant lo Blanc.

Walsh, R.G., John, K.H.; Mckean, J.R. y Hof, J.G. (1992) "Effect of Price on Forecasts of Participation in Fish and Wildlife Recreation: An Aggregate Demand Model", *Journal of Leisure Research*, 24, 2, 140-156.

Wennergren, E.B. y Nielsen, D.B. (1968) "A Probabilistic Approach to Estimating Demand for Outdoor Recreation", Working paper, Utah State University.

Witt, S.F. and Martin, C.A. (1987) "Econometric Models for Forecasting International Tourism Demand", *Journal of Travel Research*, 25, winter, 23-30.

Wolfe, R.I. (1970), Communication, *Journal of Leisure Research*, 2, 1, 85-87.

Wolfe, R.I. (1972), "The Inertia Model", *Journal of Leisure Research,* 4, 73-76.

Woodside, A. G. Y Carr, J.A. (1988) "Consumer Decision Making and Competitive Marketing Strategies: Applications for Tourism Planning", *Journal of Travel Research*, 27, 2-7.

In: Tourism Management: New Research
Editor: Terry V. Liu, pp. 123-148

ISBN 1-60021-058-9
© 2006 Nova Science Publishers, Inc.

Chapter 5

BUILDING A LONG-TERM SHARED PERSPECTIVE FOR DESTINATIONS IN STAGNATION: THE VISIONING EXPERIENCE OF KUSADASI

Atila Yuksel, Murat Hancer and Fisun Yuksel*
Adnan Menderes University, Aydın Turkey

ABSTRACT

Adopting sustainable and strategic tourism planning perspective is imperative particularly for destinations in stagnation in order to better manage their efforts for rejuvenation. Carefully crafted and implemented vision can provide such destinations with many advantages, including community building and a long-term perspective. Despite its importance, visioning exercises in the context of stagnated destinations are relatively rare. Drawing on Kusadasi case, this paper depicts the process of vision development. The experience has shown that it is not only the consensus-based vision but also the process followed in its generation matters.

Keywords: *Vision, Visioning, Nominal Group Technique, Participatory Action Research, Destination lifecycle.*

INTRODUCTION

Numerous new tourism destinations are emerging across the globe almost daily (Cooper, 2002; Ritchie and Crouch, 2000). The entry of new destinations denotes intensified competition and a probable decrease in market share for mature destinations. Due to failures of the traditional plans in achieving economic success, authorities of mature destinations are

---

* Corresponding Author: Atila Yuksel, Adnan Menderes University, Vocational School of Didim. Didim Yerleskesi, Akbuk-Didim, Aydın Turkey. Tel: + 90 256 612 5503; Fax: +90 256 612 9842; Email: ayuksel@adu.edu.tr

suggested to adopt strategic planning and to build a long-term shared perspective (Faulkner, 2002; Jamal and Getz, 1995; Ritchie, 1993, 1999; Ritchie and Crouch, 2000). "Competitiveness in this setting requires the establishment of a more strategic focus at both the individual enterprise level and for the destination as a whole" (Faulkner, 2002, p. 475). In this respect, principles of sustainable tourism have been wholeheartedly adopted by some destinations in order to ensure the viability of finite resources. The achievement of sustainable tourism objectives however hinges on two factors: i) the adoption of a participatory model, and ii) a "whole of destination" approach or a shift from a "destination marketing" to a "destination management" approach (Faulkner, 2002).

Destinations go through various cycles in their lifetimes. This implies that if appropriate counter measures are not taken, a rapid decline can be ultimate. Reversing decline can be difficult. Hence, there are a very limited number of successful rejuvenation cases, stemming from absence and/or presence of a wide array of internal and external factors. One of the contributing factors could be the absence of a vision (i.e., lack of a shared view on a preferred future). Generation (or updating) of a desirable, actionable, and effective vision is instrumental, as it acts as an important tool for direction setting for a destination at each stage of its lifecycle, and a catalyst for merging strengths of different stakeholders: "A well-designed visioning exercise has the potential to provide a 'circuit-breaker' and a 'call to action', to the extent that it can be instrumental in galvanizing opinion on the need to a fundamentally different approach from that which has prevailed in the past... a well-articulated vision that has been constructed in a manner that ensures it represents a consensus among primary stakeholders provides a focus for the strategic planning process and a vehicle for mobilizing cooperative action" (Faulkner, 2002, p. 493). The formulation and acceptance of a common, idealized vision as to what the population believes the future of that destination should be has been argued to be one of the most significant steps in the process of societal planning (Ritchie, 1999). The vision provides "an agreed upon benchmark towards which both the general community and the tourism sector can more effectively direct their efforts" (Ritchie, 1999, p. 274).

Creation of a destination vision through a participative process however is not easy. Ritchie and Crouch (2000, p.3) note that "...to develop a shared portrait of an "ideal future state" for the destination (that is, the way stakeholders envisage the destination at some loosely defined point in time in the future), the development of such a "shared" vision is not always easy within diverse, democratic societies". With few exceptions (e.g., Faulkner, 2002; Ritchie, 1993, 1999), vision development cases for tourism attractions in general and declining destinations in particular are rarely found in the tourism literature. Given the call for sustainable development based on a long-term shared perspective, the limited number of visioning exercises applied in stagnated destinations is rather curious. Using Kusadasi, Turkey as a case, this study sets out to share the experience in developing a vision and guiding values to restructure its future. This paper is organized into three sections. The literature review focuses on the concept of vision, its power, and properties and discusses vision development procedures and visioning in the context of stagnated destinations. The second section presents the research methodology employed and the steps followed in the present case of visioning. Insights drawn from the experience were outlined in the conclusion.

POWER OF VISION

Development of a vision is essential to success of an organization (Kockan and Kunkel, 1998). The role of vision cannot be confined to organizations, of course (Smith, 2003). Without a vision (or an updated vision), destinations, regardless of their newness or maturity, can rapidly lose focus, which can, in turn make it difficult to gain traction with other improvement efforts. Our experience has shown that the majority of destinations, particularly in Turkey, have not taken time to develop and/or update effective visions in any stage of their life-cycle. Predominance has been given to what sort of infrastructure would support sun- sea- sand or other booming development. Strategic planning and/or a desire to create a better or even perfect society (visioning) have not been as popular as technical details among destination authorities and planners. A vision is however not utopianism or just a series of fancy words but a meaningful model (Christenson and Walker, 2004; Shipley and Newkirk, 1998). Vision helps clarify the direction in which to proceed (Kotter, 1995, cf. Christenson and Walker, 2004). It "...has a clear and compelling imagery that offers an innovative way to improve which recognizes and draws on traditions, and connects to actions that people can take to realize" (Nutt and Backoff, 1997, p. 309). Vision refers to "an image of the future that can be discussed and perfected by those with an interest in it ... it is a glue that binds individuals together into a common goal" (cf. Hackett and Spurgeon, 1996).

Nanus (1992) describes vision as an image of a desirable future, and argues that the right vision could jump-start that future by mobilizing people into action toward achieving it (cf. Levin, 2000). Clearly articulated vision can play a key role in providing a connection to a sense of purpose and meaning greater than oneself and can serve as a beacon of inspiration during times of change and disruption (Levin, 2000). For example, Kilpatrick and Locke (1997) discovered that vision had a positive impact on employee performance and attitudes. Baum, Locke and Kilpatrick (1998) found that a vision positively affected organization-level performance as measured by growth in sales, profits, employment, and net worth (Levin, 2000). Without a vision that connects people with each other and to the places of their local environment, the desirable end-state of planning is left incomplete and opportunities for community building through civic debate are lost (Stewart et al., 2004).

PROPERTIES OF VISION

Vision is used in a variety of ways, and means so many different things to different people. It is still frequently confused with similar notions such as mission, goal, and strategy. While these denote a sense of purpose and direction, vision is different from them, as it taps people's emotion and energy (Levin, 2000; Nutt and Backoff, 1997). There is considerable agreement about the key attributes of an effective vision. It should be future oriented, compelling, bold, aspiring and inspiring, yet believable and achievable (Levin, 2000). According to Christenson and Walker (2004) a vision must be understood, motivational, credible, demanding and challenging: It must capture the core purpose, a preferred future state; make a convincing case for following the vision concept that can be internalized by stakeholders and that provides a compelling value proposition.

According to Nutt and Backoff (1997), a vision should involve inspirational possibilities that are value centered and realizable, with superior imagery and articulation. Vision should draw on an organization's values and culture (desirability). It should help people let go of the past and open them up to acting on the new possibilities that are expressed in the vision. Visions should be actionable, as people called on to carry out a vision must see a role for them to play. The possibilities and norms developed to articulate the vision mobilize people when they are understood and seen as challenging but doable (Nutt and Backoff, 1997). Others contend that people are moved to action when they see how their acts fit into the larger action plan (Gardner, 1990). People who see what they can do and how these acts can aid the vision are more apt to make the vision a reality (Nutt and Backoff, 1997). Another property of vision concerns presentation. A vision is notable when it has an uncanny ability to communicate (articulation). Commitment and enrollment are required to realize a vision (Senge 1990, cf. Nutt and Backoff, 1997). Committed people will do whatever can be done, within reason, to help implement such a vision. These two components improve when a vision has clear articulation and compelling imagery. According to Nutt and Backoff, a vision's articulation and imagery move people between the stages of noncompliance (resistance) to genuine compliance that requires both commitment and enrolment. A vision with these features can also move people who offer grudging compliance (fail to see value, just do what is expected) and formal compliance (see value, not inspired to take extraordinary steps) to the higher levels of energy produced by a vision with a powerful imagery (Nutt and Backoff, 1007, p. 314).

An examination of traditional vision statements of organizations however suggests that they fail miserably in terms of possessing the above mentioned vision qualities. Many organizations have single-sentence vision statements. These statements often comprise en vogue phrases, buzzwords and jargon that not only resemble bumper sticker slogans, but can be readily interchangeable across companies with minimal editing (Levin, 2000). The main criticism on such "vanilla visions" is that they leave so much open to varied interpretations, and they are so lofty that they do not provide a strong personal connection for the very people intended to be inspired by them (Levin, 2000). In some organizations, vision is generally described as a mission statement, formed by management, demonstrated by posters or publications, and communicated to the staff through meetings. "...it is pretended for show and may become inflexible and thus useless when circumstances change" (Holpp and Kelly, 1998, p. 50). Vision statements may be short or long, and they may be presented quite differently (Ritchie and Crouch, 2000). "What is important, is that destination stakeholders agree that the final vision statement provides both a meaningful and operational "dream" for the future of their destination - one that reflects the values of the destination stakeholders, while not ignoring the realities and constraints of the marketplace" (Ritchie and Crouch, 2000, p. 4).

VISION DEVELOPMENT

Frisch (1998) argues that winning visions do not just happen; they heavily depend on a carefully planned development process. It should be emphasized that there is currently no agreement as to the single "right way" to craft a destination vision. Its development is complex and occurs in a number of ways. There are various procedural suggestions with different prescriptions found in the literature. It is however difficult to compare these, as they all deal with several different aspects. Some visions are imposed by the leader; whereas others are co-created. Some procedures suggest involvement of consultants. The process can begin either formally or informally. Origination of the visioning idea, identification of relevant stakeholders and their priorities, undertaking workshops to develop visions and checking its validity, development of vision management and communication strategies, deployment of vision strategies, monitoring vision deployment performance and implications are the steps followed in vision generation and implementation. Undertaking a destination audit, writing and distribution of position statements based on the audit, development of vision through workshops and its implementation are the sequence of the visioning adopted in Northern New South Wales, Australia (Cooper, 2002).

Ritchie (1999) reports a conceptual framework used in visioning of Bow Valley in Banff National Park. Key components of the Banff-Bow Valley (BBV) study were public input and information gathering, research and analysis, Round Table deliberations, Task Force deliberations, and final report preparation and submission (Ritchie, 2000)[10]. Field meetings, vision building workshops, and/or story creation are techniques often used in vision development cases found in the literature. Regardless of the method, the identification and involvement of key participants and use of qualitative and/or quantitative research techniques are the two important components in the development process. The involvement of key players is crucial to the delivery of the strategic direction since they need to demonstrate consistent and visible support for the change (Hackett and Spurgeon, 1996). An understanding of the current pulse and temperature of an organization, and its weaknesses and strengths through questionnaires, interviews etc., is important in the context of long-term change (Hackett and Spurgeon, 1996).

VISIONING IN THE CONTEXT OF STAGNATED DESTINATIONS

Compared to organizations, the generation of a vision is particularly difficult in the context of stagnated tourism destinations due to different contextual, structural and situational factors: "…the adoption of strategic planning at the destination is not as straightforward as in a commercial organization where responsibilities and reporting lines are well defined"

---

[10] In the BBV, responsibilities of vision development were assigned to a five-person expert "Task Force" appointed by the Minister, which then established a formal Round Table process (Ritchie, 1999). The Round Table served as the core of consultation, advisory, and analysis of activities that provided the Task Force with the information, ideas, and insights used in the formulation of its final recommendations and report to the Minister (Ritchie, 1999). The Round Table was comprised of fourteen interest sectors and each sector had a Chair, a working committee, and supporting constituency. The information sharing and negotiation process was facilitated by a technical expert who worked with Round Table to develop procedural rules, to formulate a vision, principles and goals for the future of the region, and to put forth all the final recommendations. Interest Based Negotiations (IBN), a form of community collaboration was employed to achieve a "wise" agreement instead of traditional "positional bargaining" (Ritchie, 2000). The members of each sector held a series of meetings at which they reached consensus on a series of statements. These statements were then submitted to the IBN facilitator who had summarized the detailed interest statements after consolidation and classification of the main interest and ideas. The first phase was about achieving common understanding of each sector's major interests. The second phase of the BBV was development of a consensus based Vision on the understanding of each sector's interests. Finally core vision and its eight sub-themes were created (Ritchie, 1999, 2000).

(Cooper, 2002, p. 2). According to Faulkner (2002) and Cooper (2002), destinations in stagnation may possess some of the following features (Table 1) and these may have implications for the visioning.

Table 1. Performance Areas and Stagnation Indicators[*]

Performance Areas	Indicators
Changing markets	Growth in low-status, low-spend visitors and day visitors
	Over-dependence on long holiday market, and lack of penetration of short-stay market
	Emphasis on high volume, low-yield inclusive tour market
	A decline in visitors length of stay
	Type of tourists increasingly organized mass tourists
	A declining proportion of first time visitors, as opposed to repeat visitors
	Limited or declining appeal to overseas visitors
	High seasonality
Emerging newer destinations	Competition from emerging newer domestic and international destinations
	The destination is well know but no longer fashionable
Infrastructure	Outdate, poorly maintained accommodation and amenities
	Older properties are changing hands
	Market perceptions of the destination becoming over commercialized, crowded and "tacky"
	Tourism industry over-capacity
	Diversification into conventions and conferences to maintain numbers
	Large number of man made attractions, which started to outnumber the natural attractions that made the place popular in the first place
Business performance	Declining profits
	Lack of confidence in the tourism business community
	Lack of professional, experienced staff
	[**]*High rate of business handovers*
	[**]*Increase in victimization of tourists*
Carrying capacities	Visitor levels approaching or exceeding social and environmental carrying capacities
	Local opposition to tourism as the resort's residential role increases
Institutional environment	**Local government reorganization diluting the political power of resort**
	Demands for increased operational efficiency and entrepreneurial activity in local government
	Short-term planning horizons in local government owing to financial restrictions and a low priority given to strategic thinking
	Shortage of research data
	[**]*Increase in the number of meetings to find "a way out"*

[*]Developed by Faulkner (2002).
[**] These indicators are added by the present author to Faulkner's list.
Indicators in bold does not apply to Kusadasi on the basis of present situation.

In a stagnated destination, the level of tourist activity approaches or exceeds the limits of acceptable change in terms of social and environmental impacts. Over use and a lack of investment in management ultimately degrade resources. Due to the aging infrastructure, the destination is generally perceived as being worn-out. Generally speaking, the quality of services and facilities also begin to fall short of market expectations as a consequence of old-dated facilities. The range of products offered by the destination fails to keep up with changes in tourist demand. A fixation on product options that were successful in the past creates a form of inertia that makes providers less sensitive and adaptable to emerging markets. The emergence of newer and more competitive destinations that are catering to market demands decreases the destination's market share. Lack of profits reduces capacity to renovate and upgrade facilities and invest in staff training, resulting in a decline in standards. A reputation as a cheap destination attracts price sensitive, less desirable visitors, who engage in anti-social behavior and, in turn, discourage better quality visitors.

The nature of an institutional environment in stagnated destinations may be different from that of an emerging destination. Bramwell and Sharman (1999) argue that partnerships need to operate within a contextual environment of understanding and respect. If the partner organisations know and respect the traditions and values of each other, this works to break down barriers and facilitate interaction between stakeholders (Greer, 2002: 356). Creating an effective vision requires a deep understanding of both organizational culture and the history and trigger mechanisms that create the underlying assumptions of individuals and groups in an organization (Christenson and Walker, 2004). It requires not only enthusiasm and commitment, but also a sense of community, shared values, goals and an understanding of stakeholder interdependency. In a declining tourism destination context, the institutional environment is generally characterized by a high level of fragmentation, rivalry, conflictual relations, and organizations being overly sensitive about their authority. "Destinations are comprised of a constantly shifting mosaic of stakeholders and value systems. Each of these groups has a different view of the role and future of tourism at their destination and therefore the adoption of strategies becomes a political process of conflict resolution and consensus, all set within a local legislative context and where power brokers have a disproportionate influence" (Cooper, 2002, p. 2). Many of the resources that are so important for tourism product are 'common pool' resources, which the private sector taps free of charge and over which no single company or authority has responsibility for management (Faulkner, 2002). Bureaucracy-laden and cumbersome public institutions in charge of tourism administration generally do not keep pace with the private sector. Visions however involve change, and this in turn would invoke anxiety particularly in cumbersome public institutions because it challenges the status quo and requires expenditure of transformational energy. According to Faulkner, (2002, p. 474), "One of the underlying causes of stagnation is the inertia of entrenched management/planning practices and structures, which may have succeeded in the past but have become progressively out-of-kilter with the changing environment. This institutional inertia is reinforced by existing power relationships within the industry, and by the mindsets, comfort zones, skills, talents and egos of key decision-makers". One of the main challenges in the process of installing and implementing the new form of management and planning required to rejuvenate a destination, therefore, "involves convincing core stakeholders that the destination faces the prospect of stagnation. Furthermore, it needs to be emphasized that this can only be averted if it is realized that the approaches of the past will not work in the future" (Faulkner, 2002, p. 474).

The vision should be developed with the insights of relevant members of the organization. This process is suggested to facilitate not only group input and diversity of insights for building a credible solution, but also the development of member and team understanding. In a declining tourism destination context, the share of the natives in the total population decreases, as the destination is likely to attract people seeking jobs from outside, who are likely to bring and pursue their own culture. Increasing cultural inconsistency (different values, norms, etc) in the community may foster alienation among different culturally-segregated groups and this constitutes a formidable obstacle to collaboration required in vision development. Declining destinations tend to possess other peculiar features. The business environment is rather unstable, with a high rate of entry and exit. In a context in which people are overly concerned with present, an attempt to strategize future may not be advocated by the majority. The decline stage, which largely sets the conviction of "nothing could be done" or "nothing works", due to previous negative experiences, may act as a determining factor of people's remoteness and reluctance to vision development. Previous negative experiences in collaborative decision-making attempts may turn people off from participating in vision development at the decline stage. Turbulences and crisis however create urgency and motivation to act and make the current practices suspect. Thus, for some, the wake from decline and turbulences, calls into question aspects of current practices and strategies and this can make change seem desirable (Nutt and Backoff, 1997). Given the presence of uneven distribution of tourism income and resources between front and back fields, the majority of indigenous people may not be in favor of a future based on tourism. Based on Doxey's Irritation Index one can assume that the community in large may develop an apathy and/or hostility towards tourism when the stage of stagnation and/or decline is reached. Strategic change often requires significant resources; destinations facing a financial crisis (economic recession or decline) would be less inclined to start a search for a vision (Starbuck, 1993 cf. Nutt and Backoff, 1997). Cooper (2002) states that the stage of the destination in the life cycle is important in terms of the acceptability of a destination-wide planning exercise: "In the early stages of the life cycle for example, success often obscures the long term view, whilst in the later stages, particularly when a destination is in decline, opposition to long term planning exercises may be rationalized on the basis of cost" (Cooper, 2002, p.2).

THE RESEARCH

Reviewed literature reveals that more works need to be done to illustrate the steps and to develop prescriptive insights in order to craft effective destination visions. Using a longitudinal approach, this paper aims to depict the visioning experience of a resort town targeting rejuvenation. The consulting engagements of stakeholders with School of Tourism and Hospitality Management gave the opportunity to undertaking of such a longitudinal research, lasting seven months. Considering its suitability and advantages, the Participatory Action Research (PAR) was adopted (Fisher and Ball, 2003; Kidd and Kral, 2005; Nelson et al., 1998; Nutt and Backoff, 1997). PAR is a form of applied research that represents a fundamentally different paradigm than conventional research (Nelson et al., 1998). The term PAR is used when diagnosing and action planning are carried out in collaboration between researcher and the client (Susman and Evered, 1978). It blends the traditions of participatory research (i.e., to have a part or share in something) and action research (i.e., the bringing about of an alteration). Application of action theory shares similar objectives and seeks same type of information as participant observation. The difference between the two lies within the role that the researcher adopts. In participant observation, the researcher observes the vision as it is being created. Action theory however calls for the researcher act as a facilitator during the workshop meetings to lead the effort to create a vision for the destination (Nutt and Backoff, 1997). The PAR methodology we applied capitalizes on the strengths of these above methods.

PAR offers several advantages over other traditional research methods. It involves a high degree of cooperation between researchers and stakeholders with constant feedback loops and a commitment to using the findings and to raising all participants' consciousness about the problem in its social context (Nelson et al., 1998; Nutt and Bakcoff, 1997). In PAR, subjects participate in a process of developing research questions, designing research instruments, collecting information, and reflecting on the data in order to transform their understanding about the nature of the problem under investigation (Nelson et al., 1998). Thus, stakeholders act as both participants and coresearchers in the research process in ways that most other research approaches do not allow, and subsequently, gain a greater knowledge about themselves, their lives, and their communities (Park, 1993 cf. Nelson et al., 1998). As Gaventa (1993) suggested, PAR "attempts to break down the distinction between the researchers and researched, the subjects and objects of knowledge production, by the participation of the people-for-themselves in the process of gaining and creating knowledge" (p. 34 cf. Nelson et al., 1998, p. 886).

Researchers conducting studies perceived as having little or no relevance to the community may receive strong reactions from the participants. In such contexts, PAR approaches are likely the best way to generate knowledge and action that is meaningful for the people involved and make it more likely that researchers may be invited to contribute to those communities. PAR allows the researcher to access the understandings and narratives usually overlooked or discounted through mainstream academic approaches. It is a "living knowledge" that can be gained through PAR that can educate the researcher (Friere, 1982 cf, Kidd and Kral, 2005), inform action in other areas, and potentially greatly extend the field of inquiry through discovery of new and important information. PAR involves the development of human relationships and friendships with participants as opposed to the supposedly objective disinterest of traditional paradigms. It can be a genuine connection, an "authentic participation" that is motivating, contributes to personal growth, and reduces the barriers between peoples (Kidd and Kral, 2005). Traditional research tends to be deductive in its emphasis on hypothesis testing, whereas PAR tends to be inductive. Findings emerge during the research process and theory is grounded in the emerging findings (Chesler, 1991, cf., Nelson et al., 1998). PAR focuses on being responsive to participants' needs and perspectives, collective consciousness-raising about the issues under study, and continuous innovation and renewal (Nelson et al., 1998). In some PAR studies, the researcher facilitates a process of building a partnership among professionals, family members, consumer/survivors, and other stakeholders. Stakeholders collaborating with researchers work to develop egalitarian and authentic relationships and trust. By collaborating and sharing stakeholders' diverse knowledge and experience, PAR seeks to change the social and personal dynamics of the research situation so that it is cooperative and enhances the lives of all those who participate (Stringer, 1996, cf. Nelson et al., 1998). The stages of PAR include problem definition, fact finding, goal setting, action, and evaluation to simultaneously solve problems and generate new knowledge (Lewin cf. Nelson et al, 1998).

More specifically, researchers worked with the Vision Steering Committee from the start to devise a vision. The use of researchers as facilitators was particularly important early in the project, as community members and research staff members developed relationships and established the roles of all participants. The facilitators encouraged clear communication (e.g., using common terminology) and requested clarification when researchers or members lack the background to understand each other (Kidd and Kral, 2005). Participant observation was then utilized to observe and understand the interaction of people both in and out of meetings and how participants came to understand what they understand as they construct a vision. All sessions were recorded and observation notes were taken. The process followed and the vision that results, aspects of dialogue and the vision's consequences were then reflected upon by the researchers (i) to provide insights from the visioning process followed in Kusadasi case and (ii) to evaluate effectiveness of the use of a modified nominal group technique in destination visioning. This paper reports the visioning process. The effectiveness of the technique will be discussed in another paper.

VISIONING PROCESS AND KEY DECISIONS

Figure 1 illustrates the three main stages of the visioning process.

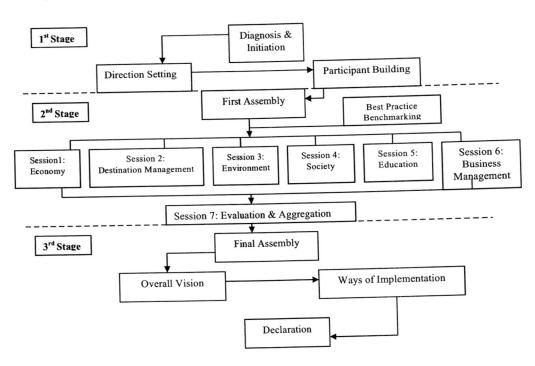

Figure 1. Visioning Stages

Stage 1. Diagnosing and Action Planning

Initiation: The first stage in Kusadasi visioning involved the introduction of the vision development idea to incrementally increasing numbers of stakeholders (i.e., individuals and institutions with an interest in Kusadasi and its future) and construction of the method for development of the vision. Different from Ritchie's (1999) study, the start of the vision development project was initiated by an association which presently has more than two thousand members in Kusadasi. More specifically, two board members of the Association brought the idea of "crafting of a vision that would guide future of Kusadasi", to the attention of the School of Tourism and Hospitality Management (STHM). Prior to its introduction to the STHM, the idea had been debated by the board members of the Association and approval was given. A series of preliminary meetings then took place in different venues involving scholars from the STHM and representatives from the Association. The main aims of these meetings were to discuss the stage Kusadasi has reached in its lifecycle, to clarify what goals were expected from the visioning project and to identify "hows" of vision generation through a participative method. Several procedures, some of which had already been applied in organizations were deliberated during meetings to which the present authors had participated. Effort was spent on development of simple and well-defined goals, as ill-defined goals and uncertainty surrounding the delivery methods stifle development of a successful vision (Christenson and Walker, 2004).

In the meetings, the members concurred that while there was inadequate quantifiable information as to where Kusadasi[11] stands in terms of its life cycle, it was apparent that the image of the town has deteriorated significantly due to a lack of planned development. Based on limited existing data and accumulated knowledge in the literature (Table 1), participants agreed that the present tourism development stage of Kusadasi exhibited many, if not all of the characteristics of stagnation (e.g., unfashionable image, high property turnover rates, lack of new investment, surplus bed capacity, etc) and this calls for taking a long-term perspective. Six themes (economy, society, education, environment, business community and local

---

[11] Coupled with Turkey's growing emphasis on international tourism during the 1980s, Kusadasi has transformed itself from a resort town visited mainly by domestic visitors into an international destination, drawing international tourists in high volumes. Located in southwest of Turkey, the town boasts of a diverse natural, historical and cultural richness and enjoys an accessible location. An international airport is an hour's drive away, a motorway connects the town to other major cities, and the town is also accessible by sea. The town is situated close to Ephesus - the Mecca of travelers visiting Turkey - and it caters not only for international and domestic holidaymakers, but also for cruise passengers and day trippers. Kusadasi has become one of the top tourist destinations in Turkey due to its beaches, natural parks, and the house of the Virgin Mary near Ephesus, which is one of the Christian centers of religious pilgrimage (Tatoglu, Erdal, Ozgur and Azakli, 2002). As of 1997, Kusadasi alone accounted for nearly 5 percent of overall tourism revenues generated in Turkey. Although the reliability of data collection is questionable, it is assumed that the town receives approximately 500.000 foreign visitors annually with the majority of tourists coming from Western Europe (Kusadasi Chamber of Commerce, 1998, 2002). Recently, the town's visitor profile has changed (e.g., more visitors from East-European countries) and a noticeable decline in tourism income continues (Ergul, Tunc and Yuksel, 2002). A recent study found that residents of Kusadasi had negative perceptions of tourism impacts on quality of environment, community attitude, and crowding and congestion (Tatoglu et al., 2002). Another study found a high level of irritation toward the state of tourism in town (Yuksel and Yuksel, 2005a). The institutional environment is rather in turmoil. Yuksel and Yuksel (2005b) identified limited information sharing particularly among local agents as a barrier to effective interorganisational relations in Kusadasi. According to Yuksel and Yuksel's study, bringing together different backgrounds for the Commercial Action Plan project constituted a formidable obstacle due to complex relationships, which involved a lack of understanding of each sector.

government) emerged from these meetings as most relevant areas for consideration in the visioning process.

Leadership: In the preliminary meetings, leadership to co-ordinate the project activities turned out to be a controversial matter. The association appeared to have been divided into two in terms of who should be the leading institution. Some asserted that the Association itself should lead the project, and define goals and methods, whereas others had considered the STHM should assume the leadership. The issue giving rise to debates was about whether the vision should be imposed by the leader organization or it should be co-developed with relevant stakeholders. Given Kusadasi's institutional environment characterized by a high extent of institutional rivalry, conflictual relationships and jealousy (Yuksel and Yuksel, 2005b), the leadership of the project by the association was opposed by the majority. Their leadership could have proven to be a major obstacle in the way of gaining a wider participation in the project. In this context, the leadership of an impartial institution, such as the STHM, having similar distance/closeness to each concerned stakeholder was argued to be instrumental and beneficial. The leadership issue however gave rise to intra-stakeholder disputes, as the negotiations were not undertaken on win-win basis. This had resulted in the Association becoming reticent and passive, and consequently underutilization of their potential contribution to the visioning process.

Vision Steering Committee (VSC): Following settlement of the leadership issue, the process (and contingency approaches) was finalized with a committee, structured to steer the project activities. The Steering Committee (VSC), composed of seven individuals, started by addressing the simple question: 'what is a vision?' A few definitions that helped to focus the VSC's thinking went as follows: 'a clear mental picture of a preferred future state', 'something that goes beyond our normal boundaries of thinking and takes us into the realm of future possibilities', 'a rational projection of the present, which generates emotion and excitement', 'something that provides focus and energy, that binds us together around a common identity and sense of destiny'. In addition to these helpful definitions, members felt the need for examples of how other organizations/destinations created their visions, and managed to achieve them (Hayhoe, 2001). Thus, scholars from the STHM searched cases from the literature and reported back to the VSC. Project in this kind requires a smooth transition of logically linked activities, each interdependent and each converging to be actioned when and where required. The VSC identified these tasks to be undertaken by individuals with skills to carry out assigned tasks. Some of the responsibilities assumed by the VSC included the development and implementation of the process for the generation of vision; training of the vision workshop team; finding out context specific means for creating enhanced awareness and achieving greater involvement of relevant stakeholders in the process; managing relations with both local and national Press and Media, and concerned public and private organizations (including tour operators).

Financing: The allocation of accessibility of sufficient funds was an important condition for the project, as resources are required to support collaborative programmes and operations (Mattessich and Monsey, 1992). One of the main responsibilities of the VSC was the finding a sponsor for the funding of the vision development project. The finding of a sponsor with no or limited relations with Kusadasi in general and other stakeholders in particular had been advocated by the VSC. Despite the efforts, a company founded in Kusadasi - one of the largest tour operators bringing considerable numbers of incoming tourists to the town - had agreed to the sponsoring of the initiative. While financial problems were resolved, this however had brought about other problems (i.e., pressure exerted by the sponsor on the selection of relevant stakeholders). The sponsor was persuaded that the vision should bring together the views of the whole community and all tourism stakeholders, and an amalgamated vision representing interests of a wider community would have a better chance of implementation (Picture 1).

Picture 1. Stakeholders participated in the vision development

Time and Venue: Meeting environments were identified as an influential factor for the success of partnership programmes (Selin andChavez, 1994). Three places were suggested for the two-day meeting: Kusadasi, Pamukkale and Antalya. Kusadasi was dismissed from the list in the first VSC meeting, as it was thought that participants would not concentrate on the workshop due to their businesses and/or other interests. Pamukkale was removed from the list. This was because the meeting place should present opportunities to observe some good practices in tourism development and city planning (i.e., what is it they do well that Kusadasi can be doing better?), particularly to those participants who had never been outside of Kusadasi. Thus, Antalya was chosen as the place for the workshop. Mid April, a time before the start of the peak season, was fixed as the date for the meetings so that participants would not turn down the invitation because of business-related concerns. Participants in the same work group traveled together and their moderators accompanied them during the journey from Kusadasi to Antalya. They were not informed as to which task group they were in or who their moderator and reporter were to prevent development of early group identity. Upon arrival to the hotel, information packs containing the aim of the workshop, details of the themes to be discussed, and meeting rules and timetable were given out. In the 1st Assembly (Picture 2), which was undertaken in an unstructured fashion, participants were specifically instructed that the reason of the workshop was to create a vision that integrates the opinions of all groups in the community. It was emphasized that people could express their views and wills freely; they were then presented with their task group, moderators and reporters. Rules, methods and objectives were restated. Following the general assembly, a full-day observation visit under the guidance of city representatives to pre-determined places in Antalya took place (Picture 3).

Picture 2. The First Assembly

Picture 3. Best practice observation visits

Group-Based Decision Making: Based on stakeholders' views during the preliminary meetings a group decision-making technique different from traditional ones was adopted for development of the vision. Considering its relative advantages over other group based decision making techniques the Nominal Group Technique (NGT) was chosen. The NGT is essentially a six-step approach to decision making (Claxton et al., 1980):

i)   participants are presented with an initial statement of the topic to be discussed;

ii) individual work precedes group discussion (i.e., silent generation of individual ideas by *group* members);

iii) round robin feedback of ideas generated during the silent generation period;

iv) unstructured group discussion and group clarification of the ideas;

v)   a polling procedure to converge to a specific solution (i.e., individual voting to rank the ideas) and,

vi) discussions of the results from the voting process.

At the first step, group members are given the opportunity to think about the problem/question presented by a leader or facilitator and to formulate possible solutions. Each participant is required to write down as many ideas as possible in answer to the question, independently and in silence. Generally ten minutes are allowed for this stage (Taffinder and Viedge, 1987). Participants are encouraged to refine their ideas before offering their ideas for recording and listing. After the members have worked alone on the problem, they are asked to present their ideas during the third step. Care is taken to ensure that each member is allowed to present ideas without any interference by other members. The best control is to prohibit discussion and merely allow the presentation of ideas. Open discussion like traditional focus group occurs during the fourth step. Each member is afforded an opportunity to clarify ideas and to ask questions of other members. It is not incumbent to clarify or justify an idea s/he has put forward. The purpose of clarification is simply to expand upon the question under review. Any ideas that appear to be duplicated in the list are marked as such and the duplication is eliminated. During the fifth step, group members choose the most important ideas presented through a nominal (anonymous) voting and rank or rate them in order of importance. Various approaches can be employed to determine the importance (Claxton et al., 1980). At the sixth step, the ideas receiving the highest rankings are presented, and ways to implement the ideas are discussed at the same or another session. These ratings or rankings can be combined to determine overall rankings or ratings. Such ratings will help give the researcher an understanding of the structure of the problem or opportunity in terms of the respondents' most important dimensions.

Among other group-based discussions, the NGT appears to be the more promising approach for developing vision. Developed by Andre P. Delbecq and Andrew H. Van de Ven in 1968, the NGT avoids many of the problems associated with brain-storming and focus groups. While not necessarily superior to Delphi for idea generation, the NGT is better suited for structured groups. The NGT is a process designed to elicit ideas from all members of the group in a relatively short period of time and is considered to be particularly beneficial in groups where participants have varying degrees of power and there is a real likelihood that participants with more power will dominate the discussion (Maxwell, 2000). It is a structured meeting that attempts to provide an orderly mechanism for obtaining information from groups of individuals who are familiar with a particular problem area. Other major advantages of the

NGT over other group problem-solving methods include: the generation of a greater number of unique ideas and elicitation of an improved quality of ideas. The emotional element is eliminated from the process since there is no interaction in the key phases. The NGT promotes a shared commitment to the group's prioritized ideas. It is a structured, sequential system for tapping the resources of individual participants in a non-threatening context. The single question provides the group with an explicit agenda whose elaboration is governed by the parameters of the NGT phases. Together with this, the listing and ranking phases provide in-built processes for documenting the progress of the group. The NGT allows individuals the opportunity to think about issues without inferences of simultaneously verbalizing the ideas. This serves to clarify member's thoughts and permits critical assessment of the value of the ideas before they are offered to the group. Another advantage of the NGT is that the outcome of the group's deliberations is both clearly documented and understood by all members (Taffinder and Viedge, 1987).

Number of participants (12 including a moderator and a reporter) was decided based on relevant literature on effective meetings (Krueger, 1994). Larger group meetings would be difficult to manage for the moderator and tend to inhibit participation by all members of the group. Facilitators were trained and two rehearsals were conducted. Following Ritchie (1999), six themes, directly or indirectly related to tourism, to comprise overall vision statement were identified by the VSC in consultation with a number of stakeholders.

Enhancing Awareness and Participant Building: This stage involved stimulation of an appropriate spirit about vision development among relevant stakeholders, and generation of awareness of and support for the project. VSC experienced a number of obstacles at this stage. Some stakeholders had shown unwillingness toward the project, as the project would have required a change in their actions. Some had objected participation due to other stakeholders that are already in the list of contacts, blamed for being responsible for the current state of Kusadasi. Some even had considered the attempt for having a vision at the stagnation stage of the town, as being futile and ridiculous. Examples of the questions often used by skeptical stakeholders were "how will this project make a difference... how would we know that this project would not be used for the benefit of a single organization... what is the difference of this from previous failed attempts of similar kind ...".

The stakeholders were found to lack a common and shared idea of what difference they could make as a result of the project. These questions signaled the problems of pseudo involvement and low commitment. Maintaining determination, commitment and stamina among participant organisations is an important condition for facilitating network relations (Yuksel, 2003). Numerous examples in the literature demonstrate that collaborations often fail to make progress as the participant organisations are unwilling to pledge their full commitment (Huxham and Vangen, 1996). Conflicts are likely to arise if commitment is not equally spread, with some organisations placing more importance on the collaboration than others (Gray, 1989; Greer, 2002). It is maintained that if a partnership is operating against a background of historical and political confrontation this could have a profound impact on the success of the relationship (Gray, 1989). In this case, the VSC confronted with the difficulty of obtaining representation across the community at the initial stages; obtaining consensus on controversial issues and the difficulty of tokenism and skepticism (Cooper, 2002).

Lack of sufficient information about the institutional environment of the town had proven to be a barrier to communication with relevant stakeholders. Informative leaflets were prepared, local broadcasting was employed and in-house/office visits were undertaken to wider spread the awareness about the project. Coordination of stakeholders and activities was difficult, particularly as stakeholders had a variety of motivations, aspirations, and agenda that might clash with the project objectives. One of the important decisions taken at this stage was the utilization of a mix of conventional and unconventional methods in the dissemination of information about the project. Experiences gained in other previous meetings shown that the use of conventional methods only (e.g., official invitation letter, telephone, advertisement in newspapers, radio broadcast) was not productive in terms of turn out for meetings. The number of participants was emphasized as an important factor that either stimulates or discourages individuals, considering participation. Thus, in addition to announcements in local newspapers and radio, personal visits/talks with individuals in their offices and homes were employed to notify individuals of opportunity to participate in the vision development. Trained moderators were teamed up and they were assigned to contact the specified names of total 96 individuals on their list. Teams reported back to the VSC about their progress and necessary measures were introduced to reach the effective number that would represent the whole community. Moderators liaised with Town Assembly and the Municipality in the participant building process. A list of all public and private organizations including associations, non-governmental organizations (NGOs) and borough headmen was obtained from the district government of Kusadasi. Following the snow-ball technique in which each individual selected from the obtained list suggested other interested people (Medeiros and Bramwell, 2000), an enlarged list containing the names of relevant stakeholders was created (Table 2).

Table 2. List of Stakeholders

Public institutions (District Governor, Directors of Security, Health, Environment, Tourism, Education)	Residents
	Headmen
	Local Press
Municipality	Farmers
Hoteliers	Fisheries
Restaurateurs	Retirees
Travel Agency	NGOs
Tour Guides	Retailers
Political Parties	Chambers
Syndicates	Associations
Students	Unions
Banks	City Council
Educators	Local Agenda 21

Phase II - Action Taking

There were seven groups consisting of ten individuals discussing the same subject at the same time in separate rooms. Task groups were allowed to meet the members of the other groups during the fifteen-minute coffee breaks. Each group started at the same time and a draft vision was produced. In each session only one topic (question) was discussed and each of the six sessions was filmed and recorded. Following six independent sessions a final session was used to aggregate the six independent visions into a meaningful compilation (overall draft vision) by each group. Then, a meeting with seven task group representatives was held to merge these seven draft vision statements to-be-subjected to an overall voting in the final assembly. The role of the moderators included introduction of the subject, provision of examples when necessary, observation of the meeting rules and facilitating the process of deduction (disaggregating) and induction (aggregation). The NGT lend individuals to consider and organize their thoughts more cautiously and this was important for productive meetings. However, one of the limitations of the NGT, experienced in one of the meetings, was its inability to exploit views of illiterate individuals. Due to their illiterateness, two individuals were excluded from discussions. The titles of the six pre-determined sub-themes (economy, local government, environment, business management, education, society) of the overall vision were not disseminated to participants prior to workshop. This was because of the possibility that some individuals could turn up with written reports that would stifle the effectiveness of the workshop meetings. Each theme was discussed an hour with sessions involving generation of a draft vision statement through a nominal voting system.

More specifically, the meetings went as follow:

i)   The facilitator greeted participants at the entrance, sit in name-reserved chairs across an I-shape table, introduced himself/herself/topic and asked participants to present themselves to the other members of the task group (Picture 4).

Picture 4. Task Group Meetings

ii) The task group was asked to consider a single question: "how an ideal Kusadasi should be in 2023" (i.e., what was their aspiration in relation to economy, education, community, local government, environment of Kusadasi in 2023). 2023 was chosen as it is the year for the centennial celebration of the foundation of Turkish Republic. Once the subject was introduced and understood, the moderator instructed the task group that they should reflect individually on the topic and to put down their individual responses on a worksheet within the allocated time for writing.

iii) Upon completion, each of the forms was collected and read aloud by the moderator, typed in a complete manner by the reporter and projected on a screen so that each participant could reflect on what the others had expressed. Participants were given enough time to read through what had been produced by the other group members and were then requested to verbally add to their own statements. At this point, participants, started at random, were allowed to explain their responses briefly so that its meaning was clear to others. This process was repeated until all participants had a chance to express. They were warned that they should not criticize what had been stated by the others but remarks of others could stimulate further ideas. Additional statements were gathered and added to the sheet.

iv) Different from the original NGT procedure and consistent with the PAR methodology, a content analysis involving both deductive and inductive approaches was employed by the participants in the examination of collected statements. Following the amendment/clarification of the statements through verbal feedback, the individuals were first asked to breakdown their statements into pieces. The moderator had given examples for this deductive analysis. Identified pieces of statements were then registered on a separate sheet, similar statements were eliminated and this process continued until all statements were analyzed. The identified similar/dissimilar statements were then counted and they were displayed to the group. Following the breaking of statements into specific pieces and counting, they were subjected to a voting. Agreement was sought and the list of statements was pruned by removal of those statements from the list that did not receive consensus. The revised list of statements was printed out and handed to each participant. An inductive approach was followed and participants through guidance of the facilitator assembled these pieces, and produced a draft vision statement based on the refined statements within the allocated time. The final draft vision was subjected to a group discussion, necessary amendments were made, agreed on and all members in the group signed the resulting statement.

Phase III – Evaluation and Declaration

v) The final session (the 7th) was designated to evaluate and aggregate separately produced draft theme-related vision statements into a single overall vision. Further amendments were made and this process had resulted in tentative overall visions produced by the seven task groups.

vi) Following a seven-hour workshop, each task group was assigned to select a spokesperson who would attend a general meeting with the representatives of the other task groups. This meeting was organized to present and discuss each group's tentative overall vision statements. The meeting was held after the dinner and the rest of the other participants were given free time to exchange views and ideas. This meeting was important in terms of reflecting on the day's work and merging separate tentative visions into one. Similar to the process employed in earlier meetings, each group's tentative visions were printed and a catalogue containing seven visions was delivered to the representatives. The similarities and differences of the seven tentative visions were identified. Consensus was sought through merging of the revised statements. A single statement was then developed by adding/removing pieces of statements and this was presented in the General Assembly to the 74 participants.

vii) Each task group sat together at I-shaped tables and was required to read the aggregated vision statement thoroughly (Picture 5 and 6). They were required to discuss the statement and record agreement and/or disagreement. They were then invited to make amendments on the statement. Amended overall statements from task groups were collected after half an hour of reflection; they were recorded and revised by the VSC without any substantial change to their content. Then, a final copy the overall vision statement was devised and subjected to an overall voting of the participants. As the statement was produced with agreement of all participants, it was unanimously accepted and presented as a declaration to the Press (Table 3).

viii) Cooper (2002) notes that many plans fail when it comes to implementation. While it is part of the planning process, the majority of planning efforts do not consider the dynamics of implementation. The roles, timelines and activities that will be put in place to secure the vision should be agreed and a monitoring system of key variables to ensure that the achievement of the vision can be tracked should be developed (Cooper, 2002). Thus, the second major objective of the workshop was identification of a method for an effective implementation of the vision. Following finalization of the overall vision statement, each group was required to respond to the question of "what actions should be taken to realize the vision" and "who should undertake such activities". They were also required to identify three obstacles in the way of vision implementation. Five key actions for implementation were identified: communication and research, formation and coordination of voluntary work groups, structuring an action-plan, monitoring and control, and resource generation. Once actions were identified and prioritized by an in-group discussion, a drawing of a coach was used to help participants determine which stakeholder(s) should undertake these activities. The gear, wheels, steer, accelerator, break, air conditioner, fuel tank, and mirrors, denoting implementation activities were highlighted on the drawing. The fuel tank stands for financing of vision implementation (resource generation), whereas the steering wheel, gear and accelerator refer to coordination of the activities. The brakes resemble control and problem solving and the air-conditioner denotes feedback and researching. The mirror signifies activities relating to monitoring and spreading of the vision through public and press relations. Following in-group and between-group discussions, organizations to pursue identified actions were agreed.

Table 3. Overall Vision Statement

We, as Kusadasi, want:

An information-based, dynamic, and sustainable **economy** prioritizing all-year around operating tourism industry, as well as, optimizing other vital industries (e.g., agriculture, fishery, shipment) in order to maximize the community welfare…

A credible, transparent, efficient, proactive, participatory and collaborative **local government** in order to stimulate and better coordinate activities of various stakeholders which have development and resource-management implications…

A customer-oriented, ethical, professional, informed, competitive, contemporary, innovative, environmentally-sensitive, socially responsive and accountable **business community** in order to promote Kusadasi as an inimitable brand…

A sustainable **natural environment** policy that strictly observes protection-utilization balance and encourages renewable energy usage for the benefit of wild-life, host community, visitors and the entrepreneurs…

A collectivist, hospitable, responsive, emphatic, informative, conscious and respectful **society** with an increased sense of community…

An innovative, contemporary, high-standard **education system** that follows principles and revolutions of Atatürk, and that "invests in people" by fostering equal opportunity and analytical thinking …

Picture 5. The Final Assembly

Picture 6. The Final Assembly

CONCLUSION

Vision development and implementation is imperative particularly for destinations in stagnation. However, visioning is complex in that it is a cyclical process; each cycle determining the other's destiny (i.e., findings informing action throughout the process). This study attempted to share the experience gained in the visioning process followed in Kusadasi case. Despite its shortcomings, largely stemming from individual and situational factors, this unprecedented exercise and synergy it created was considered successful by the participants, both in terms of the outcome and the methodology. Meaningful engagement of the community, along with industry stakeholders and relevant government agencies, is necessary so that a true consensus on the preferred directions of future development, and the actions necessary to achieve this, can be developed (Faulkner, 2002). ". It was observed that visioning was a difficult journey. It requires among other things; credible and respected leadership with perfect communication skills to align people's motivations, interests and abilities; a strong sense of community belonging and citizenship, commitment, willingness and enrolment on the part of relevant stakeholders; substantial resources; placid inter-organizational (or inter-stakeholder) relations etc. All of these conditions, conducive for generation and implementation of an effective vision, were not present in Kusadasi case. The lifecycle stage of the destination (e.g., stagnation) imposed additional obstacles on the process of visioning. Nevertheless, the process of involving the general population in decision making, which reflects the changing nature of societal decision-making (Ritchie, 1999), was beneficial. Understanding what constitutes a vision and how a vision can be created in order to make a radical change should be helpful to authorities of other similar destinations.

Availability of resources in the form of finance, venue and time and leadership of an impartial organization were the keys in the success of visioning case in Kusadasi. The importance of space required for meetings, which is often not merely a budgetary question but may also entail a symbolic element associated with the location of the meeting place, should not be underrated (Alterman, 1982). Availability and location of a meeting venue - and range of its facilities – might have important implications for perceived legitimacy of the project and participants' commitment (Alterman, 1980, Selin and Chavez, 1994). Chosen venues of meetings away from Kusadasi, accommodation and transportation availability, and types and quantities of refreshments provided during breaks/stay increased participants' commitment to and perceived legitimacy of the meetings.

The case has demonstrated that visioning is a vital tool not only for setting a direction for the destination but also for consolidating relationships, community building and communication among stakeholders. The performance of destinations in any cycle setting can be severely hampered when the stakeholders know nothing about one another. Such ignorance may lead to the unnecessary duplication of activities. Stakeholders that interact would be in a better position to know one another, and hence to adapt to the larger environment within which they live (Njoh 1993). This holds true even when such contacts mean that stakeholders are doing no more than simply talking to one another. This is because by talking to one another, individuals are likely to exchange vital information about their activities, thereby ensuring that these activities are tailored to avoid conflicts and/or unnecessary duplication of effort. Direct relations between individuals enable informal interactions. Such interaction would facilitate recognition of similarities in orientation, possible matches between goals and resources, and a dependence on each other for scarce resources (Robinson, 2000). Visioning in the Kusadasi case has generated an opportunity for stakeholders with an interest in the town's future to spend time together. The time spent together for a common purpose has appeared to have revived the spirit of team-work and restarted two-way communication. Due to the hustle and bustle of their business and daily lives, the majority of stakeholders, rarely find time to get together to discuss issues with a bearing on Kusadasi's present and the future. The so-called "physical remoteness" tends to foster psychological alienation, and this in turn results in communication gaps. As stakeholders do not frequently and adequately communicate directly with one another, this accelerates misconceptions and misunderstandings. These are detrimental to building a sense of community, which is one of the basic tenets of a successful sustainable development.

Another key component contributed to the success of visioning case of Kusadasi was the use of unconventional methods to notify individuals of opportunity to participate in the vision development. This communication strategy has resulted in achievement of full representation of the community. Proper representation has played a significant role in the vision's development by increasing the local community's sense of ownership of the project (Brandon, 1993). This involvement appears to have made the local community more supportive, confident and productive. "With this sense of ownership comes support for its implementation and ultimately, the achievements of an efficient decision" (Williams et al 1998: 865). Another important component of the present visioning case was the opportunity to observe and benchmark best practices in Antalya. As was explained earlier, Antalya has become one of the top leading destinations in the Mediterranean Rim, with best practice applications in city planning and sustainable tourism management. Participants were found to be impressed by present tourism management applications in Antalya and this has opened their horizons as to what could be achieved in Kusadasi, if wanted.

Participatory Action Research, in which diagnosis and action planning was carried out in collaboration between the researchers and stakeholders, was another significant component of the visioning case in Kusadasi. Collaboration between stakeholders and researchers to identify the problem, develop alternative courses for action, select the course of action, evaluate the stages of the action obviously benefited both the researchers and the stakeholders in terms of knowledge building. Unfamiliarity of stakeholders with the PAR at the early stages gave rise to a slight skepticism about its suitability for the project. The skepticism was replaced by confidence as the stages unfolded and appropriate structures were jointly built. Unlike traditional methods in which the researcher assumes a "disinterested observer" role, active involvement of the researcher at all stages of the visioning case built a mutual rapport between the researchers and the researched. This had resulted in production of applicable solutions. Construction of a participatory context was a key ingredient to the successful application of the PAR in this case.

The use of NGT was another success builder. The stakeholders were unhappy about traditional "passive parental meetings" in which a large number of audience just listens what is being said and asks, if found a chance, a few questions. The traditional form of meeting was considered ineffective for consensus building on matters that concern the present and future of the community. The NGT procedure was entirely different from the format to which the participants were use to. Allowing individuals to think first on a question and verbally express his/her views without intervention and/or influence of others has been enjoyed by all participants. This technique prevented the likely problems experienced in other forms of group-based decision making, including a desire to be favorably evaluated by others, attitude and preference shifts resulting from the exchange of persuasive information between group members, dominance of individuals and so on. In sum, visioning is observed to place the future of destination into the hands of community and community-based strategies should have a better chance of implementation. This form of societal planning needs to be further studied to understand its dynamics. Determinants of participation in this kind of long-term projects are another significant research avenue.

REFERENCES

Alterman, R. (1982). Planning for public participation: The design of implementable strategies, *Environment and Planning*, 9: 295-313.

Bramwell, B. and Lane, B. (2000). Collaboration and partnerships in tourism planning *in* B.Bramwell and B. Lane (eds.) *Tourism Collaboration and Partnerships: Politics, Practice and Sustainability*, pp. 1-19, Clevedon, UK, Channel View Publications.

Bramwell, B. and Sharman, A. (1999) Collaboration in local tourism policy-making. *Annals of Tourism Research*, 26 (2): 392-415.

Brandon, K. (1993) Basic Steps Towards Encouraging Local Participation in Nature Tourism Projects, in K., Lindberg and D. E., Hawkins , *Eco Tourism A Guide for Managers and Planners*, The Eco Tourism Society, 134-152.

Bristol, T and Fern, E. F. (2003). The effects of interaction on consumers' attitudes in focus groups. *Psychology and Marketing*, 20(5), 433-454.

Brown, R. and Meade, N. L. (1997). Nominal group technique for determining CEO incentive pay. *Review of Business*, 18(2), 25-32.

Christenson, D. andWalker, D. H.T. (2004). Understanding the role of vision in project success. Project Management Journal, 35(3), 39-52.

Claxton, J. D., Ritchie, J. R. B., and Zaichkowsky, J. (1980). The nominal group technique: Its potential for consumer research. *Journal of Consumer Research*, 7, 308-313.

Cooper, C. (2002). Sustainability and tourism visions. VII Congreso Internacional del CLAD sobre la Reforma del Estado y de la Administración Pública, Lisboa, Portugal, 8-11 Oct.

Ergul, A., Tunc, B. and Yuksel, A. (2002). *Kusadasi Commercial Action Plan*. Kusadasi Chamber of Commerce Publication.

Faulkner, B. (2002). Rejuvenating a Maturing Tourist Destination: The Case of the Gold Coast. *Current Issues in Tourism*. 5 (6), 472-519.

Fisher, P. A., and Ball, T. J. (2003). Tribal Participatory Research: Mechanisms of a Collaborative Model. *American Journal of Community Psychology*. 32(3/4), 207-216.

Frish, B. (1998). A pragmatic approach to vision. *Strategic Thinking*, July/August, 12.

Gaber, J. and Gaber, S. (2002). Using focus and nominal group techniques for a better understanding of the transit disadvantaged needs. *Transportation Planning and Technology*. 25, 103-120.

Gray, B. (1989) *Collaborating: Finding Common Ground for Multiparty Problems*, Jossey-Bass, San Francisco.

Hackett, M. and Spurgeon, P. (1996). Leadership and vision in the NHS: how do we create the Vision thing?. *Health Manpower Management*, 22(1), 5-9.

Hayhoe, R. (2001). Creating a Vision for Teacher Education between East and West: the case of the Hong Kong Institute of Education, *British Association for International and Comparative Education*. 31(3), 329-344.

Hegedus, D. M. and Rasmussen, R. V. (1986). Task effectiveness and interaction process of a modified nominal group technique in solving an evaluation problem. *Journal of Management,* 12(4), 545-560.

Holpp, L. (1988). Realizing the possibilities. *Training and Development Journal*. September, 48-55.

Jamal, T.B. and Getz, D. (1995) Collaboration theory and community tourism planning, *Annals of Tourism Research,* 22: 186-204.

Kidd, A. S. and Kral, M. J. (2005). Practicing participatory action research. *Journal of Counseling Psychology*. 52(2), 187-195.

Kilpatrick, A. and Silverman, L. (2005). The power of vision. *Strategy and Leadership*, 33(2), 24.

Kusadasi Ticaret Odasi (1998). *Kusadasi Ticaret [Kusadasi Commerce]*. Kusadasi Ticaret Odasi Yayin Organi. Ekim, 3.

Levin, I. M. (2000). Vision Revisited *Telling the Story of the Future. The Journal of Applied Behavioral Science*, 36 (1), 91-107.

Maxwell, J. P. (2000). Managing conflict at the county level: the use of Q methodology in dispute resolution and strategic planning. *Public Administration Quarterly*, Fall, 339-354.

Nelson, G., Ochocka, J., Griffin, K. and Lord, J. (1998). Nothing About Me, Without Me: Participatory Action Research with Self-Help/Mutual Aid Organizations for Psychiatric Consumer/Survivors. *American Journal of Community Psychology,* 26 (6), *881-912.*

Njoh, A. J. (1993) The effectiveness theory of inter-organisational relations explored in the context of a developing nation, *International Review of Administrative Sciences*, 59: 235-250.

Nutt, P. C. and Backoff, R. W. (1998). Crafting Vision. *Journal of Management Inquiry.* 6(4), 308-328.

Ritchie, J. R. B. (2000). Community roundtables for tourism-related conflicts: the dialectics of consensus and process structures. In Bramwell, B. and Lane, B. (Eds). Tourism Collaboration and Partnerships: Politics, practice and sustainability. Channel Viw Publications: London, 159-182.

Ritchie, J.R. B. and Crouch, G. I. (2000). The competitive destination: A sustainability perspective. *Tourism Management* 21, 1-7.

Ritchie, J.R. B. (1999). Crafting a value-driven vision for a national tourism treasure. *Tourism Management* 20, 273-282.

Robinson (2000) Reforming the state: Co-ordination, regulation or Facilitation *in* Robinson, D., Hewitt, T. and Harriss, J. (eds.), *Managing development Understanding Inter-organisational Relationships*, Sage Publications Ltd., pp. 167-193.

Rossiter, J. R. and Lilien, G. L. (1994). New brainstorming principles. *Australian Journal of Management.* 19(1), 61-72.

Selin, S. and Chavez, D. (1994) Characteristics of Successful Tourism Partnerships: A multiple Case Study Design, *Journal of Park and Recreation Administration,* Summer, 12 (2): 51-61.

Shipley, R. and Newkirk, R. (1998).Visioning: did anyone see where it came from? *Journal of Planning Literature*, 12(4), 407-416.

Smith, S. L.J. (2003). A vision for the Canadian tourism industry. *Tourism Management.* 24, 128-133.

Stewart, W. P., Liebert, D.,. Larkin, K. W . (2004). Community identities as visions for landscape change. *Landscape and Urban Planning* 69, 315–334.

Susman, I. G and Evered, D. G. (1978). An assessment of the scientific merits of action research. *Administrative Science Quarterly.* 23, 582-603.

Taffinder, P. A. and Viedge, C. (1987). The nominal group technique in management training. ICT, July/August, 16-20.

Tatoglu, E., Erdal, F., Ozgur, H. and Azakli, S. (2002). Resident attitudes toward tourism impacts: the case of Kusadasi. *International Journal of Hospitality and Tourism Administration*, 3(3): 79-100.

Yuksel, A. and Yuksel, F. (2005). Managing Relations in a Learning Model for Bringing Destinations in Need of Assistance into Contact with Good Practice. *Tourism Management*

Yuksel, A. and Yuksel, F. (In Pres, 2005).Clientelist Relationships: Implications for Tourism Development in the Declining Coastal Resort of Kusadasi, Turkey In Agarwal, S. and Shav, G. (Eds) *Coastal Tourism Resorts: A Global perspective.*

Yuksel, F. (2003). Centre-Local Relations and Tourism Planning in Belek, Turkey. Sheffield Halam University. Unpublished Ph. D. Thesis.

In: Tourism Management: New Research
Editor: Terry V. Liu, pp. 149-178

ISBN 1-60021-058-9
© 2006 Nova Science Publishers, Inc.

Chapter 6

THE CONTRIBUTIONS OF ECONOMIC ANALYSES TO TOURISM: A SURVEY

Jaume Rosselló-Nadal*, Antoni Riera-Font and Javier Capó-Parrilla
Centre de Recerca Econòmica (UIB-"Sa Nostra")
Departament d'Economia Aplicada, Ed. Gaspar Melchor de Jovellanos
Universitat de les Illes Balears, Palma de Mallorca, Spain

ABSTRACT

Although tourism has been studied as a phenomenon by many different disciplines (sociology, anthropology, geography etc.), over the last few years one of the most incipient new research areas is tourism economics. The generalization of econometric software packages and the adaptation of economic theory have combined to offer a deeper insight into the economics of tourism. In this context, this study reviews the most popular aspects of tourism that have been analysed by economists in recent years. After a brief introduction, tourism demand modelling and forecasting techniques are evaluated as one of the most widely considered subjects in literature. Section three reviews studies of the tourism supply and structure of the tourist industry, followed in section four by an analysis of macroeconomic issues relating to tourism, like tourism's contribution to the GDP, tourism growth, employment and prices. In continuation, section five deals with the relationship between tourism and the environment, including non–economic impacts and sustainability, while section six concludes the paper.

1. INTRODUCTION

Applying economic concepts, theories and methods to tourism not only serves to highlight the peculiarities of tourism as an economic sector, but also the limitations of economic analyses when examining some of its foremost characteristics. Tourism, as a service activity, differs from other economic activities in the sense that it is impossible to define tourism itself as a productive sector and, by extension, to identify tourism outputs as one might do with other industries. Indeed, if one defines the tourism supply, the definition is consumer oriented because, as the WTO (1994) indicates, "the tourism supply is a set of tourism products and services made available to tourists at a certain destination for their use and consumption". The definition therefore includes private services aimed at meeting the tourism demand (transport, accommodation, catering services, shopping, other recreational services, sports and cultural attractions etc.), the public infrastructure on which tourism services are based and the natural resources that also contribute to tourist satisfaction.

It is precisely the high proportion of natural resources and public services that combine to form the tourism product that hinders economic analyses of the tourist market. Given the non-rivalry and non-exclusion type characteristics of many of these inputs, the public sector is forced to intervene in order to maximize collective welfare. In this sense, activities to promote destinations, the promotion of complementary activities, and the conservation and management of natural and cultural assets are all often carried out by the public sector.

Another peculiarity of tourism is the difficulty one has in including it directly in any of the specific fields used for the general classification of economic activities. This makes it impossible to quantify tourism itself as an activity, since some of the activities it involves have a dual demand. That is, they meet the needs of both tourists and local residents alike. This raises one of the main problems: how to identify the added value and expenditure generated by the tourist industry.

All this explains the birth and subsequent development of a sub-discipline of economics known as 'tourism economics', which tries to apply economic principles and techniques used in economic analysis to the tourist industry, seen as a set of activities whose main objective is meeting the demand for tourism. Thus, the objectives of this chapter are to review theories and empirical studies within the field of tourism economics, including issues relating to the tourism demand and supply and studies of other issues more closely associated with an economic analysis of tourism such as income, employment, prices and different factors related to the sustainability of the industry.

2. TOURISM DEMAND: MODELLING AND FORECASTING

One of the fields of research that has generated the most literature in tourism economics is the analysis of the demand. In this way, although the analysis of the tourism demand can include different topics like seasonality (Ashworth and Thomas, 1999; Baum, 1999; Baum and Lundorp, 2001; Koenig and Bischoff, 2003; Lim and McAleer, 2001; Rosselló et al., 2004; Wanhill 1980; Yacoumis 1980), segmentation analysis (Chandra and Menezes, 2001; Hassan, 2000; Shaw et al. 2000) or tourism attitudes (Beaumont, 2001; Herbert, 2001; Jutla, 2000; Ryan and Huyton, 2000), the review of the literature evidences how modelling and forecasting tourism demand has been one of the most popular issues analysed by researchers. Fretchling (1996) uses the argument that tourism products and the tourist industry have different characteristics from other products or sectors as reasons why, more than any other activity, it is necessary to identify the determinants of the tourism demand for the purposes of forecasts. These reasons include the fact that tourism products cannot be stored and so any unused supply cannot be kept for a later date when there is a higher demand. Neither is it possible to separate the production process from consumption. This interaction between consumers and producers means that goods and services must be offered when there is a demand. At the same time, it must be remembered that tourist satisfaction is largely dependent on complementary services. For example, destination loyalty or the repeat visitation rate are not only dependent on tourism accommodation facilities, but, more specifically, on all the other goods and services that the tourist consumes directly or indirectly during his or her stay. Likewise, the tourism demand is extremely sensitive to natural disasters and socio-political problems like wars, terrorist attacks or natural disasters. Finally, we must also add the need for long-term investment into facilities and infrastructure able to meet the expectations of the future demand.

2.1. Modelling and Forecasting Demand

Literature highlights the existence of two big groups of quantitative methods aimed at determining and forecasting the tourism demand: univariate and causal models (Witt and Witt, 1992 and 1995). Univariate models, used primarily for the purposes of forecasting, are based on the assumption that forecasts can be made without including factors that determine the level of the variable. Thus the only information they require is the past evolution of the variable to be forecasted. Even though they take into account the theoretical weakness of these models, Witt and Witt (1992) state that in practice these methods are capable of producing very good low-cost results.

The complexity of a univariate model depends on the number of mathematical operations and implicit assumptions that are involved. *Naive* models represent simplicity. Rather than using them like true models that need evaluating, they are normally used to carry out base forecasts. Methods like Box-Jenkins, which are relatively complex given the high number of estimations that are required, are no problem now thanks to the numerous econometric programmes that are available. Forecasts obtained with more complex models normally use forecasts generated by simple univariate models to demonstrate (or reject) their superiority (Kulendran and Witt, 2001; Lim and McAller, 2001; Miller et al., 1991; Prideaux et al., 2003; Rosselló, 2001; Smeral and Wëger, 2005; Witt et al., 1992 and 2003).

Within the univariate category, a second group of models can be included that consider time to be the only variable in determining the tourism demand. Witt and Witt (1991) propose ten different functional forms that try to explain the growth of the tourism demand. Likewise, Witt and Witt (1995) propose the use of the Gomperz curve for forecasting, based on the evolutionary stage of the tourism product in the lifecycle. Finally, Chan (1993), Chu (1998a, 1998b and 2004) and Wong (1997a) focus on the strong seasonal component and propose the use of the sinusoid function for forecasting.

Nonetheless, it must be admitted that the Box-Jenkins method has always been the most widely used in literature on forecasting the tourism demand, whether it is used as a reference method or as a motive for incorporating the latest advances in this technique for use in seasonal models (Chu, 2004; Cunado et al., 2004; Gustavsson and Nordström, 2001; Kim and Moosa, 2001; Lim and McAller, 2002). In this respect, the method can often be seen to obtain superior or similar results to much more complex methodologies. In addition to the fact that most statistical packages can easily be used for estimating the model, this makes it an excellent choice when forecasting the tourism demand.

Also within the framework of univariate models, the introduction of the decomposition of structural time series (Harvey, 1989) should be mentioned. It is surprising to find that, despite the substantial flexibility that this type of model offers, no really conclusive results have been obtained to date. Thus on the one hand, González and Moral (1996), Greenidge (2001), Kulendran and King (1997), Nordström (2005), Turner et al. (1997) and Turner and Witt (2001) prove that structural time series are slightly superior to other applied methodologies whilst, on the other, Clewer et al. (1990), Kim and Moosa (2000) find that the forecasts made with this type of model are very similar to those obtained with models based on the Box-Jenkins method.

Consequently univariate models seem to offer a good alternative forecasting method with a reasonable short-term goodness-of-fit and a relatively low cost. However, they are incapable of pinpointing the determinants of the tourism demand and, as such, are not suitable for assessing the possible effects that changes in the relevant variables (consumer incomes or prices) might have on the tourism demand. For this, causal models are required.

The main characteristic of a causal model is the inclusion of a series of variables in the available data set that are considered to act as the determinants of the tourism demand. The first examples of this type of models can be found in Gerakis (1965), Gray (1966) and Laber (1969) and, given the corresponding dates, they can also be considered the first exponents of tourism economics. Following the example of these initial studies, most tourism demand models have based their estimations on a destination or region's aggregate variables. Thus the theoretical foundations on which aggregate models are based has not changed since the earliest studies, centred on the idea of a representative consumer from a certain issuing market that must take decisions that affect the number of trips they take per year and their consumption of other consumer goods (Morley, 1992; Sakai, 1988).

Despite the difficulty involved in aggregating individual tourism demands (Morley 1995), most studies have chosen to estimate aggregate models econometrically, differing in the timeframe under consideration, the variables used, the specification of the functional form and the definition of the variables. The selection of a particular variable tends to depend on the availability of data and on the researcher's goals. Thus the variable for the tourism demand is usually represented by the number of tourists, number of overnight stays, length of stay, or expenditure, although other studies have also used the aggregate income or external balance of the corresponding country (Crouch, 1994a).

Meanwhile, the independent variables normally include the consumers' approximate *income*, generally measured by using the available family income or the per capita GDP (Archer, 1980; Gray, 1982; Harrop, 1973;); the *price of the destination*, usually specified as the ratio between the consumer price indexes of the destination and country of origin, given the difficulty in finding statistical series of tourism prices (Kwack, 1972; Jung and Fujii, 1976; Rosenweigh, 1988; White, 1985); the *cost of transport* from the issuing country to the destination (Martin and Witt, 1988); the *nominal exchange rate* between the issuing country and destination (Little, 1980; Tremblay, 1989; Truett and Truett, 1987) and its volatility (Chan et al., 2005; Weber, 2001); the *price of substitute and/or complementary destinations*, usually defined in the form of an index, based on the weighted average of the prices of other destinations that compete for the same market as the destination under consideration (Uysal and Crompton, 1985; Witt and Martin, 1987); *advertising or the cost of promotion;* and other types of variables such as a *change in preferences* (Barry and O'Hagan, 1972; Crouch et al., 1992); *the capital invested in infrastructure*, which defines both the tourist industry's quality and capacity (Carey, 1989; Geyikdagi, 1995) and even *meteorological variables* (Barry and O'Hagan, 1972; Sorensen 2002).

No definitive conclusions can be reached from different meta-analyses of the results of tourism demand modelling (Crouch 1994a, 1994b, 1994c and 1996; Li et al. 2005; Lim 1997a, 1997b and 1999) with regard to the value of the parameters of those variables most often used in specifications. What does stand out is the infrequency with which econometric tests are used to examine the basic hypotheses of the linear regression model, together with the absence of serial correlation, homoscedasticity, the linear functional form, the normality of the error term, and the exogeneity of the independent variables.

Possibly, this is why more recent studies have tried to improve on specifications. Wong (1997b), for example, analyses the statistical properties of series of tourist arrivals from different countries, demonstrating an absence of stationary in most cases. The solution to this problem involves the use of the cointegration analysis, which was not widely applied to aggregate estimation models and tourism demand forecasting until the 1990s, with some of the most representative studies being made by Bonham and Gangnes (1996), Dristakis (2004), Kulendran (1996), Kulendran and King (1997), Lathiras and Syriopoulos (1998) and Syriopoulos (1995).

Within the causal model category, demand systems or tourist expenditure systems should also be mentioned, which have centred their attention on the problem of consumers faced with a choice of market goods and services. The formulation of simultaneous equation systems seeks to avoid the biases that occur with uni-equation models, when consumer decisions regarding tourism services are considered in isolation from all other consumer goods. The first applications of this methodology can be found in Kliman (1981), Taplin (1980) and Van Soest and Kooreman (1987). However, the appearance of an article by Deaton and Muellbauer (1980) lent greater weight by laying the foundations of consumer behaviour theory, leading to the adoption of the methodology and its application to the tourism demand in Divisekera (2003), Fujii et al. (1985a), Li et al. (2004), Pyo et al. (1991) and Sakai (1988). In Bakkal and Scaperlanda (1991), O'Hagan and Harrison (1984), Smeral (1988) and Syropoulos and Sinclair (1993) the model is extended to include the second-stage selection of one of a choice of destinations, so that the following third stage would correspond to the allocation of spending on goods and services in each destination.

As for aggregate models, a final mention should be made of models based on *neural networks* (Kon and Turner, 2005; Pattie and Snyder, 1996; Uysal and Roubi, 1999), designed to reproduce the data processing method used by complex decision-making systems. From a linear combination of a set of variables potentially able to determine the tourism demand, one stratum or several intermediary strata are built, which in turn combine to give a final estimation of the demand.

Nonetheless, together with aggregate models, thanks to recent developments in the field of microeconometrics, models with microdata have been gaining ground. Since the earliest applications by Morley (1992), Rugg (1973) and Witt (1982), based on discrete choice models, random utility models have been used as a tool to estimate the parameters that determine a certain choice of destination (Morley 1994a and 1994b). Different applications have attempted to tackle problems of various kinds. For example, Aguiló and Juaneda (2000) proposed a tourism expenditure model where the tourists' socioeconomic characteristics appear as determinant variables; Juaneda (1996) estimated the likelihood of a return visit by tourists; and Palmer et al. (2005) evaluated the effect of a tourist tax on vehicle hire.

3. TOURISM SUPPLY AND ORGANIZATION OF THE INDUSTRY

In terms of the supply, Smith (1987) supports the idea that, as an economic activity, tourism comprises a series of business initiatives for the provision of goods and services consumed by tourists. Thus, without forgetting the huge complexity of the tourism supply and organization of the tourist industry, the production process for tourism services and goods can be compared with other economic productive processes. By combining land, work, capital and technology, goods and services are obtained in order to meet leisure and business demands in destinations away from an individual's normal place of residence. At the same time, tourism activities take place within the framework of a highly competitive international market that has been globalized as a result of technological developments and cheaper means of transport. It might be thought that prices and amounts could be determined in this competitive market structure without the need for intervention. However, given the characteristics of tourism as an economic activity, it is not advisable to identify a market equilibrium as being a social optimum. Before analysing the organization of the tourist industry, a review will be made of some studies that have tried to analyse the tourism supply from a general point of view.

3.1. Tourism Supply

As with any market, the volume of tourists and agreed price are the result of interaction between the supply and the demand. However, as De Rus and León (1997) or Sinclair and Stabler (1997) show in their respective meta-analyses, whilst an analysis of the tourism demand has been given special attention in literature, an analysis of the tourism supply has been relegated to second place.

One reason for this disinterest is the lack of supply-related data in most destinations and the difficulty in identifying the different components that make up the tourism product, apart from transport and accommodation. For this reason, possibly, part of the existing literature has focused on determining and classifying the different components of the tourism supply (Cooper et al., 1993; Holloway, 1994) and assessing its repercussions on the other remaining sectors (Zhou et al., 1997).

Issues relating to transport (travel away from home and travel within the destination itself) have been given pride of place in literature. This is probably due to the major role that the drop in the price of air travel has played in changing tourist habits (making long-haul destinations more accessible). This has partly been the result of deregulation in Europe and the United States, allowing small airlines to enter the market, airline companies to form alliances and, more recently, new low-cost airlines to appear (Forsyth and Dwyer, 2002; Morley, 2003). In parallel, vehicle hire companies have formed alliances with airlines so that passengers of a particular airline company get cheaper rates from car-hire companies associated with that airline.

It can be seen that most studies of the supply have chosen to take a certain sector as a reference, with the hotel accommodation sector being the most common one. According to Uriel et al. (2001), this interest can be accounted for by the fact that hotels are clearly the driving force behind the specialization of tourist destinations, as well as being the sector that ends up by contributing toward the creation of stable employment and the generation of a large amount of income for workers and employers while still maintaining a considerable network of relations with other companies from the tourist sector.

Studies of the accommodation supply have mainly focused on an individual analysis of the behaviour of accommodation establishments. The most outstanding ones assess the efficiency of different hotels (Morey and Dittman, 1995; Johns et al., 1997; Anderson et al., 2000; Pestana, 2004), demonstrating the extensive applicability of data envelopment analysis techniques. Meanwhile, aggregate studies of the hotel sector in a specific region have limited themselves to describing its main features (Lundberg et al., 1995; Van Kraay, 1993) or to modelling the supply function (Borooah, 1999). In this way, the results allow causal relations to be established between different determinants and the employment variable that is used.

3.2. Organization of the Tourist Industry

The validity of the structure-behaviour-results paradigm applied to the tourist industry has been empirically proven by Davies and Downward (1996), using a sample of United Kingdom hotel companies during the period 1989-1993. With the econometric model estimated by these authors, variations in benefits in relation to sales are explained as a function of the lagged market share variables, the cyclical evolution of the unemployment rate and a concentration index.

Nonetheless, progress in industrial analyses of tourism has traditionally been limited by a lack of statistics on units of production and by how complex it is to define the limits of the sector's production system. Even so, some studies can be found that have contributed in a general way to a greater awareness of certain tourist activities by focusing on specific contexts. Sheldon (1986) makes a series of reflections on the tour-operator industry in the United States, focusing specifically on the rates applied to services in Hawaii, while Aguiló et al. (2003) analyse the structure of the German and British tour operator markets by considering the prices of tourist packages, finding evidence of market strategies and structures characteristic of an oligopolistic market.

From a theoretical perspective, Baum and Mudambi (1994) propose the use of the Ricardian model for determining income to explain the earnings of tourist companies. The model assumes that the relation between income and quality is a positive one. That is, better quality products (packages, hotels etc) stand out due to their capacity to generate higher income. The empirical evidence for the Bermuda Islands seems to support this hypothesis in the case of the hotel industry (Baum and Mudambi, 1995). On the other hand, according to previous evidence by Carey (1989 and 1992) for the luxury hotel sector in Barbados, the possible over-capacity of the industry is not ruled out, even though the results are statistically robust. The equilibrium in Baum and Mudambi's model (1994), with few suppliers and oligopolistic incomes, is possible if conjectural variations different from zero are considered, which are more likely in real market practice. However, Taylor (1996) argues that relatively low sunk costs and low barriers to entry and exit clearly make the industry similar to a contestable market, if not actually purely competitive in the case of the tour-operator industry in the UK, thus counter-arguing what Baum and Mudambi proposed in their study (1994).

Meanwhile evidence provided by Gratton and Richards (1997) seems to support the hypothesis of contestability in the case of the UK market, where the top three tour operators account for 60% of the supply, but suffer from low profit margins, competitive prices and high instability. However, the results for this market contrast with those of Germany, where, with the same concentration in the hands of the top three tour operators, entry barriers predominate thanks to controls exercised by retail distributors.

As for the price consequences of the actual structure of the market, Dijk and Stelt-Scheele (1993) suggest that the price formation of tourism services might be explained by the profit margin on unit cost rule, which has some validity in imperfect competition situations. This price-fixing rule is usually justified by an uncertain demand and long-term costs. For this reason, companies might opt to fix prices by determining a certain profit margin on short-term average costs. Thus the prices of transport, accommodation and catering activities would be determined by unit costs and the profit margin. The empirical results of this model, in the case of Holland, are not very satisfactory, due to the low statistical significance of the explanatory variables.

An alternative approach to explaining how prices are formed is the hedonic pricing model, according to which tourist destinations can be distinguished from one another by a set of characteristics that determine the equilibrium price of the market. In other words, the price of a holiday package would be explained by the destination's location, number of nights (depending on the category of hotel), characteristics of the services offered by the hotels, and a series of dummy variables for the corresponding tour operators. Estimating the equilibrium price function econometrically allows percentage price differences among destinations to be derived, together with the marginal value of an additional night's stay by hotel category and tour operator. The first applications that can be found are Sinclair et al. (1990) for coastal tourist resorts in Malaga and Clewer et al. (1992) for tourism in European cities. More recently, Aguiló et al. (2001) examined the decomposition of tourist package prices to Mallorca, while Thrane (2005) and Mangion et al. (2005) estimated hedonic pricing models for tourist packages from Norway and to the Mediterranean, respectively.

Taking a temporal approach, Taylor (1995) studied price trends in several different Mediterranean destinations, observing a progressive convergence in prices during the period under analysis (1982-1985). Taylor argued that this convergence might be due to increasing competition among destinations and to a trend toward higher visitor numbers. The need to attract more and more visitors in order to satisfy the growing supply would lead to a drop in prices in destinations with greater product differentiation.

At a global level, because the tourist industry is organized into different destinations, certain price levels are associated with certain sets of characteristics, which can be compared on a competitive basis. As Gooroochurn and Sugiyarto (2005) emphasize, there are numerous ways of measuring the competitiveness of a tourist destination. For example Campos et al. (2005), Haahti and Yavas (1983) and Kozak and Rimmington (1998 and 1999) use tourist opinions and perceptions to measure how competitive a destination is, while Dwyer et al. (1999 and 2000) and Mangion et al. (2005) use published data as a yardstick. Even so, it is important to remember that competitiveness is a complicated concept, involving various different factors that are hard to measure.

4. MACROECONOMIC EFFECTS OF TOURISM

Tourism's most outstanding positive effect is clearly its contribution to the growth of its corresponding economies, particularly if we observe the evolution of certain macroeconomic variables which show that the rise in visitor numbers to the world's leading tourist destinations has gone hand in hand with a rise in their GDPs, with growth and employment rates much higher than those of their neighbouring economies.

Analyses of the economic effects of tourism are generally based on tourist expenditure, which in turn generates increased production in order to meet the rising demand. It would be wrong, however, to limit the beneficial effects of tourism to directly observable tourist expenditure on tourism goods and services, since there are also indirect effects and these too must be included if a proper assessment is to be made.

Different examples of how to model the economic effects of tourism can be found in literature, based on income or production, although the latest trends point to the adoption of Tourism Satellite Accounts and to Computable General Equilibrium Models instead of input-output analyses and Keynesian multiplier models.

By estimating the proportion of tourist expenditure that remains in the economy, once imports and savings have been filtered, the basic Keynesian multiplier makes it easy to calculate the potential effect of an additional unit of expenditure. However, given the over-simplicity of its assumptions and its partial vision by ignoring possible interrelations over successive rounds of activity, its conclusions might not be very valid.

Thus literature also offers more sophisticated multipliers that are closer to reality, by incorporating other variables such as direct and indirect taxes and subsidies (Archer, 1976), the marginal propensity to invest (Fletcher and Archer, 1991) or categories of tourism and sector-specific expenditure (Archer and Owen, 1971). Attempts have also been made to distinguish the multiplying effects of different types of expenditure, depending on the type of tourist, so as to create multipliers divided into categories of tourism and expenditure sectors. This is the case of the ad-hoc multiplier, based on the Keynesian model, which was initially proposed by Archer and Owen (1971) and later modified in subsequent studies by Sinclair and Sutcliffe (1982) or Milne (1987). The latter studies the effect of the size of a company, showing that small companies owned by local agents generate a higher income, more employment and more public income than large companies controlled by external agents.

However, despite the progress that has been made, at this point we should highlight the criticism made by Archer (1982) about the habitual use of average tourist expenditure instead of marginal tourist expenditure as encapsulated in the definition of a Keynesian multiplier. Furthermore, this author points out that multiplier-based analyses are possibly one of the worst-used economic techniques.

As an alternative to Keynesian models, input-output models are a more powerful analytical technique for deriving the multiplying effects of tourism and their main advantage is explicit modelling of the economic system's inter-sectoral relations. Tourism activities can be included in the transactions matrix, either in the end demand as an export, or as an additional sector in the table by adding one or several rows and columns. This second option is not usually feasible, due to the complexity of segregating tourist industry purchases and sales.

In practice, most studies choose to break down economic activities related to tourism into a high number of different components (transport, accommodation, catering and attractions). Thus tourist expenditure, estimated by using visitor surveys or official statistics, is broken down by activity and included in the end demand of the corresponding sectors (Diamond, 1975; Heng and Low, 1990; Johnson and Moore, 1993; Khan et al., 1990). With an input-output analysis, it is therefore possible to derive the direct, indirect and induced effects of a variation in the tourism expenditure of an economy (Archer, 1995).

A review of studies, like those of Archer (1985 and 1995), Archer and Fletcher (1996), Briguglio (1993), Fletcher (1985), Fletcher et al. (1981), Freeman and Sultan (1997), Herce and Sosvilla (1998), Lin and Sung (1983), Manente (1999), Payeras and Sastre (1994), Santos et al. (1983), Song and Ahn (1983) etc., which analyse the economic repercussions of tourism on certain national and regional economies by using input-output analyses, highlights not just the usefulness of this methodology but also the need to use the results to apply coherent policies, just as these authors suggest.

However, despite the advantages that input-output analyses offer over Keynesian models, according to Briassoulis (1991), Fletcher and Archer (1991) and Hughes (1994), the former are subject to restrictive assumptions that can diminish the empirical validity of the results in the case of economies that specialize in tourism. That is why, in recent years, different instruments have been developed that attempt to improve input-output analyses, such as Tourism Satellite Accounts and Computable General Equilibrium Models.

A Satellite Account is merely an instrument that is used to measure the importance of the tourist industry in terms of macroeconomic variables, using information from national accounts. The main advantage of a Satellite Account is the fact that a consensus was reached regarding the corresponding accounting definitions, concepts and rules so that inter-country and inter-period comparisons can be made. As Fretchling (1999) points out, because the economic impact of tourism is estimated in a way that is coherent with the method countries use to measure income and national production, the economic implications of tourism can be properly ascertained in relation to the rest of the economy. Even so, Tourism Satellite Accounts are not a reality in most countries, although it is expected that in the near future some research will be invested in improving methods for drawing up these accounts. Some pioneering studies can be found in Cañada (2001), Holz-Eakin (2001), Mak (2005) and Suich (2002).

As for General Equilibrium Models, it should be emphasized that they manage to overcome some of the limitations of input-output instruments by allowing for production factor constraints and the existence of market interactions, although they also have limitations, such as the additional cost that they involve in comparison with input-output techniques (Adams and Parmenter, 1995 and 1999; Blake et al., 2003; Blake and Sinclair, 2003; Dwyer et al., 2003a and 2003b; Kumar, 2004; Zhou et al., 1997). Indeed there is debate about how appropriate it is to use this model when it achieves similar results to those provided by input-output techniques. Nonetheless, it is an instrument to bear in mind when estimating the real economic impacts of tourism.

Analyses of the economic effects of tourism have not just been limited to its repercussions on income. Hennessy (1994), Hansen and Jensen (1996), Iverson (2000), Purcell (1997), Sinclair (1997), Sparrowe and Iverson (1999) and Woods and Kavanaugh (1994) analyse the repercussions of specializing in tourism on the labour market, while

Ireland (1993) and Jordan (1997) demonstrate the wage differences that exist among workers of different kinds.

Finally, to conclude this section, it should be added that any attempt to assess the economic effects of tourism must also include the economic costs that tourism involves. Among these different economic costs, the one that is highlighted the most by analysts is the opportunity cost of alternative uses of scarce resources. The decision not to develop other sectors is usually associated with a scenario in which there is an excessive monoculture, exposing the destination's economy to vulnerability.

5. ANALYSES OF RELATIONS BETWEEN TOURISM AND THE ENVIRONMENT

Tourism has clearly been one of the fastest growing economic activities in recent decades. In some aspects, tourism has achieved full success. Trends in international arrivals and income from tourism show a constant increase in tourism's share of world production and employment. Not only have leading tourist destinations seen a growth in income and better employment opportunities for the local inhabitants, but there have also been big benefits in terms of the conservation of traditional crafts and the recovery of historical and natural heritage by designating certain areas natural parks, restoring buildings and historic sites and introducing quality standards to tourist resorts.

5.1. The Non-Economic Effects of Tourism

Nevertheless, this abundance of tourism services conceals something less evident: unsustainable tourism. This implies the deterioration and over-consumption of natural resources in order to maximize production, or the disappearance of the local population's cultural identity through the gradual aculturization of the destination.

Literature has not remained unaffected by these issues, as demonstrated by the high number of articles that study the socio-cultural impact of tourism on native populations, using methodologies based on the resident community's perception of the costs and benefits of tourism. Following the highly influential study by Pizam (1978), other subsequent ones have abounded, and a special mention should be made of studies by Liu and Var (1986) for Hawaii, Lindberg and Johnson (1997) for the State of Oregon (USA), and more recently by Lindberg, et al. (2001) for the Are ski resort in Sweden, and Gursoy et al. (2002) for a recreational area in the State of Virginia (USA).

Although an analysis of the perceived socio-cultural repercussions of tourism is one form of studying the relationship between tourism and the environment, a review of literature shows that it is not the only one. Indeed, this relationship can be analysed from a variety of different perspectives, depending on the approach taken by the researcher, from an analysis of the environment or physical impacts (Cessford and Dingwall, 1996; Ward and Beanland, 1996) to strictly geographical ones (Butler, 2000; Pearce, 1995; Pigram, 1980).

Although relevant studies of the environmental effects of tourism are not so numerous as those applicable to other economic sectors, we should highlight studies by Briassoulis and

Van der Straaten (1992), Cater and Goodal (1992), Davies and Cahill (2000), Green and Hunter (1992), Hunter and Green (1995), Pearce (1985), and Roberts (1983) or the monographic work by the OECD (OECD, 1980), which all detail some of the main environmental effects of tourism. To give an example, Hunter and Green (1995) point to the deterioration of types of flora and fauna in the destination, pollution, erosion, the depletion of natural resources and the visual impact as the five big groups of problems associated with the negative impacts of tourism.

5.2. Sustainability and the Carrying Capacity

The environmental effects of tourism have generated debate on a new concept, sustainable tourism, which has been the object of growing attention by governments, international organizations, academic institutions and individual researchers. A good reflection of the interest that this issue has aroused is the abundance of literature mainly motivated by an analysis of factors that can help to achieve sustainable tourism levels (Archer and Cooper, 1998; WTO, 2000).

Like its more general counterpart "sustainable development", there are problems regarding the exact definition of the term sustainable tourism. Given its appeal, it has come to be used to defend differing attitudes to tourism development. McKercher (1993) comments on how the term is used with two radically different meanings: the first alluding to the possibility of sustaining a process of tourism growth and the second directed at minimizing the impact of tourism to the benefit of the ecosystem.

One of the first studies to tackle this problem, from the viewpoint of the tourist industry, was by Pigram (1980). In it, positive, neutral and negative relations were acknowledged between the environment and tourism development. In the same year, Butler (1980) introduced the concept of a tourism lifecycle to forecast and describe the level of tourism in a certain tourist region, highlighting the different benefits and losses that occurred during each stage of tourism development.

What is true is that, from an economic viewpoint (De Rus and León, 1997; Mathieson and Wall, 1982; Romeril, 1985), natural resources are used by tourism in two senses: on the one hand, the scenery, beaches, and quality of the water and air are all part of the definition of the tourism product as basic input in the tourism production function and, on the other, the effects of tourism on the quality of the environment play an important role in terms of land use and the discharge of waste into the sea or air (Green and Hunter, 1992).

The importance of the environment as input in the tourism production function goes beyond the usual market failure problems that characterize the economic activity of any other sector, according to economists, generated by an absence of rights of ownership, no pricing or the environment's status as a public good (non-rivalry and non-exclusion). To prove this, some authors highlight the main impact of the environmental deterioration of a sector that sells its services *in situ* in conjunction with the quality of its environment as being a reduced capacity to compete (Butler, 1980; González and León, 1998; Huybers and Bennet, 2000).

It is precisely from an analysis of the factors that influence the waning appeal of a tourist destination (Tisdell, 1987) that the concept of carrying capacity emerges in the form of a set of constraints that limit further growth in visitors and services (Herath, 2002; Russo, 2002).

Attempts to define it vary extensively, depending on the perspective that is used to analyse the limits (Martin and Uysal, 1990). Physical thresholds can be used, such as basic utilities, infrastructure or natural resources, or psychological or social thresholds that cause discontent among tourists and residents (Tooman, 1997). Despite how complex it is to define the term, given the wide range of criteria (sociological, geographical, ecological and economic) that can be applied and, above all, the measurement problems it involves (Butler, 1996; Coccosis and Parpairis, 1992; Ferreira, 1999; Lindsay, 1986; McCool, 2001; Pearce and Kirk, 1986; Saveriades, 2000; Tarrant, 1996), as Martín and Uysal (1990) point out, it is a concept that should not be overlooked under any conditions.

In these circumstances, where exclusion is impossible and rights of ownership are no longer universal, the role of prices as an indicator of scarcity or as a motivating factor in the behaviour of economic agents disappears. The result is the deterioration and over-exploitation of the environment. That is why it is necessary to convert the importance of the environment in social wellbeing into monetary units and then internalize the externalities generated by tourism, thereby achieving a sustainable model of tourism development.

5.3. Cost-Benefit Analyses and Economic Assessments of the Environmental Externalities of Tourism

Cost-benefit analyses are, in fact, widely used in welfare economics in order to illustrate the social desirability of a certain project. From this perspective, together with the private financial costs and benefits of tourism, other social costs and benefits must also be taken into account in order to decide whether this is a socially desirable activity. In short, it is a question of applying the principle of equimarginality: tourism production must be taken to a point where the marginal social cost of producing an additional unit is equal to the marginal social benefit.

In this sense, a social cost-benefit analysis is a technique that can be used to determine the optimal size of a tourist industry and, in the final instance, the carrying capacity, because tourism growth is associated with a decreasing marginal social benefit (Anup, 1995; Cals et al., 1993; Canestrelli and Costa, 1991; Fisher and Krutilla, 1972; Sherman and Dixon, 1995).

Clarke and Ng (1993) suggest that, if we ignore issues of equity and assume that tourists pay for the externalities they produce, on average tourism growth always produces positive net benefits for residents. This even occurs in the case of foreign ownership of companies, since the sale of assets will have been carried out at the present discounted value of future benefits. However, the previous argument presupposes certain key assumptions whose non compliance in the real world casts doubt on the sign of the net benefits of tourism, such as the existence of unemployment (Boadway and Bruce, 1984) or big environmental costs and benefits, in which case there is the added problem of comparing costs and benefits expressed in different units of measurement.

The complexity involved in pricing environmental costs and benefits has led to the design and application of approaches and methodologies that go beyond conventional approaches to specific fields of the economy, in order to obtain a monetary indicator of the importance of the environment in social welfare for the purposes of comparison in cost-benefit analyses.

These methodologies can be classified by differentiating those that produce a direct monetary valuation and those that produce an indirect one. The first group includes the well-known contingent valuation method (Cummings et al., 1986) and bidding games. The second includes the travel cost, hedonic pricing and avoided cost methods.

The amount of research that can be found on environmental pricing techniques in leading journals in the field of environmental economics and natural resources demonstrates the interest that this issue has aroused in recent decades. However, generally speaking, the theoretical contributions far outweigh the practical applications. Consequently, more empirical headway is required, which also implies greater involvement in the introduction of policies, particularly in the case of sectoral studies like tourism.

One explanation for this gap in literature can be attributed to the big theoretical and empirical limitations that hinder the application of this type of analysis to the field of tourism.

The travel cost method, which is suited to estimating the user value of a natural resource when it is mainly visited for recreational purposes (McConnell 1985), has been used to assess the value of destinations specializing in nature or ecotourism where the main motivation for the trip is a visit to a natural area or contact with animals (Maille and Mendelsohn, 1993; Menkaus and Lober, 1996; Mercer et al., 1995; Herath and Kennedy, 2004; Pham and Tran, 2000). However, difficulties arise with the travel cost method when attempts are made to place a value on environmental attributes in destinations where there are different motivations for the trip. Firstly, there are no definite criteria for breaking down the travel cost according to the different determinants of the demand. Secondly, the trip is usually made just once a year, and so it is impossible to define the dependent variable as the number of trips made during this space of time, although this period could be extended as Mercer et al. 1995 does, or else the length of stay could be considered (Bell and Leeworthy, 1990) together with the time spent visiting the natural areas (Riera, 2000). Nonetheless, Smith and Kopp (1980) suggest that the method presents spatial constraints and so biases occur in the valuation of resources when visitors travel very long distances.

The hedonic pricing method, which prices the environmental attributes of recreational areas by taking parallel markets as references, has been used with good results in Englin and Mendelsohn (1991), Espinet et al. (2003) and Sinclair et al. (1990). However, its application to international or long-haul tourism suffers from a lack of available data. Even so, Edwards (1991) used a simplified version of the hedonic pricing method to price the conservation of the forests of the Galapagos Islands.

Finally, the contingent valuation method, which identifies potential markets by encouraging individuals to indicate their preferences with regard to the provision of natural resources, is particularly suitable in the case of tourism, even more so given its high degree of applicability and flexibility in the valuation of multiple attributes, providing that the structure of the market in question captures all the constraints that tourists find in the selection process when they choose a destination. This method is becoming more and more popular and representative examples can be found in Blakemore (2000), Bostedt and Mattsson (1994), Greiner and Rolfe (2004), Herath and Kennedy (2004), Lee et al. (1998), Lee and Chun (1999), Lee and Han (2002), León (1997), Lindberg (1995), Marangon and Rosato (1998) and Pruckner (1994)

Indeed, these studies reinforce the conviction that it is necessary to incorporate all the costs and benefits associated with tourism in order to make a correct cost-benefit analysis and ensure sustainable tourism development.

5.4. Internalizing Tourism Externalities

Once an analysis has been made of the environmental problems associated with tourism and the possibility of transforming them into monetary units, research must focus on conceptualizing these problems as externalities and correcting them in order to guarantee the continued growth of the tourist industry.

A wide range of instruments can be found in literature on economic policies for the protection of the environment (OECD 1989 and 1991; Sterner 1999), among which the most notable ones are command and control mechanisms or market-based instruments.

Economists' vigorous defence of price-based instruments can clearly be accounted for by their efficiency compared with regulatory measures. Different empirical studies show that similar environmental goals can be achieved at a much lower cost if economic instruments are applied as opposed to direct regulatory policies (Cropper and Oates, 1992).

However, despite the considerable attention that has been given to environmental policy instruments in literature, it is surprising how little emphasis there has been on the design of policies for the tourist industry, particularly since tourism is one of the driving forces behind the growth of the world economy. With the exception of some studies of the use of economic instruments to reduce the environmental effects of tourism, like that of Forsyth and Dwyer (1995), or studies of the use of taxes to correct tourism externalities, like those of Gago and Labandeira (2001), Palmer and Riera (2003) and Piga (2003), few contributions focus on the design of environmental policies in connection with tourism.

Among those studies that analyse the effects of revenue-seeking tourist taxes, many make a distinction between the incidence and exportability of the tax (Blair et al., 1987; Bonham et al., 1991; Combs and Elledge, 1979; Fujii et al., 1985b; Mak and Nishimura, 1979). When a unit tax is levied on tourism accommodation, the tax burden falls on the buyers and sellers depending on the elasticities of supply and demand. Generally speaking, levying an *ad valorem* tax on accommodation will reduce occupancy rates by raising prices. The price rise for consumers divided by the reduction in the producer price is more or less equal to the ratio between the elasticities of supply and demand. The higher the elasticity of supply compared with the elasticity of demand, the higher the tax burden on the buyers. In cases where there is an infinite elasticity of supply or zero demand, the tax burden falls exclusively on the buyers (Aguiló et al., 2005; Fujii et al., 1985b)

6. CONCLUSION

Tourism economics is in an incipient state of development, not only because this is the world's top industry but primarily due to the increasing importance that tourism flows have had on the quality of life of tourist destinations and due to progressive interaction between the industry and the environment. As this article demonstrates, priority in research has been given to modelling and forecasting the demand and these are the fields on which most contributions have focused. Aggregate uniequational models are being replaced by more complex systems, where the properties of time series are finally being explored in detail. Looking forward to the future, greater attention must be lent to microeconomic models, with more empirical applications. At the moment there seems to be a big deficit in studies that analyse the role of the environment in the formation of individual preferences and in explaining the demand.

On the supply side, a lack of data has seriously limited analyses of the tourist industry. The contributions made to date have mainly focused on theoretical aspects, with very few empirical applications. Nonetheless, as the economic importance of the tourist industry grows, databases are beginning to build up, and so the prospects for future studies of business behaviour and price fixing are hopeful.

One field of study that has also been a focus of interest for researchers is how to measure the repercussions of tourism. From Keynesian models and input-output tables to Tourism Satellite Accounts and General Computable Equilibrium Models, tourism economics has tried to quantify the effects of tourism on income, employment and the balance of payments. Given how useful these instruments are in identifying the importance of tourism in regional or national economies, we believe that, in the future, they will continue to be given attention by researchers, and an increase in the number of applications in various different contexts can be expected. Even so, significant efforts must first be made to create and systematize precise, rigorous statistical data, particularly in the case of the latest methodological contributions (Satellite Accounts and General Equilibrium Models).

One field of study that has the rosiest future prospects is an analysis of destinations' externalities and their level of sustainability. Once literature has detailed the environmental impacts of tourism, the latest advances in methodologies for assessing the economic value of the environment must be empirically tested before techniques like cost-benefit analyses or studies of the carrying capacity can be tackled with full guarantees of success. All this must be done in the hope that more efficient public intervention can be achieved both in the provision of public services and in the management of natural resources associated with tourism.

Thus by using economic sciences, tourism can be quantified, explained, managed and even forecasted. The main purpose of this study was to highlight ways in which economic theory can offer an insight into a wide range of issues that concern the tourist industry, while also indicating in which fields new theories and new applications must be developed.

ACKNOWLEDGEMENTS

The authors would like to thank different members of the Department of Applied Economics of the University of the Balearic Islands for conversations they have held with them over the years.

REFERENCES

Adams, P.A. and B.R. Parmenter (1995) "An Applied General Equilibrium Analysis of the Economic Effects of Tourism in a Quite Small, Quite Open Economy" *Applied Economics* 27(10): 985-994.

Adams, P.A. and B.R. Parmenter (1999) "General Equilibrium Models" In Valuing Tourism: Methods and Techniques" Occasional Paper n° 28. Bureau of Tourism Research: Canberra.

Aguiló, E and N. Juaneda (2000) "Tourist Expenditure for Mass Tourism Markets" *Annals of Tourism Research* 27(3): 624-637.

Aguiló, E., A. Riera and J. Rosselló (2005) "The Short-Term Price Effect of a Tourist Tax on the Demand for Tourism Through a Dynamic Demand Model. The Case of the Balearic Islands" *Tourism Management* 26(3): 359-365.

Aguiló, E., J. Alegre and M. Sard (2003) "Examining the Market Structure of the German and UK Tour Operating Industries Through an Analysis of Package Holiday Prices" *Tourism Economics* 9(3): 255-278.

Aguiló, P.M., J. Alegre and A. Riera (2001) "Determinants of the Price of German Tourist Packages on the Island of Mallorca" *Tourism Economics* 7(1): 59-74.

Anderson, R., R. Fok and J. Scott (2000) "Hotel Industry Efficiency: An Advanced Linear Programming Examination" *American Business Review* 18(1): 40-48.

Anup, S. (1995) *The Economics of Third World National Parks. Issues of Tourism and Environmental Management*, Edward Elgar, Aldershot.

Archer, B.H. (1976) "The Anatomy of Multiplier" *Regional Studies* 10: 71-77.

Archer, B.H. (1980) "Forecasting Demand -Quantitative and Intuitive Techniques". *International Journal of Tourism Management* 1(1): 5-12.

Archer, B.H. (1982) "The Value of Multipliers and their Policy Implications" *Tourism Management* 3(2): 236-241.

Archer, B.H. (1985) "Tourism in Mauritius: an Economic Impact Study with Marketing Implications" *Tourism Management* 5(2): 50-54.

Archer, B.H. (1995) "Importance of Tourism for the Economy of Bermuda" *Annals of Tourism Research* 22 (4): 918-930.

Archer, B.H. and C. Cooper (1994) "The Positive and the Negative Impacts of Tourism" In Theobald, W. (ed) *Global Tourism: the Next Decade*, Chapter 5, Ed. Butterworth-Heinemann: Oxford.

Archer, B.H. and C. Owen (1971) "Towards a Tourist Regional Multiplier" *Regional Studies* 5:289-294.

Archer, B.H. and J. Fletcher (1996) "The Economic Impact of Tourism in the Seychelles" *Annals of Tourism Research* 23(1): 32-47.

Ashworth, J. and B. Thomas (1999) "Patterns of Seasonality in Employment in Tourism in the UK" *Applied Economics Letters* 6: 735-739.

BARRY, K., and J. O'Hagan (1972) "An Econometric Study of British Tourist Expenditure in Ireland" *Economic and Social Review* 3(2): 143-161.

Baum, T. (1999) "Responses to Seasonality" *Tourism Economics* 1:299-312.

Baum, T. and B. Mudambi (1994) "A Ricardian Analysis of the Fully Inclusive Tour Industry" *The Services Industries Journal* 14 (1): 85-93.

Baum, T. and B. Mudambi (1995) "An Empirical Analysis of Oligopolistic Hotel Pricing" *Annals of Tourism Research* 22 (3): 501-516.

Baum, T. and S. Lundtorp (2001) *Seasonality in Tourism*. United Kingdom: Pergamon.

Beaumont, N. (2001) "Ecotourism and the Conservation Ethic: Recruiting the Uninitiated or Preaching to the Converted?" *Journal of Sustainable Tourism* 9(4): 317-341.

Bell, F.W. and R. Leeworthy (1990) "Recreational Demand by Tourists for Saltwater Beach Days" *Journal of Envrionmental Economics and Management* 18: 189-205.

Blair, A.R., F. Giarrantini and H. Spiro (1987) "Incidence of the Amusement Tax". *National Tax Journal* 40(1): 61-69.

Blake, A. and M.T. Sinclair (2003) "Tourism Crisis Management - US Response to September 11" *Annals of Tourism Research* 30(4):813-832.

Blake, A., M.T. Sinclair and G.Sugiyarto G. (2003) "Quantifying the Impact of Foot and Mouth Disease on Tourism and the UK Economy" *Tourism Economics* 9(4):449-465.

Blakemore, F.B. (2000) "Tourist Evaluation of Olu Deniz Beach (Turkey) Using Contingent Valuation and Travel Cost Approaches". *World Leisure Journal* 42(4): 48-55.

Boadway, R.W. and N. Bruce (1984). *Welfare economics*. Basil Blackwell.

Bonham, C.S, E. Fujiii, E. IM and J. Mak (1991) "The Impact of the Hotel Tax Room:An Interrupte Time Series Approach". *National Tax Journal* 45(4): 433-441.

Bonham, C.S. and B. Gangnes (1996) Interevention Analysis with Cointegrated Time Series: The Case of Hawaii Hotel Room Tax. *Applied Economics* 28: 1281-1293

Borooah, V. (1999) "The Supply of Hotel Rooms in Queensland, Australia" *Annals of Tourism Research* 26: 985-1003.

Bostedt, G. and L. Mattsson (1995) "The Value of Forests for Tourism in Sweden" *Annals of Tourism Research* 22(3): 671-680.

Briassoulis, H. (1991) "Methodological Issues. Tourism Input-Output Analysis" *Annals of Tourism Research* 18: 485-495.

Briassoulis, H. and J. van der Straaten (1992) "Tourism and the Environment: an Overview" In *Tourism and the Environment: regional, economic and policy Issues*, Ed. Kluwer Academic Publishers.

Briguglio, L. (1993) "Tourism Multipliers in the Maltese Economy" In Johnson, P. and Thomas, B. (eds) *Perspectives on Tourism Policy*. Russell Publishing: London.

Butler, R.W. (1980) "The Concept of a Tourist Area Cycle of Evolution: Implications for Management of Resources" *Canadian Geographer* 24(1): 5-12.

Butler, R.W. (1996) "The Concept of Carrying Capacity for Tourism Destinations" *Progress in Tourism and Hospitality Research* 2(3-4): 283-293.

Butler, R.W. (2000) "Tourism and the Environment: a Geographical Perspective", *Tourism Geographies* 2(3): 337-358.

Cals, J., A. Matas and P. Riera (1993) *Evaluación de Proyectos. Análisis de la Rentabilidad Social desde la Perspectiva del Turismo y el Ocio*. Secretaría General de Turismo, Ministerio de Comercio y Turismo: Madrid.

Campos, J., L. González and M. Ropero (2005) "Service Quality and Competitiveness in the Hospitality Sector" *Tourism Economics* 11(1): 85–102.

Canestrelli, E. and J. COSTA (1991) "Tourist Carrying Capacity: a Fuzzy Approach" *Annals of Tourism Research* 8: 295-311.

Cañada, A. (2001) *Una Nota sobre Coeficientes y Modelos de Multiplicadores a partir del nuevo sistema Input-Output del SEC95*. INE, Boletín Trimestral de Coyuntura núm. 82: Madrid

Carey, K. (1989) "Tourism Development in LDCs: Hotel Capacity Expansion with Reference to Barbados" *World Development* 17(1): 59-67.

Carey, K. (1992) "Optimal Hotel Capacity: The Case of Barbados" *Social and Economic Studies* 41(2): 102-126.

Cater, E. and B. Goodal (1992) "Must Tourism Destroy its Resource Base?" In Mannion, A.M. and Bowlby S.R. (eds) *Environmental Issues in the 1990*. John WileyandSons Ltd: Chichester.

Cessford, G. R. and P.R. Dingwall (1996) *Impacts of Visitors on Natural and Historic Resources of Conservation Significance*. Part I-Workshop Proceedings, Science and Research Internal Report, n° 156. Department of Conservation: Wellington.

Chan, F., C. LIM and M. mcAleer (2005) "Modelling Multivariate International Tourism Demand and Volatility" *Tourism Management* 26(3):459-471.

Chan, Y.M. (1993) "Forecasting Tourism: A Sine Wave Time Series Regression Approach" *Journal of Travel Research* 32(2): 58-60.

Chandra, S. and D. Menezes (2001) Applications of Multivariate Analysis in International Tourism Research: The Marketing Strategy Perspective of NTOs *Journal of Economic and Social Research* 3(1):77-98.

Chu, F.L. (1998a) "Forecasting Tourist Arrivals: Nonlinear Sine Wave or ARIMA?" *Journal of Travel Research* 36(3): 79-84.

Chu, F.L. (1998b) "Forecasting Tourism: A Combined Approach" *Tourism Management* 19(6): 515-520.

Chu, F.L. (2004) "Forecasting Tourism Demand: a Cubic Polynomial Approach" *Tourism Management* 25(2): 209-218.

Clark, H.R. and K. Ng (1993). "Tourism, Economic Welfare and Efficient Pricing". *Annals of Tourism Research* 20: 613-632.

Clewer, A., A. Pack and M.T. Sinclair (1990) "Forecasting Models for Tourism Demand in City Dominated and Coastal Areas" *Papers of the Regional Science Association* 69: 31-42.

Clewer, A., A. Pack and M.T. Sinclair (1992) "Price Competitiveness and Inclusive Tourim Holidays in European Cities" In Johnson, P., and Thomas, B. (Eds.) *Choice and demand in tourism*. Mansell: London. pp. 123-144.

Coccossis, H. and A. Parpairis (1992) "Tourism and the Environment: Some Observations on the Concept of Carrying Capacity" In Briassoulis, H. and van der Straaten, J. *Tourism and the Environment*. Kluwer: Dordrecht.

Combs, P. and B.W. Ellegde (1979) "Effects of a Room Tax on Resort Hotel/Motels". *National Tax Journal* 32: 201-207.

Cooper, C., J. Fletcher, D. Gilbert and S. Wanhill (1993) *Tourism. Principles and practice*. Pitman Publishing: London.

Cropper, M. L. and W.E. Oates (1992) "Environmental Economics: a Survey", *Journal of Economic Literature* 30: 640-675.

Crouch, G.I. (1994a) "A Meta-Analysis of Tourism Demand" *Annals of Tourism Research* 22(1): 103-118.

Crouch, G.I. (1994b) "The Study of International Tourism Demand: A Review of Findings" *Journal of Travel Research* 33(1) 12-23.

Crouch, G.I. (1994c) "Demand Elasticities for Short-Houl versus Long-Haul Tourism" *Journal of Travel Research* 33(2): 2-14.

Crouch, G.I. (1996) "Demand Elasticities in International Marketing. A Meta-Analytical Application to Tourism" *Journal of Bussiness Research* 36: 117-136.

Crouch, G.I., L. Schultz, and J. Valerio (1992) "Marketing International Tourism to Australia: a Regression Analysis" *Tourism Management* 13(2): 196-208.

Cummings, R., D. Brookshire and W. Shulze (1986) *Valuing Environmental Goods: An Assessment of the Contingent Valuation Methods.* Roowman and Allenheld: Totowa.

Cunado, L.A. Gil-Alana, F. Pérez DE Gracia. (2004) "Modelling Monthly Spanish Tourism: a Seasonal Fractionally Integrated Approach" *Tourism Economics* 10(1):79-94.

Davies, B. and D. Downward: (1996) "The Structure, Conduct, Performance Paradigm as Applied to the UK Hotel Industry" *Tourism Economics* 2(2): 151-158.

Davies, T. and S. Cahill (2000) *Environmental Implications of the Tourism Industry,* Discussion Paper 00-14 Ed. Resources for the Future: Washington.

DE Rus, G. and C. León (1997) "Economía del Turismo: Un Panorama" *Revista de Economía Aplicada* 15(V): 71-109.

Deaton, A. and J. Muellbauer (1980) *Economics and Consumer Behaviour.* Cambridge University Press: New York.

Diamond, J. (1975) "Tourism and Development Policy: A Quantitative Appraisal" *Bulletin of Economic Research* 17: 36-50.

Dijk, J.C. and D.D. Stelt-Scheele (1993) "Price Formation in tourism Industry Branches" *Annals of Tourism Research* 20(3): 716-728.

Divisekera, S. (2003) "A Model of Demand for International Tourism" *Annals of Tourism Research* 30(1): 31–49.

Dritsakis, N. (2004) "Cointegration Analysis of German and British Tourism Demand for Greece" *Tourism Management* 25(1):111-119.

Dwyer, L., P. Forsyth and R. Rao (1999) "A Sectoral Analysis of the Price Competitiveness of Australian Tourism" Working Paper, Ninth Australian Tourism and Hospitality Research Conference: Adelaide.

Dwyer, L., P. Forsyth and R. Rao (2000) "The Price Competitiveness of Travel and Tourism: a Comparison of 19 Destinations" *Tourism Management* 21(1): 9–22.

Dwyer, L., P. Forsyth and R. Spurr (2003a) "Inter-Industry Effects of Tourism Growth: Implications for Destination Managers" *Tourism Economics* 9(2):117-132.

Dwyer, L., P. Forsyth, R. Spurr and T.VAHNO (2003b) "Tourism's Contribution to a State Economy: A Multi-Regional General Equilibrium Analysis" *Tourism Economics* 9(4): 431-448.

Edwards,. S.F. (1991) "The demand for Galapagos Vacations: Estimation and Application to Wilderness Preservation" *Coastal Management* 19: 155-169.

Englin, J. and R. Mendelsohn (1991) "A Hedonic Travel Cost Analysis for Valuation of Multiple Components of Site Quality: The Recreational Value of Forest Management" *Journal of Environmental Economics and Management* 21: 275-290.

Espinet, J.M., M. Saez, G. Coenders and M. Fluvià (2003) "Effect on Prices of the Attributes of Holiday Hotels: A Hedonic Prices Approach" *Tourism Economics* 9(2): 1–13.

Ferreira, S.L.A. (1999) "The Social Carrying Capacity of Kruger National Park, South Africa" *Tourism Geographies* 1(3):325-342.

Fisher, A. and K. Krutilla (1972) "Determination of Optimal Capacity of Resource-Based Recreation Facilities" *Natural Resources Journal* 12: 417-444.

Fletcher, J. E. (1985) *The Economic Impact of International Tourism on the National Economy of Jamaica.* Report to the Government of Jamaica., WTO/UNDP JAM/84/007.

Fletcher, J. E. and B. Archer (1991) "The Development and Application of Multiplier Analysis", In C.P. Cooper. *Progress in Tourism, Recreation and Hospitality Management*, Vol. 3. pp. 28-47. Belhaven: London.

Fletcher, J.E., H.R. Snee and B. Macleod (1981) *An Input-output Study of Gibraltar*. Institute of Economic Research, University College of North Wales: Bangor.

Forsyth, P. and L. Dwyer (1995) "Problems in Use of Economic Instruments to Reduce Adverse Environmental Impacts of Tourism" *Tourism Economics* Vol. 1(3): 265-282.

Forsyth, P. and L. Dwyer (2002) "Market Power and the Taxation of Domestic and International Tourism" *Tourism Economics* 8(4):377-399.

Frechtling, D.C. (1996) *Practical Tourism Forecasting*. Butteworth-Heinemann: London.

Frechtling, D.C. (1999) Cuenta Satélite: Fundamentos, Avances y Otras Cuestiones. Instituto de Estudios Turísticos, Secretaría de Estado de Comercio, Turismo y Pymes: Madrid.

Freeman, D. and E. Sultan (1997) "The Economic Impact of Tourism in Israel: a Multi-regional Input-output Analysis" *Tourism Economics* 3(4) págs. 341-359.

Fujii, E.T., M. Khaled and J. Mak (1985a) "An Almost Ideal Demand System for Visitor Expenditures" *Journal of Transport Economics and Policy* May 161-171.

Fujii, E.T., M. Khaled and J. MAK (1985b) "The Exportability of Hotel Occupancy and Other Tourist Taxes" *National Tax Journal* 38: 169-177.

Gago, A. and X. Labandeira (2001) "Turismo y Fiscalidad Ambiental" *Papeles de Economía Española* 87: 179-186.

Gerakis, A.S. (1965) "Effects of Exchange-Rate Devaluations and Revaluations on Receipts from Tourism" *International Monetary Fund Staff Papers* 12(3) 365-84.

Geyikdagi, N.V. (1995) "Investments in Tourism Development and the Demand for Travel" *Rivista Internationale di Scienze Economiche e Commerciali* 42(5): 391-403.

González, M. and C. León (1998) "Turismo y Medio Ambiente: La Perspectiva de las Empresas Hoteleras" In Melchior Navarro, M. *El turismo en Canarias*. Fundación FYDE Caja canarias: Santa Cruz de Tenerife.

Gonzàlez, P. and P. Moral (1996) "Analysis of Tourism Trends in Spain" *Annals of Tourism Research* 23(4): 739-754.

Gooroochurn, N. and Sugiyarto (2005) "Competitiveness Indicators in the Travel and Tourism Industry" *Tourism Economics* 11(1): 25–43.

Gratton, C., and G. Richads (1997) "Structural Change in the European Package Tour Industry: UK/German Comparisons" *Tourism Economics* 3(3): 213-226.

Gray, H.P. (1966) "The Demand for International Travel by the United States and Canada" *International Economic Review* 7(1): 83-92.

Gray, H.P. (1982) "The Contributions of Economics to Tourism" *Annals of Tourism Research* 9(1): 105-25.

Green, H. and C. Hunter (1992) "The Environmental Impact Assessment of Tourism Development" In Johnson and Thomas. *Perspectives on Tourism Policy*. pp. 29-47. Mansell: London.

Greenidge, K.(2001) "Forecasting Tourism Demand - An STM Approach" *Annals of Tourism Research* 28(1): 98-112.

Greiner, R. and J. Rolfe (2004) "Estimating Consumer Surplus and Elasticity of Demand of Tourist Visitation to a Region in North Queensland Using Contingent Valuation" *Tourism Economics* 10(3):317-328.

Gursoy, D., C. Jurowski and M. Uysal (2002) "Resident Attitudes. A Structural Modelling Approach", *Annals of Tourism Research* 29(1):79-105.

Gustavsson, P. and J. Nordström (2001) "The Impact of Seasonal Unit Roots and Vector ARMA Modelling on Forecasting Monthly Tourism Flows" *Tourism Economics* 7(2): 117-133.

Haahti, A.J., and U. Yavas (1983) "Tourists' Perceptions of Finland and Selected European Countries as Travel Destinations" *European Journal of Marketing* 17(2):25-41.

Hansen, C. and S. Jensen (1996). "The Impact of Tourism on Employment in Denmark - Different Definitions, Different Results" *Tourism Economics* 2(3): 283-302.

Harrop, J. (1973) "On the Economics of the Tourist Boom" *Bulletin of Economic Research* (May): 55-72.

Harvey, A.C. (1989) *Forecasting Structural Time Series Models and the Kalman Filter.* Cambridge University Press: Cambridge.

Hassan, S.S. (2000) "Determinants of Market Competitiveness in an Environmentally Sustainable Tourism Industry" *Journal of Travel Research* 38: 239-245.

Heng, T.M. and L. Low (1990) "Economic Impact of Tourism in Singapore" *Annals of Tourism Research* 17: 246-269.

Hennessy, S. (1994) "Female Employment in Tourism Development in South-west England" In: *Tourism: A Gender Analysis*. Kinnard, V. and D. Hall. Wiley: Chichester.

Herath, G. (2002) "Research Methodologies for Planning Ecotourism and Nature Conservation" *Tourism Economics* 8(1): 77-101.

Herath, G. and J. Kennedy (2004) "Estimating the Economic Value of Mount Buffalo National Park with the Travel Cost and Contingent Valuation Models" *Tourism Economics* 10(1): 63–78.

Herbert, D. (2001) "Literary Places, Tourism and the Heritage Experience" *Annals of Tourism Research* 28(2):312–333.

Herce, J.A. and S. Osvilla (1998) *Sector Turístico y Crecimiento del Empleo en la Comunidad Autónoma de Canarias: Un Ejercicio de Prospección al Horizonte 2011* Documentos de trabajo, nº 98-02, FEDEA and Universidad Complutense de Madrid.

Holloway, J.C. (1994) *The Business of Tourism*. Pitman: London.

Holz-Eakin, D. (2001) "Capital in a Tourism Satellite Account" *Tourism Economics* 7: 223-232.

Hughes, H.L. (1994) "Tourism Multiplier Studies: a more Judious Approach" *Tourism Management* 15(6): 403-406.

Hunter, C. and H. Green (1995) *Tourism and the Environment. A Sustainable Relationship?* Routledge: London.

Huybers, T. and J. Bennett (2000) "Impact of the Environment on Holiday Destination Choices of Prospective UK Tourists: Implications for Tropical North Queensland" *Tourism Economics* 6(1): 21-46.

Ireland, M. (1993) "Gender and Class Relations in Tourism Employment" *Annals of Tourism Research* 20(4): 666-684.

Iverson, K. (2000) "The Paradox of the Contented Female Manager: An Empirical Investigation of Gender Differences in Pay Expectation in the Hospitality Industry" *Hospitality Management* 19: 33-51.

Johns, N., B. Howcroft and L. Drake (1997) "The Use of Data Envelopment Analysis to Monitor Hotel Productivity" *Progress in Tourism and Hospitality Research* 3: 119-127.

Johnson, R.L. and E. Moore (1993) "Tourism Impact Estimation" *Annals of Tourism Research* 20(3): 279-288.

Jordan, F. (1997) "An Ocupation Hazard? Sex Segregation in Tourism Employment" *Tourism Management* 18(8):525-534.

Juaneda, N. (1996) "Estimating the Probability of Return Visits Using a Surveyu of Tourist Expenditure in the Balearic Islands" *Tourism Economics* 2(4):339-352.

Jung, J.M. and E.T. Fujii (1976) "The Price Elasticity of Demand for Air Travel: Some new Evidence" *Journal of Transport Economics and Policy* 10 (3): 257-262.

Jutla, R.S: (2000) "Visual Image of the City: Tourists' Versus Residents' Perception of Simla, a Hill Station in Northern India" *Tourism Geographies* 2(4): 404 –420.

Khan, H., C.F. Seng and W.K. Cheong (1990) "Tourism Multipliers Effects on Singapore" *Annals of Tourism Research* 17(3): 408-418.

Kim, J.H. and I. MOOSA (2000) "Trend, Cycle and Seasonality in Forecasting Monthly International Tourist Arrivals in Australia" Presented at: *ISF2000. 20th International Symposium on Forecasting*. Lisboa, Portugal.

Kim, J.H. and I. Moosa (2001) "Seasonal Behaviour of Monthly International Tourist Flows: Specification and Implications for Forecasting Models" *Tourism Economics* 7(4):381-396

Kliman, M.L. (1981) "A Quantitative Analysis of Canadian Overseas Tourism" *Transportation Research* 15A(6): 487-497.

Koenig, N., and E. Bischoff (2003) "Seasonality of Tourism in Wales: A Comparative Analysis" *Tourism Economics* 9:229-254.

Kon, S.C. and L.W Turner (2005) "Neural Network Forecasting of Tourism Demand" *Tourism Economics* 11(3): 301-328.

Kozak, M., and M. Rimmington (1998) "Benchmarking: Destination Attractiveness and Small Hospitality Business Performance" *International Journal of Contemporary Hospitality Management* 10: 74–78.

Kozak, M., and M. Rimmington (1999) "Measuring Tourist Destination Competitiveness: Conceptual Considerations and Empirical Findings" *International Journal of Hospitality Management* 18(3): 273–283.

Kulendran, N. (1996) "Modelling Quarterly Tourist Flows to Australia Using Cointegration Analysis" *Tourism Economics* 2(3): 203-222.

Kulendran, N. and M.L. King (1997) "Forecasting International Quaterly Tourists Flows Using Error-correction and Time-series Models" *International Journal of Forecasting* 13: 319-327.

Kulendran, N. and S.F. Witt (2001) "Cointegration versus Least Squares Regression" *Annals of Tourism Research* 28(2): 291-311.

Kumar, P. (2004) "Economic Impact of Tourism on Fiji's Economy: Empirical Evidence from the Computable General Equilibrium Model" *Tourism Economics* 10(4): 419-433.

Kwack, S.Y. (1972) "Effects of Income and Prices on Travel Spending Abroad 1960 III-1967 IV" *International Economic Review* 13(2): 245-56.

Laber, G. (1969) "Determinants of International Travel Between Canada and United States" *Geographical Analysis* 1(4): 329-36.

Lathiras, P. and C. Siriopoulos (1998) "The Demand for Tourism to Greece: A Cointegration Approach" *Tourism Economics* 4(2): 171-185.

Lee, C., J. Lee, and S. Han (1998) "Measuring the Economic Value of Ecotourism Resources: the Case of South Korea" *Journal of Travel Research* 36:40-47.

Lee, C.K. and S. Han (2002) "Estimating the Use and Preservation Values of national Parks' Tourism Resources Using a Contingent Valuation Method" *Tourism Management* 23(5): 531-540.

Lee, H. and H. Chun (1999) "Valuing Environmental Quality Change on Recreational Hunting in Korea: A Contingent Valuation Analysis" *Journal of Environmental Management* 57: 11-20.

León, C. (1997) "Valuing International Tourism Benefits from Natural Areas" *Tourism Economics* 3(2): 119-136.

Li, G., H. Song and S.F. Witt (2004) "Modeling Tourism Demand: A Dynamic Linear AIDS Approach" *Journal of Travel Research* 43: 141-150.

Li, G., H. Song and S.F. Witt (2005) "Recent Developments in Econometric Modeling and Forecasting" *Journal of Travel Research* 44: 82-99.

Lim, C. (1997a) "An Econometric Classification and Review of International Tourism Models" *Tourism Economics* 3(1): 69-82.

Lim, C. (1997b) "Review of International Tourism Demand Models" *Annals of Tourism Research* 24(4): 835-849.

Lim, C. (1999) "A Meta-Analytic Review of International Tourism Demand" *Journal of Travel Research* 37(3): 273-289.

Lim, C. and Mcaleer (2001) "Forecasting Tourism Arrivals" *Annals of Tourism Research* 28(4): 965-977.

Lim, C. and Mcaleer (2001) "Monthly Seasonal Variations. Asian Tourism to Australia" *Annals of Tourism Research* 28(1):68-82.

Lim, C. and Mcaleer (2002) "Time Series Forecasts of International Travel Demand for Australia" *Tourism Management* 23(4): 389-396.

Lin, T. and Y. Sung (1983) "Hong Kong" In Lin, T. and Pye, E.A. *Tourism in Asia: The Economic Impact*. Pp. 1-100. Singapore University Press: Singapur.

Lindberg, K. and R. Johnson (1997) "The Economic Values of Tourism's Social Impacts" *Annals of Tourism Research* 24(2): 402-424.

Lindberg, K., T.D. ANDERsON and B.G.C. Dellaert (2001) "Tourism Development. Assessing Social Gains and Losses" *Annals of Tourism Research* 28(4): 1010-1030.

Lindberg, K.A. (1995) *Assessment of Tourism's Social Impacts in Oregon Coast Communities Using Contingent Valuation, Value-Attitude, and Expectancy-Value Models*, Dissertation: Oregon State University.

Lindsay, J.J. (1986) "Carrying Capacity for Tourism Development in National Parks of the United States" *UNEP Industry and Environment* January-May: 17-20.

Little, J.S. (1980) "International Travel in the U.S. Balance of Payments" *New England Economic Review* 42-55.

Liu, J.C. and T. Var (1986) "Resident Attitudes Toward Tourism Impacts in Hawaii" *Annals of Tourism Research* 13:193-214.

Lundberg, D.E., M. Krishnamoorthy and M.H. Stavenga (1995) *Tourism Economics*. Willey: New York.

MAIlLE, R and R. Mendelsohn (1993) "Valuing Ecotourism in Madagascar" *Journal of Environmental Management* 38: 213-218.

Mak, J. (2005) "Tourism Demand and Output in the U.S. Tourism Satellite Accounts:1998-2003" *Journal of Travel Research* 44:4-5.

Mak, J. and E. Nishimura (1979) "The Economics of a Hotel Room Tax" *Journal of Travel Research* 17(4): 2-6.

Manente, M. (1999) "Regional and Inter-regional Economic Impacts of Tourism Consumption: Methodology and the Case of Italy" *Tourism Economics* 5 (4):425-436.

Mangion M.L., A. Durbarry and M.T. Sinclair (2005) "Tourism Competitiveness: Price and Quality Tourism Competitiveness: Price and Quality" *Tourism Economics* 11(1): 45-68.

Marangon, F. and P. Rosato (1998) "The Economic Value of Wildlife (game and non-game): Two CVM Case Studies from North-Eastern Italy" In Bishop, R., and D. Romano. *Environmental Resource Valuation: Application of the Contingent Valuation Method in Italy*. Ed. Kluwer Academic Publishers: Dordrecht.

Martin, B. and M. UYSAL (1990) "An Examination of the Relationship between Carrying Capacity and the Tourism Lifecycle: Management and Policy Implications" *Journal of Environmental Management* 31: 327-333.

Martin, C.A. and S.F. WITT (1988) "Substitute Prices in Models of Tourism Demand" *Annals of Tourism Research* 15(2): 255-68.

Mason, P. (2003) *Tourism Impacts Planning and Management*. Elsevier: Oxford.

Mathieson, A. and G. WALL (1982) *Tourism: Economic, Physical and Social Impacts*. Longman ScientificandTechnical: London.

McConnell, K.E. (1985) "The Economics of Outdoor Recreation" In Kneese, A.V. and Sweeney, J.L. *Handbook of Resource and Energy Economics*, Chapter 15, North-Holland, Amsterdam.

McCool, S.F. (2001) "Tourism Carrying Capacity" *Journal of Sustainable Tourism* 9(5): 372-388.

McKercher, B. (1980) "The Unrecognized Threat to Tourism: Can Tourism Survive 'Sustanaibility'?" *Tourism Management* 14(2): 131-136.

Menkaus, S. andD.J. Lober (1996) "International Ecotourism and the Valuation of Tropical Rainforests in Costa Rica" *Journal of Environmental Management* 47:1-10.

Mercer, E., R. Kramer and N. Sharma (1995) "Rain Forest Tourism -Estimating the Benefits of Tourism Development in a New National Park in Madagascar" *Journal of Forest Economics* 1(2): 239-269.

Miller, J.J., C.S. McCahon and J.L. Miller (1991) "Foodservice Forecasting Using Simple Mathematical Models" *Hospitality Research Journal* 15(1): 43-58.

Milne, S.S. (1987) "Differential Multipliers" *Annals of Tourism Research* 14(4): 499-515.

Morey, R. and D. Dittman (1995) "Evaluating a Hotel GM's Performance : A Case Study in Benchmarking" *Cornell Hotel and Restaurant Administration Quarterly* 36(5):30-35.

Morley, C.L. (1992) "A Microeconomic Theory of International Tourism Demand" *Annals of Tourism Research* 19:250-267.

Morley, C.L. (1994a) "Discrete Choice Analysis of the Impact of Tourism Prices" *Journal of Travel Research* 33(2): 8-14.

Morley, C.L. (1994b) "Experimental Destination Choice Analysis" *Annals of Tourism Research* 21(4): 780-791.

Morley, C.L. (1995) "Tourism Demand: Characteristics, Segmentation and Aggregation" *Tourism Economics* 1(4): 315-328.

Morley, C.L. (2003) "Impacts of International Airline Alliances on Tourism" *Tourism Economics* 9(1): 31-51.

Nordström J. (2005) "Dynamic and Stochastic Structures in Tourism Demand Modeling" *Empirical Economics* 30(2): 379 – 392.

OECD (1980) *The Impact of Tourism on the Environment.* Organisation for Economic cooperation and Development: París.

OECD (1989) *Economic Instruments for Environmental Protection.* Organisation for Economic Cooperation and Development: París.

OECD (1991) *Environmental Policy. How to Apply Economic Instruments.0* Organisation for Economic Cooperation and Development: París.

O'hagan, J.W. and M.J. Harrison (1984) "Market Shares of US Tourist Expenditure in Europe: an Econometric Analysis" *Applied Economics* 16: 919-931.

Palmer, T. A. Riera and J. Rosselló, (2005) "Taxing Congestion from Tourism Transport: The Case of Rental Cars in Mallorca (Spain)" Working papers CRE n° 2005/2, Centre de Recerca Econòmica (UIB-Sa Nostra): Palma, Spain.

Palmer, T. and A. Riera (2003) "Tourism and Environment Taxes. With special reference to the Balearic ecotax" *Tourism Management* 24(6):665-674.

Pattie, D.C. and J. Snyder (1996) "Using a Neural Networking to Forecast Visitor Behaviour" *Annals of Tourism Research* 23(1): 151-164.

Payeras, M. and F. Sastre (1994): "El Multiplicador Turístico: Su Aplicación a la Economía Balear" *Papers de Turisme* 6(16): 15-29.

Pearce, D.G. (1985) "Tourism and Environmental Research: A Review" *International Journal Environmental Studies* 25: 247-255.

Pearce, D.G. (1995) *Tourism Today: A Geographical Analysis* Longman: Harlow.

Pearce, D.G. and R.M. Kirk (1986) "Carrying Capacity for Coastal Tourism" *UNEP Industry and Environment*, Jan-March: 3-7.

Pestana, C. (2005) "Measuring Efficiency in the Hotel Sector" *Annals of Tourism Research* 32 (2):456-477.

Pham, K.N. and Tran, V.H.S. (2000) *Recreation Value of the Coral-surrounded Hon Mun Islands in Vietnam.* Economy and Environment Program for Southeast Asia, International Development Research Centre.

Piga, C. A. (2003) "Pigouvian Taxation and Tourism" *Environmental and Resource Economics* 26: 343-359.

Pigram, J.J. (1980) "Environmental Implications of Tourism Development" *Annals of Tourism Research* 7(4): 554-583.

Pizam, A. (1978) "Tourism's Impacts: The Social Costs to the Destination Community as Perceived by Its Residents" *Journal of Travel Research* 20: 8-12.

Prideaux, B., E. Laws and B. Faulkner (2003) "Events in Indonesia:Exploring the Limits to Formal Tourism Trends Forecasting Methods in Complex Crisis Situations" *Tourism Management* 24(3): 475–487.

Pruckner, G. (1994) "The Economic Quantification of Natural Resources" In Peter Lang. *Evaluation of Benefits Done by the Austrian Agriculture and Forestry.* Europäischer Verlag der Wissenschaften.

Purcell, A. (1997) "Women's Employment in UK tourism. Gender Roles and Labour Markets". En: *Gender Work and Tourism.* T. Sinclair. Routledge: London.

Pyo, S.S., M. Uysal and R.W. Mclellan (1991) "A Linear Expenditure Model for Tourism Demand" *Annals of Tourism Research* 18(3): 443-454.

Riera, A. (2000) "Mass Tourism and the Demand for Protected Natural Areas: A Travel Cost Approach" *Journal of Environmentla Economics and Management* 39: 97-116.

Roberts, J. (1983) "The OECD's International Study of Tourism Impact on the Environment", In *The Impact of Tourism and Recreation on the Environment. A Miscellany of Readings.* Selected Papers from a Seminar at the University of Bradford, 1983.

Romeril, M. (1985) "Tourism and the Environment- Towards a Symbiotic Relationship" *International Journal of Environmental Studies* 25: 215-218.

Rosenweig, J.A. (1988) "Elasticities of Substitution in Caribbean Tourism" *Journal of Development Economics* 29(1): 89-100.

Rosselló, J. (2001) "Forecasting Turning Points in International Tourist Arrivals in the Balearic Islands" *Tourism Economics* 7(4):365-380.

Rosselló, J., A. Riera and A. Sansó (2004) "The Economic Determinants of Seasonal Patterns" *Annals of Tourism Research* 31(3): 697-711.

Rugg, D. (1973) "The Choice of Journey Destination: A Theoretical and Empirical Analysis" *Review of Economics and Statistics* 55(1): 64-72.

Russo, P. (2002) "The "Vicious Circle" of Tourism Development in Heritage Cities" *Annals of Tourism Research* 29(1): 165-182.

Ryan, C. and J. Huyton (2000) "Aboriginal Tourism - a Linear Structural Relations Analysis of Domestic and International Tourist Demand" *International Journal of Tourism Research*, 2(1): 15-29.

Sakai, M.Y. (1988) "A Micro-Analysis of Business Travel Demand". *Applied Economics* 20: 1481-1495.

Santos, J. S. D., E.M. Oritz, E. Huang and F. Secretario (1983) "Philippines" In Lin, T. and Pye, E.A. *Tourism in Asia: The Economic Impact.* pp. 173-240. Singapore University Press: Singapur.

Saveriades, A.(2000) "Establishing the Social Tourism Carrying Capacity for the Tourist Resorts of the East Coast of the Republic of Cyprus". *Tourism Management* 21(2): 147-156.

Sheldon, P.J. (1986) "The Tour Operator Industry. An Analysis" *Annals of Tourism Research* 13: 349-365.

Sherman, P.B. and J.A. Dixon (1995) "The Economics of Nature Tourism: Determining if it Pays" In T.Whelan (ed.), *Nature Tourism Managing for the Environment*: 89-131.

Sinclair, M.T. (1997) "Issues and Theories of Gender and Work in Tourism". En: *Gender Work and Tourism.* T. Sinclair. Routledge: London.

Sinclair, M.T. and C.M.S. Sutcliffe (1982) "Keynesian Income Multipliers with First and Second Round Effects: An Application to Tourist Expenditure" *Oxford Bulletin of Economcs and Statistics* 44: 231-238.

Sinclair, M.T. and M. Stabler (1997) *The Economics of Tourism London. Routledge Advances in Tourism.* Series Editor: Brian Goodall.

Sinclair, M.T., A. Clewer and A. PACK (1990) Hedonic Prices and the Marketing of Package Holidays: The Case of Tourism Resorts in Malaga, In Ashworth, G.J., and Goodall, B. (eds.) *Marketing of tourism places.* pp. 85-103. Routledge: London.

Smeral, E. (1988) "Tourism Demand, Economic Theory and Econometrics: An Integrated Approach" *Journal of Travel Research* 26: 38-43.

Smeral, E. and M. Wĕger (2005) "Does Complexity Matter? Methods for Improving Forecasting Accuracy in Tourism: The Case of Austria" *Journal of Travel Research* 44(1): 100-110.

Smith, S.L.J. (1987) "Defining Tourism: A Supply-Side View". Annals of Tourism Research, 14:23-43.

Smith, V.K. and R.J. Kopp (1980) "The Spatial Limits of the Travel Cost Recreational Demand Model" *Land Economics* 56: 64-72.

Song, B.N. and C. AHN (1983) "Korea" In Lin, T. and Pye, E.A. *Tourism in Asia: The Economic Impact.* Pp. 101-173. Singapore University Press: Singapur.

Sorensen N.K. (2002) "Modelling and Seasonal Forecasting of Monthly Hotel Nights in Denmark" Paper presented at ERSA 2002: Dortmund, Germany.

Sparrowe, R.T. and K.M. Iverson (1999) "Cracks in the Glass Ceiling? An Empirical Study of Gender Differences in Income in the Hospitality Industry" *Journal of Hospitality and Tourism Research* 23(1): 4-20

Sterner, T. (1999) *The Market and the Environment. The Effectiveness of Market-based Policy Instruments for Environmental Reform, International Studies in Environmental Policy Making.* Edward Elgar: Cheltenham.

Suich, H. (2002) "Development of Preliminary Tourism Satellite Accounts for Namibia" *Development Southern Africa* 19(1):105-121.

Shaw, G., S. Agarwal and P. BULL (2000) "Tourism Consumption and Tourist Behaviour: A British Perspective" *Tourism Geographies* 2(3): 264 – 289.

Syriopoulos, T.C. (1995) "A Dynamic Model of Demand for Mediterranean Tourism" *International Review of Applied Economics* 9(3):318-336.

Syriopoulos, T.C. and M.T. Sinclair (1993) "An Econometric Study of Tourism Demand: The AIDS Model of US and European Tourism in Mediterranean Countries" *Applied Economics* 25: 1541-1552.

Taplin, J.H.E. (1980) "A Coherence Approach to Estimates of Price Elasticites in the Vacation Travel Market" *Journal of Transport Economics and Policy* May19-35.

Tarrant, M.A. (1996) "A Crowding-Based Model of Social Carrying Capacity" *Journal of Leisure Research* 28(3): 155-168.

Taylor, E. (1995) "Measuring Changes in the Relative Competitiveness of Package Tour Destinations" *Tourism Economics* 1 (2): 169-182.

Taylor, E. (1996) "Oligopoly or Contestable Markets in the UK Package Tour Industry?" *The Services Industries Journal* 16(3): 379-388.

Thrane, C. (2005) "Hedonic Price Models and Sun-and-Beach Package Tours: The Norwegian Case" *Journal of Travel Research* 43(3): 302-308.

Tisdell, C.A. (1987) "Tourism, the Environment and Profit" *Economic Analysis and Policy* 17(1): 13-30.

Tooman, L.A. (1997) "Multipliers and Life Cycles: a Comparison of Methods for Evaluating Tourism and its Impacts" *Journal of Economic Issues,*31(4): 917-932.

Tremblay, D. (1989) "Pooling International Tourism in Western Europe". *Annals of Tourism Research* 16(4): 477-91.

Truett, D.B. and L.J. Truett (1987) "The Response of Tourism to Initernational Economic Conditions: Greece, Mexico, and Spain". *The Journal of Developing Areas* 21(2): 177-190.

Turner, L.W and S.F. Witt (2001) "Forecasting Tourism Using Univariate and Multivariate Structural Time Series Models" *Tourism Economics* 7(2): 135-147.

Turner, L.W., N. Kulendran and H. Fernando (1997) "Univariate Modelling Using Periodic and non-Periodic Analysis: Inbound Tourism to Japan, Australia and New Zealand compared" *Tourism Economics* 3(1): 39-56.

Uriel, E., Monfort, V.M., Ferri, J., and J. Fernández DE Guevara (2001) *El Sector Turístico en España*. CAM: Valencia.

Uysal, M. and J.L. Crompton (1985) "An Overview of Approaches Used to Forecast Tourism Demand" *Journal of Travel Research* Spring: 7-15.

Uysal, M., and M.S. Roubi (1999) "Artificial Neural Networks versus Multiple Regression in Tourism Demand Analysis" *Journal of Travel Research* 38: 111–118.

Van Kraay, F. (1993) *Tourism and the Hotel and Catering Industries in EC*. Atholone Press: London.

Van Soest, A. and Kooremn (1987) "A Micro-Econometric Analysis of Vacation Behaviour" *Journal of Econometrics* 2: 215-226.

Wanhill, S.R.C. (1980) "Tackling Seasonality: A Technical Note" *Tourism Management* 1:243-245.

Wanhill, S.R.C. (1983) "Measuring the Economic Impact of Tourism" *The Services Industries Journal* 3(1): 9-20.

Ward, J.C. and R.A. BEANLAND (1996) *Biophysical Impacts of Tourism*. Centre for Resource Management, Information Paper n° 56, Lincoln University.

Weber A.G. (2001) "Exchange Rate Volatility and Cointegration in Tourism Demand" *Journal of Travel Research* 39: 398-405.

White, K. (1985) "An International Travel Demand Model: U.S. Travel to Western Europe" *Annals of Tourism Research* 12(4): 529-45.

Witt S.F., H. Song and P. Louvieris (2003) "Statistical Testing in Forecasting Model Selection" *Journal of Travel Research* 42:151-158.

Witt, S.F. (1982) "A Binary Choice Model of Foreign Holiday Demand" *Journal of Economic Studies* 10(1): 46-59.

Witt, S.F. and C.A. Martin (1987) "Deriving a Relative Price Index for Inclusion in International Tourism Demand Estimation Models: Comment" *Journal of Travel Research* 25(3): 23-30.

Witt, S.F. and C.A. Witt (1991) "Tourism Forecasting: Error Magnitude, Direction of Change Error, and Trend Change Error" *Journal of Travel Research* 30 (2): 26-33.

Witt, S.F. and C.A. Witt (1992) *Modelling and Forecasting Demand in Tourism*. Ed. Academic Press.

Witt, S.F. and C.A. Witt (1995) "Forecasting Tourism Demand: A Review of Empirical Research" *International Journal of Forecasting* 11(3):447-475.

Witt, S.F., G.D. Newbould and A.J. Watkins (1992) "Forecasting Domestic Tourism Demand: Application to Las Vegas Arrivals Data" *Journal of Travel Research* 31(1): 36-41.

Wong, K. (1997a) "The Relevance of Business Cycles in Forecasting International Tourist Arrivals" *Tourism Management* 18 (8): 581-586.

Wong, K. (1997b) "An Investigation of the Time Series Behaviour of International Tourist Arrivals" *Tourism Economics* 3(2): 185-200.

Woods, R. and R.R. Kavanaugh (1994) "Gender Discrimination and Sexual Harassment as Experiences by Hospitality-Industry Managers" *The Cornell H.R.A. Quaterly* February: 16-20.

WTO (1994) *Recomendaciones Sobre Estadísticas de Turismo.* World Tourism Organitzation: Nueva York.

WTO (2000) *Measuring Economic Impacts of Tourism Report. Tourist Satellite Account: Methodological References.* Enzo Paci World Conference on the Measurement of the Economic Impact of Tourism. World Tourism Organitzation: Niza, France.

Yacoumis, J. (1980) "Tackling Seasonality – The Case of Sri Lanka" *Tourism Management* 1: 84-98.

Zhou, D., J.F. Yanagida, U. Chacravorty and P. Leung (1997) "Estimating Economic Effects from Tourism" *Annals of Tourism Research* 24: 76-89.

In: Tourism Management: New Research
Editor: Terry V. Liu, pp. 179-210

ISBN 1-60021-058-9
© 2006 Nova Science Publishers, Inc.

Chapter 7

COST, BENEFITS AND RISK ASSESSMENT FOR IMPROVING PERFORMANCE OF THE MARINE TOURISM INDUSTRY

Petros Lois[1] and Jin Wang[2]*

[1]Assistant Professor, School of Business, Intercollege, Nicosia, Cyprus
[2]Professor of Marine Technology, School of Engineering,
Liverpool John Moores University, UK

ABSTRACT

This contribution examines the different categories of cruise ship costs. Attention is focused upon capital, and running and operating costs, in the hope that they can be reduced to improve the performance of the company. The costs are examined in the context of the different cost categories aboard the cruise ship, including the five phases of cruise operation from the time the passengers embark to when they last depart. A cost-benefit analysis is carried out in order to identify the cost elements arising from each cost category involved in the examined operation phase, namely cruising, and to estimate the benefits for each cost element. Risk analysis is another issue that is examined. Risk assessment techniques are studied and the risk criteria for determining whether a risk is acceptable or not, are established. The proposed cost, benefit and risk assessment methodology is developed in the light of decisions of the cruise companies about the safe, economic, efficient and effective operation of their cruise ships. A test case is finally used to demonstrate the application of the proposed methodology.

INTRODUCTION

The cruise ship and the associated items bought for its future operations are generally capitalised, that is, they are considered to be a long-term acquisition and therefore not something consumable. The initial outfit of a new ship may include some items which are

---

* Assistant Professor, School of Business, Intercollege, Nicosia, Cyprus, E-mail: plois@cytanet.com.cy

normally considered to be consumables but are included initially as capital costs, such as the chart outfit and the original lubricating oil charge [Downard J. M., 1997].

However, once one considers the capital costs and setting up of departments on the ship and ashore, it remains for the total costs of running the ship, i.e. the "Running Costs", to be estimated. They can then be presented to senior management and operators for inclusion in their voyage costs calculations. According to John M. Downard [Downard J. M., 1997], it is at this stage that an allowance for the ship's depreciation and any interest charges are often added to the running costs, although these are outside the control of the ship manager. Capital items, shown as assets in the Balance Sheet, can be reduced by the cost of depreciation at each accounting period until paid for and considered fully used, but will be shown as an asset at a nominal or resale value. The interest charges, which influence the cost of bank loans, are paid on an annual basis and in accordance with the agreement made between the owner of the company and the banks or financial institutions.

The economics of ship operation today warrant close attention by management to ensure that the service provided is viable, competitive and best suited to the market requirements, having regard to safety, statutory obligations and service standards. It is necessary for each cruise line to ascertain the steps that can be taken in order to enhance quality when it is associated with high cost. Cruise lines can consider the valuation of quality in the market for cruising services and analyse the way that demand and supply factors interact to determine the equilibrium level of quality.

The ability to make wise decisions is critical to a successful business enterprise. In today's complex world, business decisions are seldom simple or straightforward. Components of a good decision-making process include [American Bureau of Shipping, 2000]:

(i) *Identification of a wide range of potential options*. In the cruise shipping industry, the companies may identify a wide range of potential options. Examples may include the options to buy new or second-hand ships, merge with another company, charter part or all of their fleet to another company etc..

(ii) *Evaluation of each option's relative merits*. Having identified the potential options, the companies may evaluate the relative merits of each option and carry out a comparison between those options, using a cost-benefit analysis.

(iii) *Determination of appropriate levels of input* (i.e. risk). As options are valuated, it may be critical to determine and analyse the appropriate levels of input (i.e. risk) introduced with each option. The analysis can address financial risks, health risks, safety risks, environmental risks and other types of business risks.

(iv) *Timely and rational decision-making methods*. The companies may use rational decision-making methods at the most appropriate time. An appropriate analysis method (i.e. cost, benefit and risk assessment) will provide information, which may be critical to good decision-making, and may often clarify the decision to be made.

(v) *Effective communication and implementation of the decision, which is made*. The results from the cost, benefit and risk assessment can be effectively communicated to a company, and once the decision has been made as to which of the options will be implemented, responsibility for the option should be assigned to a responsible person. The required resources will need to be made available to the responsible person who should be given specific targets to achieve.

Risk assessment is typically applied as an aid to the decision-making process. As options are evaluated, it is critical to analyse the level of risk introduced with each option. The information generated through risk assessment can often be communicated to the organisation to help affected parties understand the factors, which influence the decision. Risk assessment is not a new field. Formal risk assessment techniques have their origins in the insurance industry [American Bureau of Shipping, 2000]. Since the 1980s, more and more governmental agencies have required the industry to apply risk assessment techniques. For instance, the U.S. Environmental Protection Agency requires new facilities to describe "worst case" and "expected" environmental release scenarios as part of the permitting process [American Bureau of Shipping, 2000]. Also, other industries such as Maritime, Offshore Oil and Gas Sectors, and many researchers have applied risk assessment techniques in their fields [Arnold K., 1997; Henley E. J., 1992; Sohal B., 1999; Wang J., 1999; Wang J., 1994].

THE GENERIC CRUISE SHIP COST CATEGORIES

A cost is the value of the economic resources used as a result of producing or doing something [Harper W. M., 1995]. Cost, therefore, can be mathematically stated as:

Cost = Usage × Price

This means that costing involves ascertaining both a usage figure and a price figure. Costs can relate to things other than cost units. They can refer to individual parts of the organisation. Any part of an organisation to which costs can be charged is called here a cost category.

The relevant formal safety assessment studies carried out on containerships [Wang J., Foinikis P., 2001] and on cruise ships [Lois P., Wang J., Wall A. D., Ruxton T., 2004] offer a useful guide to developing a generic cruise ship cost category model.

The generic cruise passenger ship consists of all technical, engineering, operational and environmental networks that interact during the transportation of passengers. This model has been broken into two basic levels of the cruise ship operations, which are described as follows:

Hotel Facilities

a) Passenger: passenger cabins, public areas, stairways and halls, outdoor spaces.
b) Crew: crew cabins, common spaces, service, stairs and corridors.
c) Service: passenger service, catering facility, hotel services.
d) Task related: car decks, tender boats, stern marina, special attractions.
e) Entertaining: casino, swimming pools, cabaret shows, disco, shore-excursion office.
f) Others: shops, beauty saloon, Internet, self-service, laundrettes, medical centre, photo shop, sporting club.

Ship Facilities

a) Comfort systems: air conditioning, water and sewage, stores.
b) Machinery: engine room, pump room, steering and thrusters.
c) Tanks and voids: fuel and lubricated oil, water and sewage, ballast and voids.
d) Outdoor decks: mooring, crew.
e) Safety systems: lifeboat, life raft, sprinkler system and fire fighting equipment, detectors and alarms, low level lighting, life jackets.
f) Navigation and radar systems: bridge navigation equipment, bridge radio/satellite equipment, passenger radio/satellite equipment.
g) Others: car decks, tender boats, stern marina, special attractions.

One way to identify the cost elements charged to different cost categories aboard the cruise ship is to combine the two generic functions mentioned previously in the different phases of cruise operations. Figure 1 shows the five phases of operation of a cruise ship that will be assessed.

It is also important to classify the ship and hotel generic functions into different cost categories, and describe the services or facilities offered to the passengers and crew during the five operation phases.

The total costs of the ship's cruise are derived from all the departments which are involved in the cruise operation phase. Some costs incurred during the cruise may belong to an individual cost category, and, in some cases, there are costs that belong to more than one cost category. To combine the costs of the different departments, the cost for a hypothetical cruise ship may be classified as shown in Table 1.

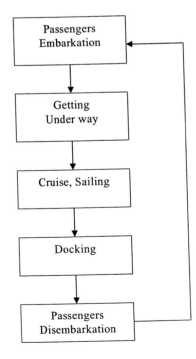

Figure 1. Operation Schedule

Table 1.Classification of costs

Cost categories	Cost elements
Ship related costs	Port costs
	Bunkers
	Insurance
	Repairs and maintenance
	Stores – deck and engine
Crew related costs	Crew wages, overtime, vacation, sickness
	Social security
	Insurance
	Training
Passenger related costs	Food and hotel
	Entertainment
	Security
	Insurance
Administration and general costs	Communication
	Medical
	General

ANALYSIS OF COSTS AND BENEFITS

Taking into consideration the cruise operation phases and the classification of cost categories, it is essential to identify the cost elements of the different cost categories, to carry out an analysis of them, and to study the benefits associated with each cost element. It would be important to propose an approach in order to synthesise the above factors for rational decision-making. Probably a classical example is the development of cost-benefit analysis. This model can be applied in the cruise market as a tool to synthesise the competition factors quantitatively and qualitatively [Lois P., Wang J., Wall A. D., Ruxton T., 2001]. Cost-Benefit Analysis (CBA) is an economic evaluation tool used to compare the total costs against the total benefits of different activities. Within the context of policy development, CBA attempts to quantify the total costs and total benefits of a given policy option in order to determine if the policy is worth pursuing.

The steps of the proposed cost and benefit model are shown in Figure 2 and are described as follows:

1. Operation Phases

This step will identify and assess the different phases of the cruise ship operation. The assessment can either be conducted for all the operation phases or on particular phases individually. For example, the assessment will be carried out only during the sailing phase of the ship's operation.

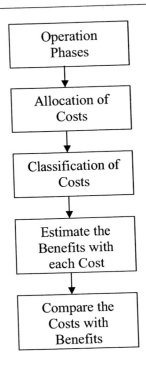

Figure 2. Cost and benefit model

2. Allocation of Costs

The next step is to allocate the cost elements to:

a) Different operation phases.
b) Different cost categories.

Allocation means allotting to a cost category those overheads that result solely from the existence of that cost category [Harper W. M., 1995]. The information with regard to different cost categories and the services or facilities provided by each department on-board a cruise ship can be based on expert judgement deriving from the experience in the cruise market if other alternative methods do not produce satisfactory results.

3. Classification of Costs

The elements assigned to each cost category will then be classified into the following categories:

a) Capital costs.
b) Running costs.
c) Voyage costs.

These three categories of costs will also be sub-divided into "Fixed" and "Variable". "Fixed" costs remain constant at all levels of operation, while "Variable" costs vary with operation levels.

The subject of costs is an important element of the economic analysis. Despite some differences in definition, costs are seen as expenditure by the producers to generate goods or services. In general, there are numerous criteria of cost classification. The most important is the division of costs into "Fixed" and "Variable" costs. Fixed costs, which are sometimes called fixed overheads or indirect costs, are the costs, which do not increase or decrease when a different number of units are produced. Variable costs increase when more units are produced and decrease when fewer units are produced [BPP Publishing, 1997].

a. Capital Costs

Capital costs are the actual costs of the ship. They are a sunk cost in the short term and, at least, they must be regarded as a fixed cost. The annual capital cost may be considered to include depreciation and interest on capital. It may be modified by including the effects of loans, interest, tax and capital allowances (i.e. depreciation for tax purposes). A capital cost may be turned into a variable cost by means of a short term "lease" or "bareboat charter" [Evans J. J., Marlow P. B., 1997].

For the purposes of voyage estimating, annual capital cost may be considered as equivalent to depreciation. This is commonly calculated by the "straight line" method where annual depreciation is simply the capital cost of the ship divided by the projected economic life. For example, if the cost of capital of a cruise ship is £3 million and the projected economic life is 20 years, then the depreciation is as follows:

$$Depreciation = \frac{£3 million}{20 years} = £150,000 \ per \ year$$

Depreciation does not include return on capital or profit, so that Net Profit = Gross Profit (i.e. Revenue – Operating Costs) – Depreciation. Depreciation is a non-cash flow item and is, therefore, not included in the calculation of present values. This is because it does not reflect additional cash spent, and so is not a relevant cost. Depreciation is only deducted from Gross Profit in order to arrive at Net Profit.

b. Running Costs

These comprise certain costs that are incurred, provided that the vessel is in service. Essentially, they do not vary with the specific voyage and are time-related. Although these costs are in some sense fixed, they are predominantly variable with output [Evans J. J., Marlow P. B., 1997]. For example, the running costs in port are related to the time taken in loading and discharging (output), while at sea they are related to the number of miles steamed (output). Running costs, in broad terms, are considered to comprise the following [Chrzanowski I., 1999]:

i) Crew's salaries and leave allowances.
ii) Training and travelling expenses.

iii) Insurance (hull and machinery): This covers total loss as well as damage to hull from collision and it also covers certain third party claims.

iv) Maintenance of hull and equipment including painting and cleaning.

v) The supply of consumable stores, paints and cleaning materials for deck, cabin, galley and engine room.

vi) Food and beverage for crew.

vii) Administration expenses.

viii) Protection and Indemnity (i.e. P and I Clubs).

ix) Surveys and dry-docking expenses.

The running costs are calculated on an annual basis and then divided by the number of days to establish cost per day for each ship. This can be used to make comparisons between the cruise ships and also with previous years.

c. Voyage Costs

These are costs connected with running the ship under normal operating conditions [Chrzanowski I., 1999], and include the following:

a) Fuel costs: in transit and in port in tons per day and per hour.

b) Port dues and charges: pilotage, port authority dues, etc..

c) Agency expenses: all costs connected with the services rendered to the ship by the ship's agents.

The costs normally borne by the shipowner under different types of charter party are shown in Figure 3. Other costs are normally borne by the charterer.

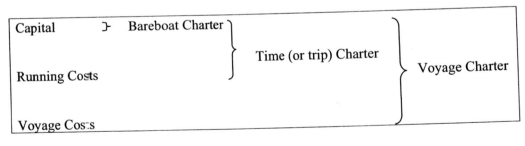

Source: Chrzanowski I., (1999)

Figure 3: Costs to the operator associated with a ship

4. Estimate of Benefits with each Cost Element

This step will examine the possible benefits (from taking cost reduction and control measures) that can be estimated with each element of costs. In particular, the cost elements arising from each cost category involved in the examined phase of operation, i.e. cruising, will be identified and then, the possible benefits will be estimated for each cost element. The estimate of the possible benefits will be obtained based on Table 2.

Table 2. Cost and benefit estimates

Cost categories	Cost elements	Benefits
Ship-related costs	a. Port costs	1. Reduced pilotage, tug and berthing fees.
		2. Fewer unnecessary costs.
		3. More efficient ship documentation.
		4. More efficient passenger documentation and handling.
		5. More efficient use of money.
	b. Bunkers	1. More efficient bunkering policy.
		2. More efficient routeing and speed.
		3. More efficient itinerary planning.
		4. More efficient machinery.
	c. Insurance	1. Fines for stowaways and breaches of immigration laws, drug related offences and personal injury claims are covered by the insurance company.
	d. Repairs and maintenance	1. Effective use of capital and operational funds through tight budgetary control.
		2. Greater availability of machinery and equipment.
		3. Less expensive emergency repairs.
		4. Effective use of labour, time and maintenance equipment.
		5. Higher staff morale.
		6. Increased forecasting ability and highlighting of weaknesses.
	e. Stores	1. Cruise company may make significant cost savings in the purchase of stores for ship and passenger use through bulk purchasing contracts, by tightening inventory control and the use of computerised systems.
Crew-related costs	a. Crew wages, vacation, sickness and overtime	1. Reduction in crew costs through choice of flag and nationality of crew.
		2. Reduction in the number of crew by installing automated machines, which may lead to improved productivity.
	b. Social security	1. Employ crew who are subject to less overheads in the form of social security payments or leave benefits.
	c. Insurance	1. Increased level of comfort and satisfaction of crew.
	d. Training	1. Avoid training through the employment of crew with technical knowledge and experience.
Passenger-related costs	a. Food and hotel	1. Increased sales revenue.
		2. Improved quality service.
	b. Entertainment	1. Provision of quality products.
		2. Increased level of satisfaction of passengers.
	c. Security	1. Increased passenger safety.
	d. Insurance	1. Increased level of comfort and satisfaction of passengers.
Administration and general costs	a. Communication	1. Effective communication.
	b. Medical	1. Effective handling of injured and sick passengers.
	c. General	1. Provision of quality products.

5. Comparison of Costs with Benefits

This step is to compare the sum of the costs with the sum of the benefits. This comparison will enable the analyst to carry out an investigation of the possible areas of cost reduction and control.

6. Risk Assessment and Management

Risk analysis is a decision-making tool. It is the cornerstone for decision-making under uncertainty [Yoe C., 2001]. The model of risk analysis comprises risk assessment and risk management.

Risk assessment is the process of gathering data and synthesising information to develop an understanding of the risk of a particular enterprise [American Bureau of Shipping, 2000]. To gain an understanding of the risk of an operation, the following three questions must be answered [Farqharson J., 2003]:

a)   What can go wrong?
b)   How likely is it?
c)   What are the impacts?

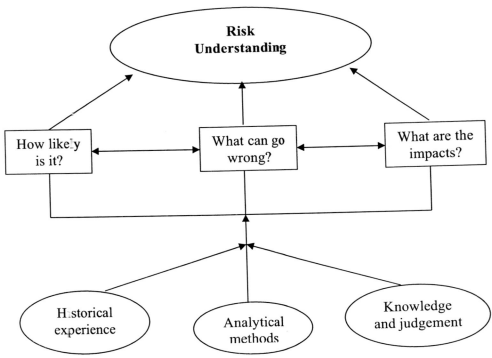

Source: American Bureau of Shipping (2000)
Figure 4. Elements of risk assessment

Qualitative answers to one or more of these three questions are often sufficient for making good decisions. However, as managers seek more detailed cost/benefit information upon which to base their decisions, Quantitative Risk Assessment (QRA) methods may be used [American Bureau of Shipping, 2000; Kuo C., 1998]. QRA is the use of numerical estimates of hazards so as to make a calculated evaluation of the risks [Parker C. J., 1999]. Figure 4 illustrates the elements of risk assessment.

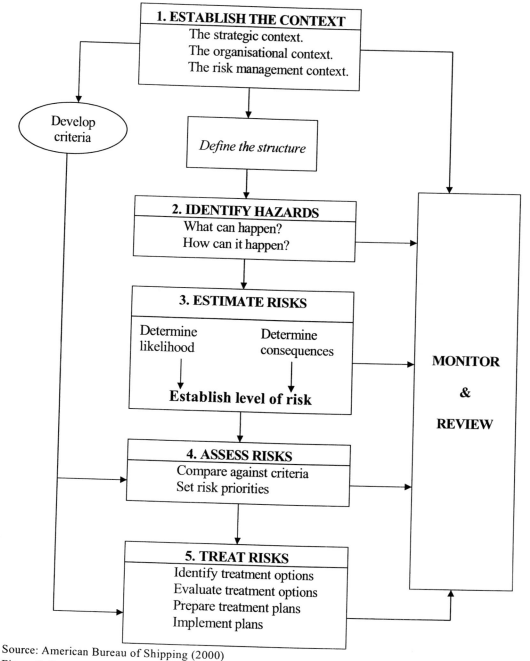

Source: American Bureau of Shipping (2000)

Figure 5. Structure of risk assessment and management

Risk management is defined as a systematic approach of studying policies, procedures and practices to the tasks of identifying possible hazards as well as analysing, evaluating, treating, and monitoring the associated risks. This can be applied to any stage in the life of a policy, programme, project, activity or asset. It can also be applied at all levels of the organisation [State Records New South Wales, 2000]. Risk management does not mean that risks can be prevented or avoided completely. Rather it enables the organisation to reduce the impact of the risks to an acceptable level and to make contingency arrangements. The level of risk relates to the likelihood of something happening (i.e. frequency or probability) and the potential consequences (i.e. magnitude of possible effects).

The level of risk is influenced by any controls, or measures to minimise the likelihood of the occurrence of each significant hazard and/or its consequences. The main economic reason for introducing risk management is the savings in costs by reducing risks [Toft B., 1999]. There are six steps to assessing and managing risks, and an effective risk management requires all six of them [Microsoft Project Plan, 2002; Plan B Systems Incorporation, 2001]. These are:

(1) Establish the context.
(2) Identify hazards.
(3) Analyse the risks associated with the hazards.
(4) Evaluate and prioritise the risks.
(5) Treat the risks.
(6) Monitor and review.

The level of information needed to make a decision varies widely. In some cases, after identifying the hazards, qualitative methods of assessing frequencies and consequences are satisfactory to enable risk evaluation. In other cases, a more detailed quantitative analysis is required [American Bureau of Shipping, 2000].

The generic process shown in Figure 5 can be applied at any stage in the life of a cruise ship.

1. Establish the Context

This step should:

a) Identify relevant stakeholders, including passengers and resource providers.
b) Define the scope and depth of the risk management process. It is necessary to consider if the risk management process is to cover the company's wide issues, or be limited to a specific function.
c) Establish risk criteria. The risk criteria are used to decide if risks are acceptable in Step 4 of Figure 5.

2. Identify Hazards

This step requires identification of hazards, which arise not only from the external environment but also from internal sources. Unidentified hazards can pose a major threat to the cruise company. It is therefore important to ensure that the full range of hazards is identified. Key strategies for effective hazard identification are as follows:

a) Examine all sources of hazards from the perspective of all stakeholders, both external and internal. By identifying each source, the company can consider the contribution each makes to the likelihood and the consequences of the hazard.

b) Access good quality information to identify hazards and understand the likelihood and consequences. The information should be as relevant, comprehensive, accurate and timely as resources will permit. Existing information resources should be accessed and, where necessary, new information developed.

c) Ensure that managers, staff and passengers identifying the hazards are knowledgeable with regard to the company's operation policy.

The most possible methods that can be used in order to identify hazards include:

i)   Interview [Plan B Systems Incorporation, 2001].
ii) Survey and questionnaire [Plan B Systems Incorporation, 2001].
iii) Brainstorming [Kuo C., 1998; Microsoft Project Plan, 2002].
iv) Working experience [Parker C. J., 1999].
v)   Expert knowledge [Microsoft Project Plan, 2002; Parker C. J., 1999].
vi) History failure analysis [Kuo C., 1998].
vii) Incident, accident and injury investigation [American Bureau of Shipping, 2000].
viii)Decision Trees [American Bureau of Shipping, 2000].
ix) SWOT (Strengths, weaknesses, opportunities, threats) analysis.
x)   HAZOP analysis [Kuo C., 1998].

In addition, the possible sources of hazards may be the following:

i)   New activities and services.
ii) Economic activities.
iii) Socio-political activities.
iv) Personnel/human behaviour.
v)   Misinformation.
vi) Technological activities.
vii) Operation (the activity itself).
viii)Health and safety.
ix) Natural events.
x)   Security (including theft, fraud and terrorism).

A risk assessment should concentrate on all significant possible areas of impact relevant to the ship or activity. These may include:

a) Assets and resources.
b) Cost, both direct and indirect.
c) Passengers.
d) Government/port authorities.
e) Environment.
f) Timeliness of activities, including start-time, downstream or follow-up impacts.

3. Analyse the Risks Associated with the Hazards

In this step, the level of risk is established by analysing the likelihood (i.e. frequency or probability) and consequences (i.e. magnitude of the possible effects). Likelihood and consequences should be viewed not only within the context of current controls, which may detect hazards or prevent undesirable risks but also in the absence of such controls. This will serve either to demonstrate the importance of existing controls and thus justify their continuation, or to identify those controls which are no longer necessary or cost-effective.

A preliminary screening of the identified hazards can be done to exclude the extremely low risks from the review. There are three methods used to determine the level of risk: qualitative, semi-quantitative and quantitative [American Bureau of Shipping, 2000]. In this contribution, due to the high level of uncertainty, a qualitative method is used where scales are employed to assess the consequence and likelihood of events occurring.

Table 3. Likelihood (i.e. frequency)

Likelihood	F	Description
Almost Certain	1	The event is expected to occur in most circumstances
Likely	2	The event may occur monthly
Moderate	3	The event may occur every season
Unlikely	4	The event may occur every five years
Rare	5	The event may occur only in exceptional circumstances

Table 4. Consequences

Consequences	S	Description
Extreme	1	Loss of lives, loss of vessel, extreme environmental impact, huge financial loss.
Very High	2	Extensive injuries, serious vessel damage, major financial loss, major environmental damage, missed voyages.
Medium	3	Medical treatment required, medium vessel damage, some environmental damage, high financial loss.
Low	4	First aid required, cosmetic vessel damage, no environmental damage, medium financial loss.
Negligible	5	No injuries, low financial loss.

Table 3 shows the five parameters that should be considered when determining the likelihood of an event occurring. In determining the consequences of a particular hazard, both the number of people involved and the possible cost to the ship together with possible damage to the environment need to be considered (both in terms of financial liability and damage to reputation). The scales used for this purpose are clearly shown and described in Table 4.

4. Evaluate and Prioritise the Risks

Acceptance of risk is basically a problem of decision-making and is inevitably influenced by many factors such as type of activity, level of loss, economic, political and social factors, confidence in risk estimation, etc.. The HSE (Health and Safety Executive) framework for decisions on the tolerability of risk is shown in Figure 6 where there are three regions: intolerable, ALARP (As Low As Reasonably Practicable) and broadly acceptable.

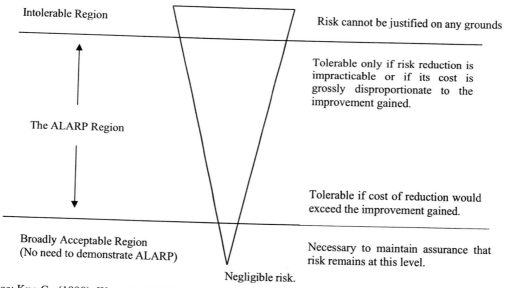

Source: Kuo C., (1998), Wang J., (2002)

Figure 6. The HSE framework for decisions on the tolerability of risk

Table 5. Risk matrix (to determine risk level)

Likelihood	Consequences				
	Extreme	*High*	*Medium*	*Low*	*Negligible*
Almost certain	Severe	Severe	High	Major	Trivial
Likely	Severe	High	Major	Significant	Trivial
Moderate	High	Major	Significant	Moderate	Trivial
Unlikely	Major	Significant	Moderate	Low	Trivial
Rare	Significant	Moderate	Low	Trivial	Trivial

Tolerability criteria are based on the principle that above a certain level, a risk is regarded as intolerable and cannot be justified in any ordinary circumstance. Below a certain level, the risk is considered as "broadly acceptable", but it is necessary to maintain assurance that risk remains below this level. Between these two levels is the so called "tolerable region" within which an activity is allowed to take place provided that the associated risks have been made ALARP.

Having considered the likelihood and consequences of individual hazards, the importance of risks can be determined using Table 5.

The following guide can be used to describe the level of risk:

Severe:	Must be managed by senior management with a detailed plan.
High:	Requires detailed research and management planning at a senior level.
Major:	Requires senior management attention.
Significant:	Requires specific allocation of management responsibility.
Moderate:	Must be managed by specific monitoring or response procedures.
Low:	Must be managed by routine procedures.
Trivial:	Unlikely to need specific application of resources, or can be managed through cheap and immediate solution.

It would also be useful to link up the risk matrix shown in Table 5 with the HSE risk criteria. This link can be shown in Table 6. The three risk regions shown in Table 6 can be briefly described as follows:

I = Intolerable, T = Tolerable, N = Negligible

Table 6. HSE risk criteria

Likelihood	Consequences				
	Extreme	*High*	*Medium*	*Low*	*Negligible*
Almost certain	I	I	I	T	N
Likely	I	I	T	T	N
Moderate	I	T	T	T	N
Unlikely	T	T	T	N	N
Rare	T	T	N	N	N

5. Treat the Risks

A combination of risk control options may be appropriate in treating risks. Such options include [Queensland University of Technology, 2001]:

a) Avoiding the risk.
b) Reducing the level of risk.
c) Transferring the risk.
d) Ignoring the risk.

Avoiding the risk involves the decision not to proceed with the policy, project, function or activity that would incur the risk, or to choose an alternative means of action that achieves the same outcome without such risk.

Reducing the level of risk involves the reduction of the likelihood or consequences of hazardous events, or both. The likelihood of possible hazardous events may be reduced through management controls, organisational arrangements or influence over external environment.

Transferring the risk involves shifting responsibility for a risk to another party. Risks may be transferred by contract, legislation, administrative processes and insurance. Risks may be transferred in full or they may be shared with another party. As a general principle, risks should be allocated to a party, which can exercise the most effective control over them.

Ignoring the risk involves the ignorance of events where they are assessed to have minimal consequences and little likelihood of occurring.

Risk treatment options should be evaluated on the basis of the extent of risk reduction, and the extent of benefits or opportunities created. A number of options may be considered and applied either individually or in combination. Selection of the most appropriate option involves balancing the cost of implementing each option against the benefits derived from it. The cost of treating risks needs to be commensurate with the benefits obtained. The cost-benefit analysis should determine the total cost impact of the hazardous events, and the cost of options for managing those risks. Other factors, such as political or social costs and benefits, should also be taken into account.

Table 7. Treatment plans

Level of risk	Ignorance	Transfer	Reduction	Avoid
Severe	1	1	2	3
High	1	2	3	3
Major	1	2	3	3
Significant	1	2	3	3
Moderate	1	3	3	3
Low	2	3	3	3
Trivial	3	3	2	1

The main purpose of this step is to determine the appropriate control strategy for the hazardous events that have been identified. Table 7 shows how the different levels of risk can be controlled. The numerical notations in Table 7 can be found in Table 8. In Table 8, rating 1 represents "not possible", which means that the risk cannot be controlled by the particular action or treatment plan. Rating 2 represents "possible" meaning that the risk may possibly be controlled in some circumstances, and rating 3 represents "probable", which means that the risk can be controlled by the particular actions or treatment plans.

Table 8. Action assignment

Assign a rating of:	If the action to be taken is:
1	Not possible
2	Possible
3	Probable

6. Monitor and Review

Monitoring and review are essential for managing risk. Cruise companies should continually monitor risks and the effectiveness of the plan, strategies and management systems that have been established to control implementation of the risk treatments. Risk needs to be monitored and reviewed periodically to ensure that changing circumstances do not alter risk priorities. Few risks remain static. Functions and processes change, as can the political, social and legal environment and goals of a company. Accordingly, cruise companies should re-examine the risk context to ensure that the way in which risks are managed remains valid.

A PROPOSED COST-BENEFIT RISK ASSESSMENT METHODOLOGY AND A CASE STUDY

Having analysed the cost, benefit, and risk assessment models, a cost-benefit risk assessment will be carried out. The proposed methodology may be an important tool for cruise companies in studying their ships' costs, estimating the benefits associated with each cost element, investigating the possible areas of cost reduction and control, and assessing the ways in which hazardous events may influence costs. The procedures involved in the process are described as follows:

(1) Define, or breakdown the plan/process into its elements by drawing a flowchart or list of activities and events.
(2) Study the cost and benefit associated with each element.
(3) Model cost elements. The cost elements are classified into four categories, namely ship, crew, passenger-related costs, and administration and general costs. In this step, a possible annual rise for each cost element is estimated and a controllability factor is used. A controllability factor is a level within which each cost element can be controlled and is expressed in percentage terms. Areas of possible control are also exercised.
(4) Rank the cost elements in terms of impact of their potential success/failure on the whole process and assign weighting values to each element. This can be done by estimating the average controllability factor for each cost element and then assigning relative values to the cost elements being considered.
(5) Estimate the likelihood and consequences of possible hazards. In this step, the importance of risks to a cruise company will be determined. The analysis will determine the tolerability of the risk level.
(6) Propose control measures to reduce the risks associated with significant hazards.

A test case is conducted in order to demonstrate its feasibility and is limited to one phase of operation only, namely cruising. This is because a full-scale trial application would be too large in volume.

The test case is based on a hypothetical cruise company, namely "Byzantium Cruise Lines". The company has acquired a passenger cruise vessel from "Ex Builders". The ship will be used to perform seven-day cruises in the Eastern Mediterranean. Its main technical characteristics are as follows:

Overall Length:	175 m
Gross Tonnage:	17,000 tons
Net Tonnage:	12,000 tons
Cabin Capacity:	462
Berth Capacity:	1,200

Step 1: Define the Plan/Process

The first step will break down the process into certain elements by drawing a list of associated activities/systems during the phase of cruising, and also the cost categories that can exist. Table 1 shows the cost categories that exist on a generic cruise ship and all the possible associated cost elements during a cruise operation.

Step 2: Study the Costs and Benefits

The purpose of the second step is to study the cost and benefit associated with each element identified in Step 1. The total costs of the ship's cruising include capital, running and voyage costs as shown in Figure 3. The costs of cruising can then be divided into four cost categories. These are:

a) Ship-related costs.
b) Crew-related costs.
c) Passenger-related costs.
d) Administration and general costs.

Table 2 shows an analysis of the costs incurred under each category, and also the possible benefits associated with each cost element.

Step 3: Model Cost Elements

The third step is to model cost elements, and to investigate the possible areas of cost reduction and control.

Table 9 identifies the cost elements of a cruise ship and also attempts to forecast their annual rise over the five-year period 2003-2007 in percentage terms.

The table is subjective, depending upon an assessment of recent movements of the individual cost elements involved. In the third column, an estimate of the possible average annual control (i.e. controllability factor), which might be exercised over the cost element, is given. For example, Table 9 shows that the cruise company can expect to control 10% of port costs. The last column of the table identifies some of the possible areas where control might be exercised. The forecasts were obtained from the financial statements and cash budgets of the Cyprus cruise companies. The controllability factors were obtained by calculating the fluctuations in cost elements and by comparing the financial results from year to year.

Table 9. Control areas with controllability factor

Cost elements	Forecast annual rise (%)	Controllability factor-% (Possible Average Annual Control)	Areas of possible control
Ship-related costs			
Port costs	10	2-10	Adjusting cruise itinerary, agency costs, lobbying authorities for reduction of taxes.
Bunkers	5	5-10	Improving machinery efficiency, adjusting grade of oil, adjusting cruise itinerary.
Insurance	10-30	5-10	Accident/casualty avoidance, extent of cover.
Repairs and maintenance	5-15	5-10	Improved crew productivity, budgeting and inventory control of spares.
Stores	5	5-10	Inventory control, computerisation, re-use of lube oil.
Crew-related costs			
Crew wages, overtime, vacation and sickness	5-15	2-10	Selection of crew with low pay, reduction in crew with more efficient employment, renegotiated contracts.
Social security	5	2-7	Extension of offshore terms of employment
Insurance	5-15	5-10	Effective work, safety and healthy organisation.
Training	7-10	5-10	Use of on-board training systems and use of staff with experience.
Passenger-related costs			
Food and hotel	3	3-8	The standard of service provided on-board.
Entertainment	5	4-10	The cruise product offered.
Security	10-25	5-15	Involvement of all company personnel, efficient use of surveillance equipment.
Insurance	5-15	5-10	Passenger comfort and satisfaction.
Administration and general costs			
Communication	5-20	5-10	Efficient use of communication systems, data exchange by electronic equipment.
Medical	5-10 10-20	5-10	Increasing prices charged to passengers, more effective use of medical equipment.
General		5-15	Documentation control, budget monitoring, project planning scheduling, reassessment of company's goals.

Step 4: Rank the Cost Elements

The purpose of this step is to rank the cost elements as so to reflect the impact of their potential success on the whole process. Table 9 can be used to rank the cost elements starting with those having the highest controllability factor. Then, a measurement weighting system can be used to assign relative values to the cost elements being considered. Before the weighting values can be used, it would be necessary to estimate the average controllability factor. It is assumed that the largest average controllability factor is 10%. This is shown in Table 10.

Table 10. Average controllability factor (%)

Cost elements	Controllability factor (%)	Average (%)
Ship related costs		
Port costs	2-10	6
Bunkers	5-10	7.5
Insurance	5-10	7.5
Repairs and maintenance	5-10	7.5
Stores	5-10	7.5
Crew related costs		
Wages, vacation, sickness and overtime	2-10	6
Social security	2-7	4.5
Insurance	5-10	7.5
Training	5-10	7.5
Passenger related costs		
Food and hotel	3-8	5.5
Entertainment	4-10	7
Security	5-15	10
Insurance	5-10	7.5
Administration and general costs		
Communications	5-10	7.5
Medical	5-10	7.5
General	5-15	10

The following are the weighting values to the cost elements being considered, based upon their importance to the cost control policy of the cruise company:

1	2	3	4	5
Least important			Most important	

The weighting system is used in order to help cruise companies, especially in the Cyprus cruise region, to make costing performance reviews more meaningful. This system can also be used by cruise companies with different controllability factors.

The above results can then be used to find the weights to each cost element.

Class intervals (%)-Average controllability	Weighting system
0-2	1
2.1-4	2
4.1-6	3
6.1-8	4
8.1-10	5

Using the above weighting system, the cost elements will correspond to the weights shown in Table 11. Multiple expert judgements can also be incorporated into the above analysis.

Table 11. Weighting factors

Cost element	Average controllability (%)	Weights
Ship related costs		
Port costs	6	3
Bunkers	7.5	4
Insurance	7.5	4
Repairs and maintenance	7.5	4
Stores	7.5	4
Crew related costs		
Wages, vacation, sickness and overtime	6	3
Social security	4.5	3
Insurance	7.5	4
Training	7.5	4
Passenger related costs		
Food and hotel	5.5	3
Entertainment	7	4
Security	10	5
Insurance	7.5	4
Administration and general costs		
Communications	7.5	4
Medical	7.5	4
General	10	5

It is obvious that all costs involved in the operation of the cruise ship are important. Table 11 shows that, according to the case examined, the most important cost elements are "Security" of passengers from passenger-related costs and "General" from administration and general costs. There is a growing cost element in ensuring passenger security against unlawful acts and terrorism. Some of this cost falls directly upon the shipowner in taking security measures on his ship, some arises ashore and must be met through port dues and other means. International Maritime Organisation (IMO) has produced a resolution recommending that ship companies, port authorities, cruise operators, governments and crew should take measures in order to prevent unauthorised acts against passengers, and this is being put into law around the world. "General" includes shore operating expenses for offices, subscriptions, seminars, media costs, advertising, brochures, public materials and other marketing material. "General" expenses are of great importance because they are spent for the smooth and efficient operation of the cruise company and its ship. Marketing costs depend on the structure of the market within which the cruise company is operating. Success in marketing is dependent upon weighting forecast returns against the cost of advertising and promotion. "Communication" costs are also important. The introduction of satellite communications has led to a revolution in the manner in which information may be transferred to and from cruise ships. These costs can be controlled by an efficient use of communication systems installed ashore and on-board cruise ships. Another area that needs attention is that of medical services. Cruise ships must necessarily provide medical services because passengers, crew and staff may suffer illness or injury during a cruise operation. Therefore, the cruise company will have to cope with medical costs since medical supplies and equipment must be provided aboard at all times. These medical costs can be controlled by the effective use of medical equipment and increasing prices charged to passengers for providing such services.

From Table 11, it can be seen that "Insurance" as a passenger-related cost is also important. This may be because there is an increasing concern in passenger safety because of unlawful acts and terrorism.

Ship-related costs are also of great importance. "Stores" depend upon the size, type, area of operation and the company's purchasing and accounting policies. The cruise company may make significant cost savings in the purchase of stores for its cruise ship through bulk purchasing contracts, by tightening inventory control and the use of computerised systems. "Bunker costs" depend on various factors including the amount of time spent at sea, the speed adopted, the efficiency of the main machinery, and the grade and cost of fuel used. Reliability will be a great consideration in the choice of engine design, rather than economy and flexibility. The cost of "Repairs and maintenance" depends on the age of the cruise ship and machinery, and the repair and maintenance policy followed by the cruise company. The company can make sure that all the national and international rules and regulations are obeyed. The legislative obligations of maintaining a cruise ship to a certain standard of safety may lead to a minimum cost requirement. "Insurance" is also of paramount importance. It includes hull and machinery cover, PandI cover, passenger claims deductible, war risk, crime and loss of earnings cover. Insurance cover is largely provided on the basis of the ship owner's track record. However, underwriters are seeking to limit their risk by ensuring the quality of the items they are insuring. Age and condition of the owners' existing fleet are important to the hull and machinery underwriter for the purpose of determining a premium. In PandI insurance, emphasis is placed on the actual condition and operational standard of the cruise ship. Other areas that need to be considered include fines for stowaways, drug-related offences and personal injury claims.

Of the crew-related costs, "Training" and "Insurance" are the most important. Although officers are required to hold certificates to fill certain positions in the cruise ship, some companies require them to undergo additional training. Such training may include shipboard management, ship handling simulation, safety and survival courses. The costs of these courses can be high but the benefits to the company are considered to be worthwhile. Crew can also be required to undergo training courses. This would enable them to carry out their duties in an effective and efficient manner and also help passengers in serious accidents. Training of crew and officers is necessary because, in many instances, crew have not responded professionally to accidents and could not prevent loss of the ship and lives. "Insurance" is also necessary for a cruise company to insure its crew and staff. Insurance costs can be high, but a healthy cruise company can reduce or control such costs by providing efficient and effective safety training to its crew and staff.

Step 5: Estimate the Likelihood and Consequences of Possible Hazards

The purpose of this step is to establish a risk assessment by analysing the likelihood and consequences of possible hazards. The events that will be examined are chosen in the way described above, and include the following:

a) Machinery defects.
b) Poor maintenance.
c) Poor operation.
d) Poor housekeeping.
e) Inadequate training.
f) Delays in activities.
g) Crew and passenger casualties.
h) Material casualties.
i) Environmental impact.

The examination of the frequencies and the consequences of the events occurring is carried out using the "Likelihood and Consequences Scales" as explained in Tables 3 and 4. Having considered the likelihood and consequences of individual hazardous events, the importance of risks to the cruise company can be determined. This is clearly shown in Table 12. Having investigated the hazardous events, as shown in Table 13, the company can decide if the associated risks are acceptable. This can be done by connecting the risk matrix in Table 12 with the HSE risk criteria (i.e. intolerable, tolerable, negligible) as shown in Table 6.

Table 13 shows that poor housekeeping and delays in activities are in the "negligible" region. Poor maintenance, poor operation, inadequate training, crew and passenger casualties, material casualties, and environmental impact are included in the "tolerable" region, while machinery defects are in the "intolerable" region.

Table 12. Risk matrix results

Events	Frequency (F)	Consequence (S)	Level of risk
Machinery defects	F2	S2	High
Poor maintenance	F3	S3	Significant
Poor operation	F1	S4	Major
Poor housekeeping	F1	S5	Trivial
Inadequate training	F4	S2	Significant
Delays in activities	F1	S5	Trivial
Crew and passenger casualties	F3	S4	Moderate
Material casualties	F3	S3	Significant
Environmental impact	F5	S1	Significant

Table 13. Qualitative risk matrix

Events	Level of risk	Region
Machinery defects	High	Intolerable
Poor maintenance	Significant	Tolerable
Poor operation	Major	Tolerable
Poor housekeeping	Trivial	Negligible
Inadequate training	Significant	Tolerable
Delays in activities	Trivial	Negligible
Crew and passenger casualties	Moderate	Tolerable
Material casualties	Significant	Tolerable
Environmental impact	Significant	Tolerable

It is stated that risks, which fall within the ALARP region, will require a cost-benefit analysis. Even if risks fall within the ALARP region, they may still be acceptable if risk reduction measures are proven to be not cost-effective.

It is important, after the decision on the acceptability of risks and before the proposal of possible control measures, to determine the appropriate control strategy for the hazardous events that have been identified and shown in Table 13. For this purpose, it is necessary to combine Tables 7 and 8 with Table 13. The results of this combination analysis show the most probable control strategies that may be followed for each hazardous event. These are shown in Table 14.

Table 14. Probable control strategies

Events	Level of risk	Probable control strategy
Machinery defects	High	Reduction or Avoid
Poor maintenance	Significant	Reduction or Avoid
Poor operation	Major	Reduction or Avoid
Poor housekeeping	Trivial	Ignorance or Transfer
Inadequate training	Significant	Reduction or Avoid
Delays in activities	Trivial	Ignorance or Transfer
Crew and passenger casualties	Moderate	Transfer, Reduction or Avoid
Material casualties	Significant	Reduction or Avoid
Environmental impact	Significant	Reduction or Avoid

Step 6: Propose Control Measures to Reduce the Risks Associated with the Significant Hazards

Having considered the risk levels and the appropriate control strategy for the hazards shown in Table 13, it is important to propose control measures to reduce the risks associated with the intolerable hazards. An attempt will also be made to suggest control measures for the reduction of the hazards that fall within the tolerable region.

The methods and measures that will be considered are partly based on the analysis carried out previously and shown in Table 9, partly on expert judgement, and partly on the authors' experience. The proposed methods and measures have been effectively used by a cruise company in Cyprus. They can also be used by any Cyprus cruise company, since cruise ships operating from Cyprus have similar features. The list of the proposed methods and measures is not exhaustive. The measures were proposed by considering the current status of the Cyprus and Mediterranean cruise market.

A. Machinery Defects

This hazard is in the intolerable region (Table 13) and the methods suggested are outlined under the following three headings:

Management:

a) Ensure that the machinery of the ship is subject to the rules of classification societies, who also widely act on behalf of "Flag States" in the survey and certification of equipment required under the relevant conventions.
b) Ensure that all crew members involved take special training on the proper use of the machinery.
c) Devise a policy on systematic repairs and maintenance of the machinery and ensure that it is communicated to all concerned.

Engineering:

a) Adopt a computerised engineering system for preventive maintenance.
b) Install a machinery monitoring system to provide data when the vessel is in service.

Operation:

a) Implement a procedure for inspecting hull and machinery before departure and have alternative ways of verifying that this has been effectively done.

The following control measures refer to the hazardous events that fall in the tolerable region (Table 13):

B. Poor Maintenance

Management:

a) Devise a policy on systematic maintenance of machinery and other equipment used for the operation.
b) Ensure that all crew members concerned are familiar with the company's policy and regulations.

Engineering:

a) Install a system for measuring the performance of active machine equipment objectively.

b) Perform analyses to identify potential areas of machinery failure and modify the design accordingly.

Operation:

a) Implement audit procedures to ensure that maintenance is effectively done.
b) Update maintenance-related documentation on a regular basis.

C. Poor Operation

Management:

a) Ensure that all staff and crew members are provided and are familiar with the ship's operation rules and regulations.
b) Ensure segregation of duties (i.e. appropriate allocation of duties and responsibilities) to crew and staff members.
c) Adjust cruise itinerary and destinations.
d) Devise a policy for evaluating the employees' work.

Engineering:

a) Install a computerised system to ensure proper and efficient use of operation equipment.
b) Provide the crew with special training and use simulator systems for practising navigation in difficult situations.

Operation:

a) Implement procedures for supervising the work of on-board personnel.
b) Deal with passengers' comments and complaints arising from questionnaires.
c) Carry out surveys of critical operation areas to identify possible failures.
d) Try to improve the standard of service provided on-board.

D. Inadequate Training

Management:

a) Ensure that all crew members take special training in the operation of a cruise ship and its activities.
b) Ensure that training is done regularly in an effective and efficient manner.
c) Establish a set of procedures or standard methods to be used in training courses.

Engineering:

a) Introduce new technology techniques in training crew members.

b) Install fire fighting, safety and survival equipment to prevent serious accidents and damage.

c) Install a continuous monitoring system to ensure efficiency and effectiveness in training methods and equipment.

Operation:

a) Install language teaching equipment to assist in overcoming the language barrier between officers and crew of different nationalities.

b) Implement a procedure for inspecting training equipment before use and keep spare parts in case of breakdown.

c) Ensure that specified training requirements are followed so as to avoid inadequate training.

E. Crew and Passenger Casualties

Management:

a) Devise a policy on safe loading and training of crew members and passengers.

b) Install a public address system to use for reminding crew and passengers of the company's and ship's policies, especially in emergency situations.

c) Designate a safety officer with the appropriate knowledge and experience to deal with safety and fire matters.

d) Ensure that the ship operates in accordance with the international safety regulations.

Engineering:

a) Install appropriate equipment for fire fighting.

b) Maintain a medical centre in order to avoid undesired situations.

c) Install security systems to avoid violence and bomb threats.

Operation:

a) Perform inspections and train people in the ship's procedures and in the use of equipment.

b) Implement a system to ensure that procedures are followed by crew and passengers during the cruise.

c) Observe the machines on a regular basis to ensure that they work properly.

F. Material Casualties

Management:

a) Devise a policy on safe loading of materials and supplies and ensure that it is communicated to all concerned.

b) Adopt a policy of limiting the quantity of items to be taken onto the gangways.
c) Ensure that materials are kept safely aboard while the ship sails.

Engineering:

a) Install a continuous monitoring system to provide data on loading levels and distribution.
b) Install high technology equipment to prevent fire and flooding situations.

Operation:

a) Ensure that all the procedures for loading materials are properly followed.
b) Enforce no-smoking policy to prevent material casualties.
c) Ensure that the safety officer, other vessels and local port authorities are promptly notified in cases of material casualties.

G. Environmental Impact

Management:

a) Set up an environmental policy, which will be in compliance with the international regulations on environmental issues.
b) Establish on-board anti-pollution measures and ensure that crew and passengers are fully aware of them.

Engineering:

a) Use cleaning materials on-board and inspect public areas on a regular basis.
b) Maintain a system of providing health and sanitation facilities.

Operation:

a) Ensure that the ship operates according to the international environmental regulations (ISM Code).
b) Ensure that the anti-pollution measures are used in an effective and efficient manner.
c) Implement a system to check any changes or additions made in the ISM Code on environmental issues.

CONCLUSION

This contribution has attempted a critical assessment of cost and risk levels as it applies to cruise passenger ships. Cost assessment has covered the possible elements in the cost categories of a generic cruise passenger vessel. A cost-benefit analysis is also carried out in order to study costs and the possible benefits. Risk assessment techniques are studied and the risk criteria to decide whether a risk is acceptable or not, are established. A test case study is used in order to demonstrate the feasibility of the proposed approach.

This contribution has also attempted to portray the current status of cost and risk assessment in the Cyprus and Mediterranean cruise shipping industry and to provide some information to guide those who would like to apply cost and risk assessment techniques.

According to the analysis carried out earlier in this chapter, the cruise companies operating in the Cyprus and Mediterranean cruise regions classify their costs into four categories. These are shown in Table 9. In the ship-related cost category, "Insurance" has the higher annual percentage increase followed by "Repairs and maintenance". Insurance cost is very high for cruise ships operating in the Cyprus and Mediterranean regions because it is placed on the actual condition and operational standard of the fleet, which is very old. Since the cruise ship fleet is old, the cruise companies are enforced to repair and maintain their ships more frequently, and as a result the cost element of repairs and maintenance increases from year to year. Of the crew-related costs, "Insurance" and "Training" are the most important. The training is necessary companies in the examined cruise regions because most of the crew and staff are not skilled and they have communication problems. Although the training costs are high, the benefits obtained from training are considered to be worthwhile. Insurance costs are also high, but a cruise company can control those costs by providing efficient work safety training to its crew and staff. "Security" is the most important cost element in the category of passenger-related costs. This is because the cruise companies invest large amounts in this field due to the phenomenon of terrorism and unlawful acts. Of the administration and general cost category, "General" costs have the higher annual increase. The companies pay attention to this element, and ensure smooth and efficient operation of their ships.

The possible areas of controlling costs are shown in Table 9, and the possible events (i.e. hazards) that may give rise to cost elements are explained above. This contribution has also attempted to propose control measures for the reduction of hazards, which may help cruise companies operating in the Cyprus and Mediterranean regions to reduce or control the cost elements described earlier.

The thoughtful application of cost and risk assessment techniques can improve the decisions made by a cruise company and result in improved performance in a number of areas by reducing cost and risk exposure. As awareness of cost and risk assessment increases, the benefits, which can be realised through its application, will continue to increase.

Cost and risk assessment can be a useful tool to help cruise companies in the Cyprus and Mediterranean cruise region to make good decisions about the safe, economic, efficient and effective operation of their cruise ships. The decisions need to be considered in the light of the company's strategic investment. This should be consistent with the company's long-term objectives, which can usually be the maximisation of profits for the shareholders, and the welfare of its passengers and personnel. Since there may be a high degree of risk and uncertainty in the cruise industry, a detailed evaluation of future benefits will need to be examined. It is therefore essential to carry out an investigation and evaluation of the principal methods to decide if a capital investment project is of value to a cruise company.

REFERENCES

American Bureau of Shipping (ABS) (2000), Risk assessment techniques, applications for the marine and offshore oil and gas industries, *Guidance Notes*, USA, 5, 11, 15-45.

Arnold K. (1997), Risk assessments of offshore platforms, Draft Report (7th Draft*), Panel for Marine Board of National Research Council*, USA.

BPP Publishing (1997), Cost accounting systems, Certified Accounting Technician (CAT), *Interactive Text*, UK, 15.

Chrzanowski I. (1999), Costs of shipping operations, *Fairplay Publications*, London, 69-70.

Downard J. M. (1997), Running costs, *Ship Management Series*, Fairplay Publications, UK, 18, 91.

Evans J. J., Marlow P. B. (1997), Ship's costs, quantitative methods in maritime economics, 2nd Edition, UK, 94.

Farqharson J. (2003), When and how should quantitative risk assessment techniques be used?, Internet Paper, www.jbta.com/qratechniques.html., 15 March.

Harper W. M. (1995), Cost and management accounting, *The M and E Handbook Series*, London, 9-10, 86-87.

Henley E. J. and Kumanoto H. (1992), Probabilistic risk assessment, *IEEE Press*, New York, USA.

Kuo C. (1998), *Managing ship safety*, Lloyd's of London Press Ltd, London, UK.

Lois P., Wang J., Wall A. D., Ruxton T. (2001), "Fundamental considerations of competition at sea and the application of cost-benefit analysis", Tourism Today, *The Journal of the College of Tourism and Hotel Management*, No. 1, Cyprus, Summer, 89-102.

Lois P., Wang J., Wall A. D. and Ruxton T. (2004), "Formal safety assessment of cruise ships", *Tourism Management*, Vol. 25, Issue 1, 93-109.

Microsoft Project Plan (2002), Risk assessment and management, http://www.projmgr. org/risk.pdf, March.

Parker C. J. (1999), Managing risk in shipping companies, managing risk in shipping, *A Practical Guide*, Published by the Nautical Institute, UK, 8, 12.

Plan B Systems Incorporation (2001), Continuous risk management, http://www.pbsi.ca/html/ continuous-risk-management.htm.

Queensland University of Technology (2001), QUT risk management system operational guide, http://www.qut.edu.au/admin/mopp/Appendix.html, 16 March.

Sohal B. (1999), *"Risk assessment applied to special trade VLCC operations: A case study"*, Presented at Safety Risk Assessment in Shipping Conference, Athens, Greece, IIR Ltd, May.

State Records New South Wales (2000), Forms, guides, checklists and templates records keeping risk analysis, Exposure Draft, http://www.records.hsw.gov. au/publiscsector/ DIRKS/exposure-draft/risk-assessment.htm, February.

Toft B. (1999), Advantages of risk assessment, managing risk in shipping, *A Practical Guide*, Published by the Nautical Institute, UK, 8.

Wang J. (1994), *Formal safety analysis methods and their application to the design process*, PhD Thesis, Engineering Design Centre, University of Newcastle upon Tyne, UK.

Wang J. (1999), "A review of design for safety methodology of large marine and offshore products", *IMechE Journal on Process Mechanical Engineers*, Vol. 212, Part E, 251-266.

Wang J. (2002), "A brief review of marine and offshore safety assessment", *Marine Technology, SNAME*, Vol. 39, No. 2, April, 77-85.

Wang J. and Foinikis P. (2001), "Formal safety assessment of containerships", *Marine Policy*, Vol. 25, 143-157.

Yoe C. (2001), *Risk analysis: ecosystem restoration cost risk assessment*, A Report submitted to U.S. Army Corps of Engineers, Institute for Water Resources, Alexandria, USA, June, 3.

In: Tourism Management: New Research
Editor: Terry V. Liu, pp. 211-224

ISBN 1-60021-058-9
© 2006 Nova Science Publishers, Inc.

Chapter 8

A STUDY OF TECHNICAL EFFICIENCY OF INTERNATIONAL TOURIST HOTELS IN TAIWAN

Kuo-Liang Wang and Tai-Sen He
Department of Economcis, National Chengchi University, Taipei, Taiwan

ABSTRACT

Based on the survey data of Taiwan's international tourist hotels in 2002, this paper first uses the DEA to access technical efficiency of each international tourist hotel, and then applies the Tobit censored regression model to investigate the relationship between technical efficiency and firm-specific characteristics. The DEA evaluation results show that international tourist hotels in Taiwan could have reduced inputs by at least 15 percent, on average, and still have produced the same level of outputs. The mean scale efficiency measure implies that the inefficiency is mainly from wasting resources instead of inappropriate production scale. The regression results show that an international tourist hotel's size has a positive impact on its technical efficiency. The impact of an international tourist hotel's service concentration on technical efficiency is positive. An international tourist hotel's degree of concentration in guest type is positively related with technical efficiency. International hotels located in Taipei are more technically efficient than those located in other areas. International hotels located in resort areas are more technically efficient than those located in other areas.

Keywords: Data Envelopment Analysis; Technical Efficiency; Tobit Censored Regression Model

I. INTRODUCTION

Since the end of the first oil crisis in 1977, the government deregulated the entry barriers and encouraged the setup of Taiwan's international tourist hotels. The number of Taiwan's international tourist hotels increased from 21 in 1976 to 44 in 1985, and to 62 in 2002. However, Taiwan's competitiveness of international tourism, compared to other Southeast

Asian countries, has been continuously losing ground since mid-1979 (Wang and Wu, 2003). During the period of 1989-2002, the growth rate of the number of guest rooms is 44.93% while the growth rate of international arrivals is 36.04%[12]. This phenomenon indicates that the expansion of supply significantly exceeds that of demand. It would make market competition stiffer. Therefore, the average profitability of Taiwan's international tourist hotel industry in 2002, in terms of operating profit margin and net operating margin[13], are 0.16% and -8.20%, respectively. Besides, individual international tourist hotels' profitability is significantly different from each other. The highest operating profit margin is 38.25% while the lowest is −56.65%. The standard deviation is 18.99%. These facts imply that some firms may adopt superior managerial strategies and thus have better performance than others. Consequently, individual hotels have to continuously improve their managerial efficiency in order to survive in the market.

The above phenomena indicates the significance of the ability to quantify efficiency and motivate our great interest in assessing and analyzing managerial efficiency of Taiwan's international tourist hotels. Therefore, this paper will first evaluate the efficiency of individual international tourist hotels, and then investigate firm-specific characteristics that are related to variation in their efficiency.

In the economic literature, productive/managerial efficiency comprises two parts: the technical (physical) and allocative (price) parts (Farrell, 1957). The former is measured by determining the maximum feasible reduction of inputs for the given levels of outputs (an input-conserving orientation), or by determining the maximum feasible expansion of outputs for the given levels of inputs (an output-augmenting orientation). In addition, taking the reference technology exhibiting different types of returns to scale into consideration[14], the technical efficiency can be decomposed into two components, purely technical efficiency and scale efficiency (Banker et al., 1984). The latter refers to the ability to combine inputs and outputs in optimal proportions at the prevailing prices. The measurement of the latter requires information on input prices that are often difficult to obtain or measure accurately in the international tourist hotel market. Hence, the analysis in this paper will be mainly focused on technical efficiency.

The approaches to evaluate technical efficiency can mainly be divided into parametric approach and non-parametric approach. The later is also known as data envelopment analysis (DEA) developed by Charnes et al.(1978). The advantage of DEA is that it does not require a pre-specification of a parametric functional form and several implicit or explicit assumptions about the production correspondences. However, it is more sensitive to data errors (Ahn and Seiford, 1992). There is no simple rule to determine which of these two approaches best describe the true nature of data. The DEA approach is used in this paper for two reasons. First, we use the census data collected and carefully checked by the Bureau of Tourism, Ministry of Transportation and Communications to eliminate data errors. Second, previous studies related to hotel industry do not provide a clear model of input transformation, which discourages us from adapting parametric approach to avoid misspecification error.

---

[12] According to the Operating Report of International Tourist Hotels in Taiwan, international visitors include foreign visitors and overseas Chinese.
[13] Operating profit margin is operating profit divided by revenues for that period; net operating margin is net operating income divided by revenues, expressed as a percentage.
[14] DEA models can be classified as CCR model and BCC model. CCR model assumes that reference technology exhibits constant returns to scale. BCC model relax this assumption and variable returns to scale is assumed.

DEA has been applied to many industries to evaluate technical efficiency, including profit sector and non-profit sector (Seiford, 1996). However, it is relatively rare regarding to hotel industry. Morey and Dittman(1995) used data for 54 hotels of a hotel chain in U.S. and found that managers were operating at 89% efficiency. Anderson, Fok and Scott (2000) used data of 48 hotels listed in Ward's Business Directory of U.S. private and public companies. They found that managers were operating at 42% efficiency. Hwang and Chang (2003) used data for 45 Taiwan's international tourist hotels in 1998 and found that resort hotels are more efficient than city hotels; sources of customers (foreign or domestic visitors) may have positive relationship with efficiency; and hotels participating in international chains are more efficient than those not. But, they used CCR model, instead of BCC model, so they were unable to decompose overall technical efficiency into purely technical efficiency and scale efficiency. Moreover, their choice of input-output variables may violate the principle of exclusivity[15] suggested by Thanassoulis (2001). Hwang and Chang (2003) included both the number of full-time employees and salary expenses as input variables. Nevertheless, it is appropriate to exclude salary expenses from operating expenses to avoid double counting. In addition, they might neglect some relevant firm-specific characteristics, such as firm size, service concentration, and location, which are further investigated in this paper.

In addition to this section, the rest of this paper is organized as follows. Section II will first construct the empirical model of data envelopment analysis to evaluate individual international tourist hotels' technical efficiency. Then, a censored regression model will be established to explore the relationship between technical efficiency and firm-specific characteristics. Data description, interpretation of the efficiency-evaluation and the Tobit censored regression results will be presented in Section III. Section IV concludes this paper.

II. EMPIRICAL MODELS

2.1. Efficiency Evaluation Model

The DEA approach introduced by Charnes et al. (1978) uses a mathematical programming technique to determine a piecewise linear envelopment surface from the observed levels of inputs and outputs of decision making units (DMUs). The envelopment surface is referred to as the efficient frontier. DMUs which construct the frontier are termed efficient; DMUs which do not lie on the frontier are termed inefficient. The distance between the former and the later provides a measure of efficiency and inefficiency.

As mentioned above, there are input-oriented and output-oriented models to evaluate the productive efficiency in the DEA approach. Lovell(1993) suggested that if producers are required to meet market demand, and if they can freely adjust the input usage, then input-oriented model seems appropriate. On the contrary, if they cannot freely adjust the input usage, output-oriented model is proper. Theoretically, due to fixed budget and staffs, output-oriented model is commonly used in public sector. Private sector, not subject to these constraints, is evaluated by input-oriented model. The input-oriented DEA model is adapted in this paper since international tourist hotels belong to private sector in Taiwan.

---

[15] Exclusivity means that every input should not be counted more than once.

Suppose that there are n DMUs in a market, each using m inputs and producing s outputs. Let x_{ij} and y_{ij} denote the ith (i=1,2,......,m) input usage and the rth (r=1,2,......,s) output production of the jth (j=1,2,......,n) DMU. According to Fare et al. (1985), under the assumptions of the reference technology exhibiting constant returns to scale (CRS) and free disposability of inputs, the kth DMU's technical efficiency measure (F_k) can be gauged by solving the following problem (Model I):

$$F_k = \min_{\theta_k, \lambda_1......\lambda_n} \theta_k \ . \tag{1}$$

$$\text{subject to} \sum_{j=1}^{n} \lambda_j x_{ij} \le \theta_k x_{ik}, i = 1,2,......,m \ . \tag{2}$$

$$\sum_{j=1}^{n} \lambda_j y_{rj} \ge y_{rk}, i = 1,2,......,s \tag{3}$$

$$\lambda_j \ge 0, j = 1,2,......,n \ . \tag{4}$$

where λ_j is the weight of the jth DMU's production action used. Just as the Model I describes, the technical efficiency is evaluated in terms of the feasibility of its inputs usage radical reduction. If the inputs usage radical reduction is feasible, then optimal $F_k < 1$; otherwise, $F_k = 1$.

The technical efficiency measure (F_k) evaluated above is not only influenced by the pure technical inefficiency, but also by the inappropriate production scale chosen. To decompose these two inefficient factors, the reference technology assumption of the Model I is relaxed to those of variable returns to scale (VRS) by imposing the constraint (Banker et al., 1984):

$$\sum_{j=1}^{n} \lambda_j = 1 \tag{5}$$

Thereafter, technical efficiency measure F_k(VRS) is produced. Since F_k(VRS) excludes the production scale impact, it is regarded as the kth DMU's pure technical efficiency measure, and the scale efficiency measure(SE_k) corresponding to the kth DMU is defined as the ratio of F_k to F_k(VRS), that is

$$SE_k \equiv F_k \Big/ F_k (VRS) \tag{6}$$

Obviously, $0 \le F_k \le F_k (VRS) \le 1$. It implies that $SE_k \le 1$. If $SE_k = 1$, then the kth DMU is scale-efficient; if $SE_k < 1$, then the kth DMU is scale-inefficient.

In the choice of input and output variables, this paper will consider the operating characteristics of international tourist hotels and refer to previous literature to select appropriate input-output mixes. Moreover, since the results of DEA efficiency evaluation are sensitive to the choice of variables, the stability test suggested by Kirjainen and Loikkanen(1998) will be used to examine whether the efficiency evaluation results are stable among different input-output mixes. According to the test, the values of the Pearson correlation coefficients among different input-output mixes should, at least, be positive to conclude that efficiency evaluation results among different input-output mixes are stable and the choice of input-output variables is appropriate.

2.2. Regression Model

In the existing studies, efficiency in production has been linked with a number of firm-specific attributes. These attributes include firm size, service concentration, location, etc. (Cheng et al., 2000; Tsaur, 2001; HwangandChang, 2003; Wang et al., 2003). Factors which capture the firm's long-term strategic consideration in the industry, for example, whether to participate in an international tourist hotel chain, is also considered. Consequently, the regression models for examining the relationship between each efficiency measure and firm-specific attributes in this paper can be built as follows:

$$F(VRS) = f(FS, H, GC, TAIPEI, RESORT, CHAIN)$$
$$(?) \ (?) \ (+) \qquad (+) \qquad (?) \qquad (?)$$

$$(7)$$

where FS is firm size, which is measured by total revenues. H is the service concentration, which is the sum of the squared ratios of revenues from each revenue to total revenues. GC is the degree of concentration in some type of guests, which is the sum of the squared ratios of the number of individual visitors to that of total visitors and the number of group visitors to that of total visitors. The dummy variable TAIPEI=1 indicates that an international tourist hotel is located in Taipei City; otherwise, TAIPEI=0. The dummy variable RESORT=1 indicates that an international tourist hotel is located in resort area; otherwise, RESORT=0. The dummy variable CHAIN=1 indicates that an international tourist hotel participates in an international hotel chain; otherwise, CHAIN=0. The notation under each dependent variable indicates its expected sign. Since the values of dependent variable F(VRS) all lie between 0 and 1, equations (7) is a censored regression model.

Fundamentally, the theoretical foundation for the relationship between efficiency measures and firm-specific attributes can be illustrated as follows:

Firm Size (FS)

Theoretically, international tourist hotels can enjoy economies of scale as their sizes expand. In addition to cost aspects, economies of scale may also exist in establishing brand names. However, improper managerial decision to expand firm size may lead to idle capacity and deficiency since the distinction between peak and off-peak periods is obvious. Therefore, the relationship between the firm size and its technical efficiency is ambiguous and needs to be empirically tested.

Service Concentration (H)

By specializing in a single product (service), international tourist hotels can increase their efficiency due to employees' familiarity with their simple and routine work (Boumol et al., 1982; Eaton and Eaton, 1995; Wang et al., 2003). Therefore, service concentration is expected to have a positive impact on technical efficiency because of gains from specialization. As the degree of service concentration goes up, gains from specialization will come up, but the economies of scope may disappear gradually. The former effect will raise a firm's technical efficiency; the latter effect will reduce the firm's technical efficiency. As a result, the relationship between service concentration and technical efficiency is hard to determine without further empirical investigation.

Concentration in Guest Type (GC)

International tourist hotels' guests can be divided into two types: individual and group guests. An essential part of individual guests are business travelers while group guests are basically visiting travelers (Hwang and Chang, 2003). These two types of guests have different needs and put emphasis on different services (Chu and Choi, 2000). If an international tourist hotel is focused mainly on one type of guests, no matter individual or group guests, it will enjoy cost reduction and saving from providing uniform services. As a result, the relationship between concentration in guest type and technical efficiency is expected to be positive.

Location (TAIPEI)

In 2002, 42.86% of international tourist hotels are located in Taipei City. Thus, the degree of competition among hotels located in Taipei City is higher. Generally, the pressures of competition will enhance the firm's efficiency (Leibenstein, 1996). Hence, it is reasonable to expect that the positive relationship exists between the location dummy and technical efficiency.

Resort (Resort)

Basically, international tourist hotels can be categorized into urban and leisure hotels (Hwang and Chang, 2003). Leisure hotels are located in resort areas with popular visiting spots that would attract local and foreign visitors. However, because usually located in less-populated area, they face more fluctuating demand in peak (weekends and vacations) and off-peak periods (Baum and Mudambi, 1995). This may cause difficulties in reducing input waste during off-peak periods. The former effect will enhance hotels occupancies; the latter may decrease hotels' technical efficiency. As a result, the relationship between the location dummy and technical efficiency is indeterminate.

Participating in International Hotel Chains (CHAIN)

In the past decade, some international tourist hotels in Taiwan have participated in international hotel chains in order to attract foreign visitors from their international reputation and improve efficiency from their managerial experience. In 2002, 18.03% of international tourist hotels in Taiwan were members of international hotel chains. However, the franchisers require all their members to satisfy higher standard in services and facilities. It would definitely increase operating costs. Therefore, the relationship between the dummy variable and technical efficiency is also indeterminate.

III. DATA DESCRIPTION AND EMPIRICAL RESULTS

3.1. Data Description

The data used in this paper are based on the survey data among all Taiwan's international tourist hotels that run their businesses in 2002. The survey was conducted by the Bureau of Tourism, Ministry of Transportation and Communications, ROC. There were 62 international tourist hotels in Taiwan by the end of 2002. In addition, international tourist hotels that did not run their businesses for the whole year of 2002 are not included in the sample to ensure the homogeneity of the observations. After deleting unqualified and incomplete observations, the actual sample size for this paper is 56.

Table 1. Input-output Mixes

	Alternative input-output mixes			
	M1	M2	M3	M4
Output variables:				
Revenues from accomdation service	*		*	
The number of guests		*		*
Revenues from food and beverage service	*	*	*	*
Revenues from other services	*	*		
Input variables:				
Number of employees	*	*	*	*
Number of guest rooms	*	*	*	*
Total areas of meal department	*	*	*	*
Operating expenses	*	*	*	*

In choosing input and output variables, this paper considers the operating characteristics of international tourist hotels and refers to the previous literature to select appropriate input-output mixes (Tsaur, 2001; Hwang and Chang, 2003). Three outputs and four inputs are chosen to form four alternative input-output mixes in the efficiency analysis (Table 1). On the output side, the outputs of international tourist hotels are classified into three broad categories: accommodation service, food and beverages service as well as other services[16].

---

[16] Other services include store rental, auxiliary guest services, night clubs, etc.

Table 2. The Descriptive Statistics of the Relevant Variables

	Mean	Std. Dev.	Maximum	Minimum
Revenues from accomdation service	220370204.371	215215695.479	1245741793.796	7804522.689
Number of guests	95399.357	58855.250	287236.000	6092.000
Revenues from food and beverage service	257240945.737	252623249.245	1078896281.369	526757.000
Revenues from other service	51718659.893	74333873.522	341746725.000	0.000
Number of employees	333.589	241.977	989.000	26.000
Number of guest rooms	311.946	160.954	873.000	50.000
Total areas of meal department	1038.625	784.391	3727.000	48.000
Operating expenses	224902403.429	195851481.750	957942737.000	8955856.000
Total revenues (FS)	529329810.000	515597339.953	2550224684.000	15379118.000
Service concentration (H)	0.478	0.092	0.934	0.334
Guest type concentration (GC)	0.637	0.159	1.000	0.500
Taipei city (TAIPEI)	0.429	0.499	1.000	0.000
Resort hotels (RESORT)	0.125	0.334	1.000	0.000
Participating in international chains(CHAIN)	0.180	0.388	1.000	0.000

Note: Revenues and expenses are measured in terms of NT dollars

On the input side, four types of inputs are distinguished: the number of employees, the number of guest rooms, total areas of meal department and operating expenses. Accommodation service can be measured by revenues (M1 and M3) or the number of guests (M2 and M4). Besides, due to the heterogeneity of other services among international tourist hotels, this paper excludes this output variable in M3 and M4.

In the regression analysis, FS is measured by an international tourist hotel's total revenues. An international tourist hotel's H is the sum of the squared ratios of revenues from each service to total revenues. Theoretically, the value of H lies between 0 and 1. Since international tourist hotels in the sample provide at most three categories of services, H is actually in a range of 1/3 to 1, with the value 1/3 representing balanced development of services and a higher value representing a higher service concentration. An international tourist hotel's GC is the sum of the squared ratios of the number of individual guests to that of total guests and the number of group guests to that of total guests. Since there are only two categories of guests, GC is actually in a range of 1/2 and 1, with the value 1/2 representing balanced types of guests and a higher value representing an international tourist hotel's focusing on one specific type of guests. The descriptive statistics of the relevant variables for both efficiency and regression analyses are presented in Table 2.

3.2. Empirical Results

Efficiency evaluation results. The efficiency evaluation results for each efficiency measure are summarized in Table 3. The mean overall efficiency measures of international tourist hotels in four input-output mixes are between 0.787 and 0.845. It implies that international tourist hotels could have reduced inputs by 15.5%~21.3%, on average, and still have produced the same level of outputs. The percentage of international tourist hotels operating on the frontier is between 23.2 (13 out of 56 in M1) and 35.7 (20 out of 56 in M4). The overall technical efficiency can be further decomposed into two factors: purely technical efficiency and scale efficiency. The mean purely efficiency measures of international tourist hotels in M1-M4 are between 0.787 and 0.846, which are almost the same as overall technical efficiency measures. In addition, the mean scale efficiency measures are closely to 1 (0.998-0.999). These two results imply that the inefficiency is mainly from wasting resources instead of inappropriate production scale. That is, most of international tourist hotels in Taiwan have an ample space to improve.

Since the DEA efficiency evaluation result is sensitive to the choice of input-output variables, this paper performs stability test. The results are shown in Table 4. The Pearson correlation coefficients are between 0.374 and 0.835. It implies that the results of efficiency evaluation among M1-M4 are stable and thus the choice of input/output variables is appropriate.

Regression results. The regression technique is then used to explore the relationship between technical efficiency and firm-specific characteristics. Since there is a non-negligible proportion of observations reaching the maximum efficiency measure of one, the ordinary least square technique applied to a censored regression model may yield estimates that are asymptotically biased toward zero (Greene, 1981). Therefore, by referring to McCarty and Yaisawarng (1993), Cheng et al.(2000) and Wang et al. (2003), the Tobit regression model will be used to estimate Equation (7). Initially, this paper uses the purely technical efficiency

measures of all four input-output mixes as the dependent variable to run regression analysis
for Equation(7), respectively. M4 has the highest adjusted R-squared value of 0.437,
indicating that it has the best explanation power. Therefore, only the Tobit censored
regression results of M4 are reported in Table5. The variance inflationary factor (VIF) is also
used to test the degree of multicollinearity among independent variables[1]. Since the VIF value
of each independent variable in the regression model of this paper is within the range of 1.135
and 1.589, there is almost no multicollinearity problem among these variables.

Table 3. Summary of International Tourist Hotels' Technical Efficiency Measures

	M1			M2		
	Fk	Fk(VRS)	SE	Fk	Fk(VRS)	SE
Mean	0.806	0.807	0.999	0.845	0.846	0.999
Std. Dev.	0.154	0.154	0.005	0.157	0.158	0.005
Max.	1	1	1	1	1	1
Min.	0.413	0.413	0.971	0.478	0.478	0.965
Number of Obs.	56	56	56	56	56	56
On the Frontier	14	15	32	20	20	42
	M3			M4		
	Fk	Fk(VRS)	SE	Fk	Fk(VRS)	SE
Mean	0.787	0.787	0.999	0.824	0.826	0.998
Std. Dev.	0.153	0.153	0.006	0.167	0.167	0.006
Max.	1	1	1	1	1	1
Min.	0.426	0.426	0.953	0.335	0.335	0.963
Number of Obs.	56	56	56	56	56	56
On the Frontier	13	13	41	17	17	44

Table 4. Summary of Stability Test Results

CRS	M1	M2	M3	M4
M1	1.000	0.558	0.784	0.399
M2	0.558	1.000	0.382	0.831
M3	0.784	0.382	1.000	0.566
M4	0.399	0.831	0.566	1.000
VRS	M1	M2	M3	M4
M1	1.000	0.549	0.783	0.390
M2	0.549	1.000	0.374	0.835
M3	0.783	0.374	1.000	0.554
M4	0.390	0.835	0.554	1.000

Notes: The values in the table are Pearson correlation coefficients

---

[1] The VIF value is equal to 1 for each independent variable with no correlation with each other, but the VIF value
may be even more than 10 for the independent variable highly correlated with each other (Greene, 2000).

Table5. Tobit Censored Regression Results

Parameter	Estimate	Standard Error
Intercept	0.074	0.141
FS	<0.001***	<0.0001
H	0.688***	0.216
GC	0.328***	0.124
TAIPEI	0.084*	0.046
RESORT	0.202***	0.058
CHAIN	0.004	0.068
Log Likehood	18.842	
Adj. R-square	0.437	
Sample Size	56	

***, **, * represent that the coefficients are significantly different from 0 at the 0.001, 0.005, 0.1 levels, respectively.

The regression results show that firm size has a positive impact on technical efficiency at the 0.01 significant level. That is, international tourist hotels exploit economies of scale as their sizes expand. There exists a positive relationship between the international tourist hotel's service concentration and technical efficiency at the 0.01 significant level. That is, international tourist hotels with higher service concentrations do enjoy higher technical efficiency duo to the existence of gains from specialization. Concentration in guest type has a positive impact on technical efficiency at the 0.01 significant level. It implies that international tourist hotels with higher degree of guest concentration, no matter concentrated in individual or group guest, have higher technical efficiency due to saving from providing uniform services. The coefficient of the TAIPEI dummy variable is positive at the 0.1 significant level, implying that international tourist hotels located in Taipei City are more efficient than those located in other areas. A possible explanation for the result is that stiff competition among hotels in Taipei City causes international tourist hotels to improve their efficiency to survive in the market. The coefficient of the RESORT dummy variable is positive at the 0.01 significant level, implying that international tourist hotels located in resort areas are more efficient than those in other areas. Two possible explanations for this result are given as follows: First, popular visiting spots help international tourist hotels to attract guests and to enjoy better occupancies. Second, the international tourist hotels may adopt superior managerial strategies, such as flexible pricing and working hours to reduce input waste and improve their efficiency during off-peak periods. The coefficient of the CHAIN dummy variable is positive but insignificant, implying that international tourist hotels participating in international hotel chains do not enjoy higher technical efficiency than those not. This result may indicate that although joining international hotel chains could attract foreign visitors via their international marketing chain and benefit from their managerial experience, the required standard services and facilities may increase input usage and associated costs of Taiwan's international tourist hotels. As a result, this strategy does not necessary improve international tourist hotels' technical efficiency.

IV. CONCLUSIONS AND SUGGESTIONS

After the government deregulated the entry barriers and encouraged the setup of Taiwan's international tourist hotels in 1977, the number of Taiwan's international tourist hotels increased from 21 in 1976 to 44 in 1985, and to 62 in 2002. During the period of 1989-2002, the growth rate of international arrivals, 36.04% was slower than that of the number of guest rooms, 44.93%. To survive in the market, it is crucial for international tourist hotels in Taiwan to improve their efficiency. Based on the survey data of Taiwan's international tourist hotels in 2002, the DEA evaluation results show that the mean overall technical efficiency measures of international tourist hotels in Taiwan are between 0.787 and 0.845, implying that they could have reduced inputs by at least 15 percent, on average, and still have produced the same level of outputs. The overall technical efficiency can be further decomposed into two factors: purely technical efficiency and scale efficiency. The mean scale efficiency measure is closely to 1, implying that the inefficiency is mainly from wasting resources instead of inappropriate production scale. The regression results show that an international tourist hotel's size has a positive impact on its technical efficiency. The impact of an international tourist hotel's service concentration on technical efficiency is positive. An international tourist hotel's degree of concentration in guest type is positively related with technical efficiency. International hotels located in Taipei City and resort areas are more technically efficient than those located in other areas of Taiwan. Whether international tourist hotels participate in international chains or not does not influence their technical efficiency significantly.

The empirical evidence of this paper could provide some implications and suggestions for international tourist hotels in Taiwan to improve their efficiency. First, since the efficiency can enhance with expansion of the firm size, it may provide small-to-medium-sized international tourist hotels incentives for mergers or acquisitions to expand their operational scales. Second, it is suggested that international tourist hotels may adopt the specialization strategy under consideration of efficiency improvement. Third, the positive influence of concentration in guest type on efficiency suggests that international tourist hotel can apply the strategy of market segmentation to improve efficiency. Finally, international tourist hotels might have to reconsider whether to participate in international hotel chains since this strategy does not necessarily improve their technical efficiency.

ACKNOWLEDGEMENTS

Financial support from the National Science Council under NSC 92-2416-H-004-036 is acknowledged. The authors are grateful to the Tourism Bureau of Taiwan for its kind help with data collection.

REFERENCES

Ahn, T. and Seiford, L. M. (1992), "Sensitivity of DEA to models and variables sets in a hypothesis test setting: The efficiency of university operations", Ijiri, Q.(ed.), *Creative and Innovative Approaches to the Science of Management*, New York.

Anderson, R. I., R. Fok and J. Scott (2000), "Hotel Industry Efficiency: An Advanced Linear Programming Examination," *American Business Review*, January 2000, 40-48.

Banker, R. D. , A. Charnes, and W.W. Cooper (1984), "Some Models for Estimating Technical and Scale Inefficiencies in Data Envelopment Analysis," *Management Science*, Vol. 30, 1078-1092.

Baum, T. and R. Mudambi (1995), "An Empirical Analysis of Oligopolistic Hotel Pricing," *Annals of Tourism Research*, Vol.22, No.3 ,501-516.

Baumol, W. J., J. C. Panzar and R. D. Willig (1982), *Contestable Markets and the Theory of Industry Structure*, Harcourt Brace Jovanovich, New York.

Charnes, A., W.W. Cooper and E. Rhodes (1978), "Measuring the Efficiency of Decision Making Units," *European Journal of Operations Research*, Vol. 2, 429-444.

Cheng, T.W., K.L. Wang and C.C. Weng (2000), "A Study of Technical Efficiencies of CPA Firms in Taiwan," *Review of Pacific Basin Financial Markets and Policies*, Vol.3, No.1, 27-44.

Chu, R.K.S. and T. Choi (2000), "An importance Performance Analysis of Hotel Selection Factors in the Hong Kong Hotel Industry": A Comparison of Business and Leisure Travellers", *Tourism Management*, Vol.21, 363-377.

Eaton, B. C. and D. F. Eaton (1995), Microeconomics, Englewood Cliffs, Prentice Hall, New Jersey.

Färe, R. S. Grosskopf and C. A. K. Lovell (1985), *The Measurement of Efficiency of Production*, Kluwer-Nijhoff, Boston.

Farrell, M.J. (1957), "The Measurement of Productive Efficiency," *Journal of the Royal Statistical Society*, Series A, CXX, Part 3:253-290.

Greene, W. H. (1981), "On the Asymptomic Bias of the Ordinary Least Squares Estimator of the Tobit Model", *Econometrica*, Vol. 49, 505-513.

Greene, W.H. (2000), *Econometric Analysis*, 4th edition, Prentice Hall.

Hwang, S. N., and T. Y. Chang (2003), "Using data envelopment analysis to measure hotel managerial efficiency change in Taiwan.," *Tourism Management*, 24, 357-369.

Kirjavainen, T. and H. A. Loikkanen (1998), "Efficiency Differences of Finnish Senior Secondary Schools: An Application of DEA and Tobit Analysis," *Economics of Education Review*, Vol.17, No. 4,377-394.

Leibenstein, H. (1966), "Allocative efficiency vs. X-efficiency," *American Economic Review*, Vol. 56. No. 3,392-414.

Lovell, C. A. K. (1993), "Production Frontiers and Productive Efficiency," in *The Measurement of Productive Efficiency: Techniques and Applications*, edited by H. O. Fried, C. A. K. Lovell and S. S. Schmidt, Oxford University Press, New York, 3-67.

McCarty, T.A. and S. Yaisawarng (1993), "Technical Efficiency in New Jersey School Districts," in *The Measurement of Productive Efficiency: Techniques and Applications,-* edited by H. O. Fried, C. A. K. Lovell and S.S. Schmidt, Oxford University Press, New York, 271-87.

Morey, R. C. and D. A. Dittman (1995), "Evaluating a Hotel GM's Performance, " *Cornell Hotel and Restaurant Administration Quarterly,* October, 30-35.

Seiford, L. M. (1996), "Data Envelopment Analusis: The Evolution of the State of the Art(1978-1995)", *Journal of Productivity Analysis*, Vol. 7, 99-137.

Thanassoulis, Emmanuel (2001), *Introduction to the Theory and Application of Data Envelopment Analysis: A Foundation Text with Integrated Software*, Kluwer Academic Publishers, Boston.

Tsaur, S.H. (2001), "The Operational Efficiency of International Tourist Hotels in Taiwan," *Asia Pacific Journal of Tourism Research*,Vol.6, 73-81.

Wang, K.L., Y.T. Tseng and C.C. Weng , (2003), "A Study of Production Efficiencies of Integrated Securities Firms in Taiwan," *Applied Financial Economics*, Vol. 13, 159-167.

Wang, K.L., C.S. Wu (2003), "A Study of Competitiveness of International Tourism in the Southeast Asian Region," in *Trade in Services in the Asia-Pacific Region* edited by T. Ito and A.O. Krueger, Chicago Press: Chicago and London.

INDEX

resolution, 46, 147, 200
resource management, 72
resources, x, 3, 27, 44, 46, 48, 53, 56, 58, 60, 71, 72,
    73, 94, 124, 128, 129, 130, 134, 138, 144, 145,
    162, 180, 191, 192, 194, 211, 219, 222
responsibility, 29, 31, 56, 129, 180, 194, 195
responsiveness, 16, 30, 31
retail, 11, 30, 31, 67, 81, 156
retirement, 80
retrieval, 74
returns, 54, 55, 67, 68, 201, 212, 214
returns to scale, 212, 214
revenue, 50, 163, 187, 215
rights, 28, 43, 53, 58, 160, 161
risk, ix, 20, 179, 180, 181, 188, 189, 190, 191, 192,
    193, 194, 195, 196, 201, 202, 203, 207, 208, 209,
    210
risk assessment, ix, 179, 180, 181, 188, 189, 191,
    196, 202, 208, 209
risk management, 188, 190, 209
risk-taking, 20
rule of law, 58
RVS, 15

S

safety, 7, 70, 180, 181, 187, 191, 198, 201, 206, 207,
    208, 209, 210
sales, 125, 155, 157, 187
salinity, 67
sample, viii, ix, 2, 17, 19, 22, 24, 26, 65, 70, 76, 77,
    78, 79, 82, 87, 91, 94, 96, 100, 101, 105, 106,
    109, 112, 114, 115, 116, 155, 217, 219
sampling, 19, 49, 76, 87, 106
sanctions, 8
satellite, 182, 201
satisfaction, 2, 5, 9, 10, 12, 32, 33, 34, 35, 94, 95,
    104, 116, 150, 151, 187, 198
savings, 157, 190
scandal, 50
Scandinavia, 78
scarce resources, 57, 145, 159
scarcity, 161
scattering, 86
scheduling, 198
scholarship, 28
school, 17, 48
search, 20, 24, 36, 46, 49, 94, 130
seasonal component, 151
seasonality, 128, 150
secondary data, 86
security, 16, 22, 23, 28, 32, 70, 183, 187, 198, 199,
    200, 206

segregation, 205
self, vii, 1, 22, 23, 24, 27, 28, 29, 81, 112, 115, 181
self-control, 22, 24, 28
self-esteem, 23, 28
sensitivity, 116
separation, 17, 103
series, 55, 59, 86, 96, 100, 125, 127, 133, 152, 153,
    154, 155, 156, 171
service provider, vii, 1, 2, 4, 5, 10, 12, 13, 14, 15, 16,
    31, 33, 94
service quality, 2, 5, 13, 14, 16, 32, 33, 34
services, vii, 1, 2, 4, 5, 9, 12, 13, 14, 16, 22, 30, 32,
    33, 52, 66, 69, 94, 98, 99, 107, 150, 151, 153,
    154, 155, 156, 159, 160, 180, 181, 182, 184, 185,
    186, 191, 201, 216, 217, 219, 221
sewage, 182
shape, 7, 140
shareholders, 52, 208
shares, 52, 130
sharing, 44, 82, 131
shortage, 50, 57
sign, 161
similarity, 102
simulation, 73, 101, 106, 201
Singapore, 6, 36, 170, 171, 172, 175, 176
sites, 9, 49, 50, 51, 54, 61, 73, 79, 88, 89, 97, 159
skills, 14, 28, 57, 58, 74, 129, 134
smoking, 207
social acceptance, 28
social attributes, 28
social behavior, 129
social class, vii, 1, 28, 31, 44
social context, 131
social control, 42
social costs, 89, 161, 195
social desirability, 161
social group, 56, 58
social network, 27
social norms, 27, 29
social order, 27
social problems, 56
social psychology, 34, 89
social relations, 3, 56
social relationships, 3
social security, 187
social security payments, 187
social standing, 31
social status, 30
social structure, 61
social welfare, 161
software, ix, 149
South Korea, 171
Southeast Asia, 4, 7, 174, 212, 224

transport, 6, 9, 53, 54, 67, 95, 108, 112, 115, 150, 152, 154, 156, 158
transportation, 6, 145, 181
treaties, 6
trees, 88
trend, 5, 63, 75, 156
trial, 196
Turkey, 45, 61, 63, 123, 124, 125, 133, 148, 166
turnover, 133

U

uncertainty, 31, 32, 133, 188, 192, 208
unemployment, 155, 161
unemployment rate, 155
uniform, 216, 221
unit cost, 156
United Kingdom (UK), 5, 38, 74, 77, 78, 79, 85, 120, 146, 155, 165, 166, 168, 169, 170, 174, 176, 179, 209
United Nations, 52
United States, 29, 30, 32, 154, 155, 169, 171, 172
universe, 30
universities, 50
updating, 124
urban areas, 7, 53

V

Valencia, 119, 121, 122, 177
validity, 16, 127, 155, 156, 158
values, vii, 1, 5, 9, 10, 11, 12, 15, 19, 22, 27, 28, 29, 34, 35, 45, 46, 58, 59, 69, 73, 111, 112, 114, 115, 116, 124, 126, 129, 130, 196, 199, 215, 220
variable(s), vii, viii, 1, 10, 14, 16, 17, 22, 24, 26, 32, 33, 65, 72, 91, 93, 105, 106, 107, 108, 109, 111, 112, 115, 117, 142, 151, 152, 153, 155, 156, 157, 158, 185, 212, 213, 214, 215, 217, 219, 220, 221, 223
variance, 17, 22, 24, 26, 105, 106, 110, 111, 220
variation, 158, 212
varimax rotation, 17, 22
vector, 105
vegetation, 72, 78, 97
vehicles, 46, 51, 73
vessels, 207
victimization, 128
Vietnam, v, vii, 1, 2, 3, 4, 5, 6, 7, 8, 9, 13, 15, 16, 18, 19, 20, 21, 33, 34, 35, 36, 37, 38, 39, 174

village, 48, 49, 51, 53
violence, 206
vision, ix, 51, 58, 66, 123, 124, 125, 126, 127, 129, 130, 131, 133, 134, 135, 136, 137, 138, 139, 141, 142, 144, 145, 147, 148, 157
voice, 44, 50
volatility, 152
voting, 137, 140, 142
vulnerability, 159

W

wages, 183, 187, 198
Wales, 169, 171
war, 3, 24, 201
water, 71, 72, 78, 86, 99, 100, 160, 182
water quality, 99
weakness, 151
wealth, 28, 30, 78
wear, 86
welfare, 24, 82, 143, 150, 161, 208
welfare economics, 161
well-being, 29
Western countries, 2, 8, 43, 45, 58, 59, 60
Western Europe, 133, 176, 177
wetlands, 77
wilderness, 74, 89
wildlife, 73, 78, 89
winter, 122
withdrawal, 13
words, viii, 13, 27, 47, 91, 93, 95, 96, 107, 109, 117, 125, 156
work, 2, 11, 20, 24, 28, 29, 31, 32, 47, 53, 54, 55, 57, 60, 67, 93, 100, 105, 108, 110, 129, 131, 135, 137, 142, 145, 154, 160, 198, 205, 206, 208, 216
workers, 17, 20, 50, 155, 159
working hours, 221
writing, 127, 141
WTO, 6, 39, 150, 160, 168, 178

Y

yield, 85, 128, 219

Z

Zone 1, 62